The Schools in College Street in 1928.

Dame Allan's Schools

Newcastle upon Tyne
1705 - 2005

E.D. Smith

Dame Allan's Schools

ISBN 0-9551275-0-5

Printed by Prontaprint, Newcastle

PREFACE

From Elizabeth Fallaize, Professor of French, Fellow of St John's College and Pro-Vice-Chancellor (Education) in the University of Oxford

I am delighted to be invited to provide a preface to this history of my old school. I feel the school played a very significant part in encouraging me at an early age to have confidence in my own future. I think that began with my interview with Miss South, who I remember took the ambitions of a nine-year-old extremely seriously. I was very proud of the uniform and posed on my parents' front door step for a photograph, which shows me standing stiffly to attention in an oversize blazer and straw hat. I threw myself into gymnastics, netball and hockey but it was French that really captured my imagination when we began studying it with Miss Brass. I absolutely loved it and took an unaccustomed lead in my family's dealings with hotels when we made a trip to France that summer. This eventually led to degrees in French at Exeter University and so on to my present chair at Oxford in 1990. From September 2005, I take up the post of Pro-Vice-Chancellor (Education) in the University. Miss Hornsby and Miss Brass would no doubt have been astonished had they known where it would all lead.

Congratulations on the Tercentenary, and may the Schools continue to flourish.

Elizabeth Fallaize

From Sir David Lumsden, formerly Principal of the Royal Academy of Music

My recent visit to Dame Allan's Schools Tercentenary Concert in The Sage was for me a mind-blowing experience. The consistently high standard of the performances, the eclectic choice of programme, its professional presentation, the magic of the new auditorium – all added up to an overwhelming feeling of excitement and inspiration and deep admiration for what is happening in the Schools now. But they also brought to mind again my own time at Dame Allan's, 60-odd years ago, the happy atmosphere then, despite World War II raging around us, the lifelong friendships forged, the fundamental and benign influence of a dedicated, skilful band of teachers, whose names and personalities are ingrained in my heart and mind and who are vivid and alive to this day. In short, the School was the most important formative influence of my life, from which everything else has flowed.

For this I am eternally grateful and I hope and believe that the present generation of pupils will benefit similarly. Good luck to them all, and blessings on the School for its next 300 years.

David Lumsden

This book is dedicated to all who by their lives have sustained and enhanced Eleanor Allan's Foundation through three centuries of change, and to those who seek to do so in the future.

"The great lesson for a school like this is that it has history. You enter not in a new life or a mushroom growth, but into something that has been going on for more than two centuries. Its traditions are all about you…Strong with the strength that made England great, a school like this will exert a real power over the days to come if we learn from it those lessons which it teaches by its very existence and its long-enduring vitality."

From a sermon preached by the Revd J. Neville Figgis, Litt. D., Honorary Fellow of St Catharine's College, Cambridge, on the occasion of the Annual Service on 29 January, 1912, in St Peter's Church, Newcastle

"I'd hope he'd go on with Willie to Newcastle. There's a place called Dame Allan's there…She must have been a very good woman to have a school named after her. Aye, she must. I've heard that's a good place for an education."

From Bill Bailey's Daughter, *by Catherine Cookson. 1988*

Contents

Newcastle upon Tyne in 1745, dominated by St. Nicholas's Church, with the medieval bridge (1250, repaired 1339, destroyed 1771) and the Gothic All Saints' Church. (Samuel and Nathaniel Buch).

Chapter One

THE ALLANS AND THE FOUNDATION

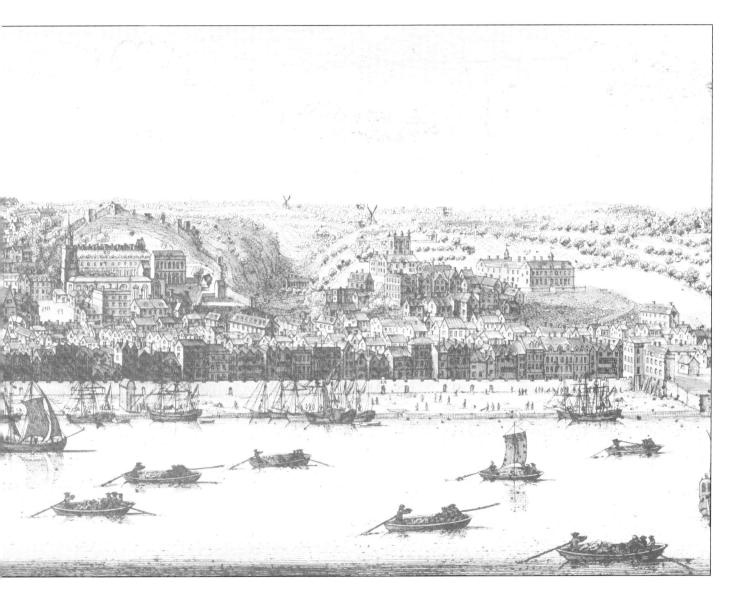

At the beginning of the Eighteenth Century Newcastle was a very different place from the Newcastle of today. Its medieval walls and street plan survived virtually intact, and although there was growth outside the walls, it was not substantial. The population has been estimated at around 18,000, and a great many of them were crowded into the narrow streets of the town. There can be no doubt the smell was considerable, and living conditions very bad for many of the townspeople. Daniel Defoe, visiting in 1727, says "the buildings (are) very close and old... Not the pleasantest place in the world to live in... The fires make such a smoke that we saw it ascend in clouds over the hills four miles before we came to Durham, which is at least sixteen miles from the place." Celia Fiennes visited some thirty years earlier in 1698, and her view was quite different: "it most resembles London of any place in England, its buildings lofty and large of brick mostly or stone; the streetes (sic) are very broad and handsome and very well pitch'd." In fact, these two travellers seem to have looked at things in very different ways, and the truth probably lies between them. Some streets will have been wide and some very narrow; it depended where you looked. Defoe noted "the poor, of which the town has always a prodigious number", but a glance at the splendid Seventeeth Century houses, timber-framed, with large windows and five storeys high, still standing in Sandhill (e.g. Bessie Surtees' House) shows the prosperity of the merchant class.

Newcastle had had a mayor since 1216 and had become a county in 1400. Coal was of course king, but there was much other trade too. The trade in coal had started in the Thirteenth Century and mining, as distinct from quarrying, had started in the Fifteenth Century. Coal was brought downriver by keels, but primitive railway tracks evolved in the Seventeenth Century to assist in bringing coal down to a point where it could be loaded on colliers for London and elsewhere.

The view of the town from the south by Samuel and Nathaniel Buck in 1745 gives a good impression of a compact town and busy port, the river spanned by its picturesque medieval bridge with gate, chapel, houses and shops, and the skyline broken by the great steeple of St Nicholas's, the mother church of the town.

Armorial bearings of Merchant Adventurers

The Allan family came from south Yorkshire. Leonard Allan, a yeoman, had a son John born at Brampton, but the family removed at some point to north Yorkshire. John was apprenticed to John Lewen, described as a boothman or corn merchant. His indenture is dated 2 July, 1647, and he was enrolled on 3 March the next year. On 23 September, 1657, he was admitted to the Company of the Merchant Adventurers of Newcastle. He married Eleanor, the daughter of William Luck, a local goldsmith. Although not a member of the goldsmiths company, William was a skilled man; in 1635, for example, he was commissioned to make a new silver seal for the Town Court. He was clearly a man of substance, since when he died in 1649, he was buried near the east end of All Saints' Church. He had married in 1612, and his wife Margaret bore him nine children, several of whom died in childhood. Ellinor (as spelt in the parish register) was baptised on 21 June, 1629, in All Saints' Church[1].

It was usual to baptise a healthy child some three days after birth. John and Eleanor Allan seem to have settled on the north side of The Side, and established a general merchant's shop. They had a daughter Ann in 1651, and on 3 June, 1660, their son Francis was also baptised in the same church. There also seems to have been another son, Peter, who died in childhood.

In 1679, John Allan died. He had been a rather unsuccessful general merchant; we do not know why. However, his widow and the children were more successful, and when the daughter married a wine cooper and moved to London, mother and son, apparently specialising in tobacco, ran a thriving business. In 1706, the business was on the south side of The Side and thus in the Parish of St Nicholas; earlier they had lived in All Saints' Parish, possibly only across the road in The Side, which was in that parish. Celia Fiennes had observed that in Newcastle the "shops are good and are of distinct trades, not selling many things in one shop as is the custom in most country towns and cittys.". Perhaps that was the key to their success. Early sources also speak of their frugality. Another Allan family – probably related – are recorded as "tobacco pipemakers". Eleanor's brother Richard was described as a "Dr of Physick" in the town.

Their enterprise caused them to look for an investment, and on 20 July, 1700, Francis bought the lease of a farm at Wallsend for twenty-one years (see framed section) from the Dean and Chapter of Durham. He died on 17 February, 1705/6[2], and was buried in St. Nicholas's churchyard. There is a record of the payment for his gravestone to the church wardens for "Mr ffrancis Allan Lair stone – 6s 8d." He had not married and it is evident that he and his mother had discussed how their property might eventually be used. We know nothing about their shop, whether they owned it or rented it, whether they lived above it (almost certainly) and whether they had resources in addition to the Wallsend Farm lease. Francis Allan's will, dated 6 March 1704/5, made several specific bequests, and the rest was left to his mother. His wish was that the income from the Wallsend farm should be used "for charitable purposes." We do not know whether he favoured the foundation of a charity

[1] Not the present building above the quayside, which was not built until 1786-96 but its medieval predecessor which had become unsafe.
[2] 1705/6. At this time the new year was regarded as starting on 25 March (cf financial year and academic year today). Thus a date in early 1706 was expressed as 1705/6 or even 1705.

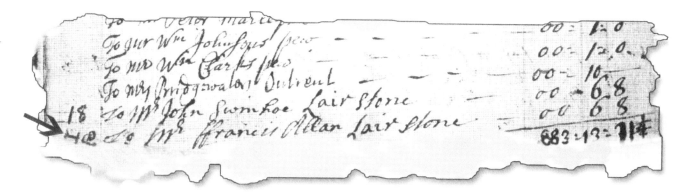

Entry in St Nicholas's account book for lair stone viz., grave stone, for Francis Allan. 1706

Extract from Eleanor Allan's will

school, but since the matter was dealt with so speedily on his death, it is highly likely. Only three days elapsed before Eleanor Allan passed the lease of the Wallsend Farm to three trustees by deed of gift. The agreement was that Mrs Allan should receive the income from the farm until her death, when the money should be applied to the foundation of charity schools for the parish of St Nicholas and the chapelry of St John the Baptist. The executors of their wills were William Proctor, George Henderson and John Ord, all men of substance and standing in the town. William Proctor was sheriff in 1684 and George Henderson was sheriff in 1695 and mayor in 1700, while John Ord had just anonymously founded and endowed the charity school at St John's Church, the rules for which were to be the pattern for the new school. (See Appendix 5 for full text of the indenture and the edited St John's rules).

An immediate task of the trustees was to pay Mrs Alice Wild 1s 2d each Saturday morning, and that can only be for her services as a teacher. It is likely that Eleanor Allan found that she could live on part of the Wallsend income – she was earlier noted for her frugality – and that she was eager to see the school up and running in her own lifetime. Moreover, there must have been pressure to open a charity school for St. Nicholas's, since St. John's had just acquired a charity school for boys, with the intention as soon as possible to make provision for girls. In January 1707/8 St Andrew's opened its own school for thirty boys, founded by Sir William Blackett. In 1709 All Saints' charity school was set up by public subscription for about forty boys and twenty girls. It would have looked inappropriate for the mother church of Newcastle to be the only one *not* running a school, and thus the likelihood is that Mrs Wild was developing a small school of younger children until such time as the full

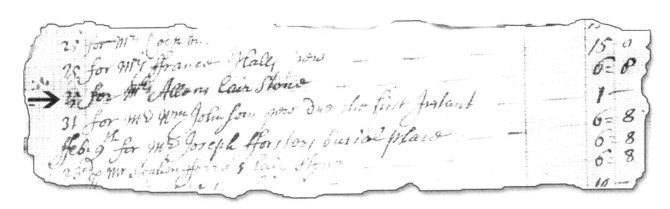

Entry in St Nicholas's account book for lair stone, viz., grave stone, for Eleanor Allan. 1709

foundation could be realised. It is likely that it would be mixed, and perhaps little more than a superior dame's school.

It is said that Eleanor Allan "was strongly importuned to revoke this deed" but by whom or for what reason we do not know. It is also said that she took no notice of this and "did not meddle with the farm". Perhaps her tenants at Wallsend were less than happy with the changed arrangements: negotiating with a highly educated group of trustees might have seemed daunting after Eleanor and Francis Allan. She died on 21 January, 1708/9, at the age of 79,[3] and was buried two days later in St Nicholas's churchyard. A new board of trustees came into being. In addition to the three original trustees, it consisted of the Vicar of Newcastle, (the Revd Nathaniel Ellison, D.D.), the Mayor of Newcastle (George Whinfield), the perpetual curate of St John the Baptist's (the Revd Andrew Bates), the curate of All Saints' (the Revd Richard Musgrave), the curate of St Andrew's (unknown) and the lecturer or afternoon preacher of St Nicholas's (the Revd Dr Robert Tomlinson, who was also Rector of Whickham and Prebendary of St Paul's Cathedral).

They appointed James Dixon as the master of the boys' school with a salary of £20, with £1.10s for rent and £1 for coals. Mrs Dorothy Wild – probably the daughter of Alice Wild – was appointed as mistress, with exactly half the payments to the master. Mr Dixon was to teach forty boys to read and write English and "to cast accompt", viz., practical arithmetic. Mrs Wild was to teach twenty girls "to read, knit and sow plain work"; the master was to teach them to write. The children were to be drawn from the parish of St. Nicholas and the chapelry of St John, and were to attend from 7.00am in summer or 8.00am in winter to 11.00am, and from 1.00pm to 4.00pm. They were required to attend church regularly. The surplus of the income after the payments to the two teachers was to be used in "charitable and necessary uses about the Schools", in the education and teaching of the children and in putting out the boys as apprentices and the girls to domestic service. When children left the school, they were given two volumes: a Bible and Prayer Book bound together and *The Whole Duty of Man*[4] "plain bound". At a slightly later date Lewis's *Explanation of the Church Catechism* was also given. The sums of £2 for boys and £1 for girls were to be paid "in binding out any apprentice or putting out a girl to service. The rules for St John's School, drawn up by John Ord who was deeply involved in both schools, were followed closely: the edited text is the second part of Appendix 5. St John's Charity School had been provided with a schoolhouse by the Corporation of Newcastle, who also maintained it. They also assisted All Saints' School very considerably. There is no evidence to suggest any such help for St Nicholas's School.

It would be useful to consider at this point the sudden development of education in Newcastle. As the Eighteenth Century began, there were only the grammar school, a municipal school at St Ann's Chapel and an unknown number of small private schools, some run by elderly women scarcely literate themselves but others by highly educated clergy and similar. Newcastle was prosperous as industry started to stir itself and was in need of better educational provision. Brand, writing in 1789, speaks of a national rise of charity schools beginning around 1688, founded by Anglicans "with the view of opposing and defeating the pernicious effects of the seminaries set up by the Papists during the reign of King James the Second"[5].

Baillie (1801) speaks in similar terms of such institutions set up "during the short and inglorious reign of that furious bigot James II". The language seems excessive to the modern reader, but there is no denying the strength of feeling against Roman Catholicism at that date, and that may have played a part. Certainly there was concern nationally about Jacobitism. For example Edmund Gibson, Bishop of London, as late as the 1720s, is concerned about it in London charity schools, and saw it as an urgent task to rectify matters. The charity school was seen as "a bulwork of the 1689 settlement – as 'a fortress and a frontier garrison against popery which flourished on mass ignorance'".[6] However, a growing social conscience, coupled with a realisation that a workforce that was literate and numerate was more useful and thus more profitable, may have played a larger part. Perhaps the presence in the community in Newcastle of a number of caring individuals – John Ord particularly springs to

---

[3] Her mother also lived to a similar age or perhaps rather older.

[4] *The Whole Duty of Man* is a devotional book written c1658, probably by Richard Allestree (1619-81), Regius Professor of Divinity at Oxford. It was extremely popular.

[5] He was right about the great increase in charity schools, many of them endowed. In the diocese of Lincoln, for example, there were by 1713 some 200 such schools.

[6] Joan Simon, in "Education in Leicestershire 1540-1940", quoting the Revd White Kennett, a supporter of S.P.C.K.'s charity schools campaign at this period.

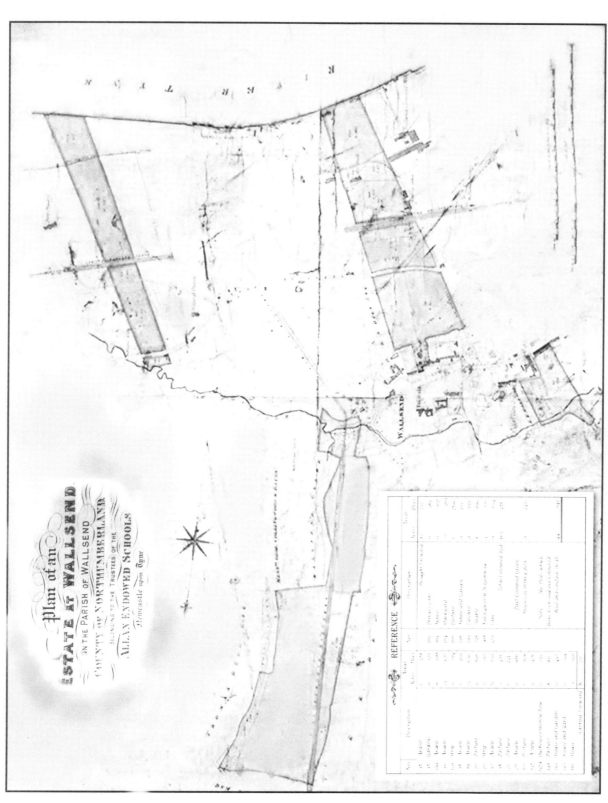

mind – was the catalyst. Whatever the stimulus, between 1705 and 1709 the four church charity schools were set up, in 1712 the Brethren of Trinity House opened a boys' school and another was later created at the Unitarian Chapel in Hanover Square.

The St Nicholas' Charity Schools thus began their first century.

Village Farm, Wallsend, facing the Green. Now demolished.

VILLAGE FARM, WALLSEND

Some independent schools have rich endowments that have enabled them to ride every storm with ease. This is not quite true of Dame Allan's, but the original endowment of the Village Farm at Wallsend was to provide the Schools with a modest but regular income from 1709 (and perhaps 1706) to 1922. This may well have been decisive in their survival, since it gave the trustees and, later, governors the independence that comes of a steady income. I propose to trace the history of the estate in one place in this book.

On 20 July, 1700, Eleanor and Francis Allan bought the leasehold of the estate from James Burfield, whose family had held it for over seventy years. The land was the property of the Dean and Chapter of Durham, and the lease excluded timber and mineral rights. The rental was £16 19s 5d, and the lease was for twenty-one years. Soon after the purchase of the lease, Francis Allan renewed in his own name only the lease from the Dean and Chapter. In his will he left the lease to his mother, and when he died on 17 February, 1705/6, it passed to her. She promptly vested the lease in trustees.

The Allans never lived at or farmed Wallsend Farm; it was simply an investment. The practice was to surrender the old lease and to take a new lease for seven years at the end of every fourth year, when a fine was demanded of one and a half times the full value. Thus in 1829, for example, the trustees paid £328 5s 5d, effectively to cover the next four years. The rent from the tenant was calculated according to the average price of wheat, and paid every six months. The income for the year 1828-9 was £280. The trustees had to plan on a four-year basis to allow for the payment to the Dean and Chapter. Clearly the arrangement worked to the advantage of the Schools and since one family held the tenancy from 1735 until 1881, it seems they were content with the arrangement too. In the first nine years of the lease, the income was on average just under £80 per annum from three tenants, Anthony Bolton, Ann Jefferson and Peter Reed.

On 9 January, 1867, the trustees acquired from the Dean and Chapter the freehold of all the Wallsend estate. This enabled the sale of thirty-five acres in 1868-69 in two lots totalling £11,738 11s 9d for the proposed new school building.

The estate covered in total 137 acres, in four sections:

> a) The Village Farmhouse and attendant buildings, facing the village green opposite the Hall and next to the Grange, was the residence of the tenant farmer, and was rebuilt by one of them, William Robert Swan, around 1835. In addition there were five more houses on or close to the Green. Behind these houses stretched 43 acres of arable land in a tapering strip down to the north bank of the Tyne. This land was bisected by the Newcastle to Tynemouth turnpike road, and later by the Newcastle – Tynemouth railway. The section between the railway and the river was developed in 1847 by Mr John Allan (no relation), who was a chemical manufacturer. He built an alkali works and jetty on the site; the Swan Hunter shipyard partly occupies the spot today. The trustees sold the land on which the factory stood to Mr Swan in 1868. The rest of the arable land, i.e., between the Village Farmhouse and the railway, was sold by the trustees in 1897 to Messrs Lawson Brothers.

> b) A terrace of eleven houses at Shiney Row and eight acres of arable land, through which the Wallsend Burn flowed. These were sold in 1899 to W. H. Thompson.

> c) Two houses and 25 acres in a strip between the Newcastle-Tynemouth Turnpike just east of the parish church, and the Tyne. Most of the land was sold before 1881; the houses and a small area of land were sold about 1900.

> d) An area of 60 acres, an irregular strip running north from the Wallsend Burn, and traversed in its full length by the Killingworth Wagonway. In the late Nineteen Century,

the Corporation of Wallsend rented two sections of this land, one for an Infectious Diseases (Fever) Hospital and the other for a Small Pox Hospital, yielding by the time of their sale £105 a year.

The land was valued at £8500, and with the permission of the Board of Education it was sold in 1921 to the Battle Hill Estate Company. The next year Wallsend Farmhouse and buildings were also sold for £1600 to Mr S J Long. The farmhouse was pulled down some twenty years ago to make way for sheltered housing. Finally, the Board approved of the sale of part of Threap Moor to the Thermal Syndicate Ltd. for £357. Strangely, one small area of land, described as "4/28th shares of Threap Moor", was still in the Schools' possession in 1948, but was sold the next year for only £173. After 243 years the Schools' link with the Wallsend Farm came to an end: the farm had served them well.

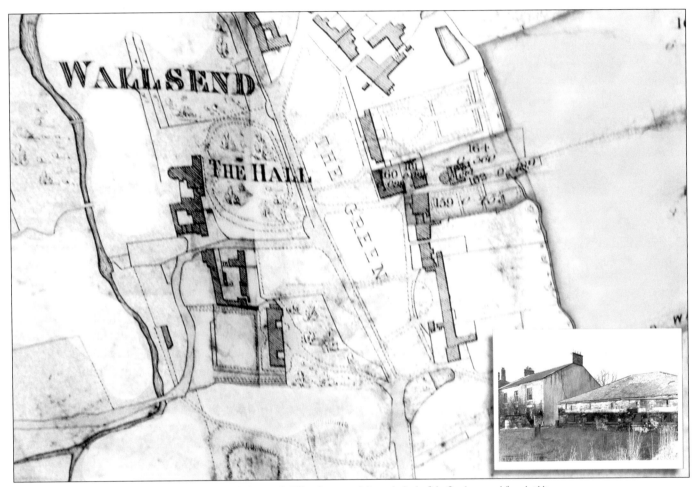

The Green, Wallsend, c1880, showing the Village Farm in red. Inset: the back of the farmhouse and farm buildings

Chapter Two

St Nicholas's Charity School,
Sustained by Charity, Church and Corporation,
1709 - 1821

The Schools were fully opened on 1 May, 1709; some of the pupils would be Mrs Alice Wild's existing pupils. Just as we do not know the location of Mrs Wild's school, we do not know for certain where the twin schools were housed. The earliest reference to their location is as late as 1778, when they are described as being at the foot of the Flesh Market, to the north of St Nicholas's Church. It is however likely that this was the site of 1709 too.

James Dixon stayed only eighteen months, and he was succeeded by John Watson, who added to his duties by teaching the children to sing psalms, for which he was paid an additional £1 a year. He too left after a similar spell and was replaced by Samuel Mowbray – the third master in under four years. The reason for this inauspicious start is unlikely to have been the pay, modest though it was, since similar schools seem to have paid much the same. Dorothy Wild stayed until 1723, but of course she may have had little choice about changing jobs. Her departure at this point was because she married on 4 November, 1723; married women were normally barred from being schoolmistresses. Strangely, there was a succession of singing masters in the 1720s – Matthew Richardson, George Simpson, Ralph Wilkinson and Edward Reed – and each of them also left after only a short spell. The financial situation, handled by one of the trustees, John Ord[1], as honorary treasurer, seems to have been quite satisfactory, with an average annual income from the three Wallsend tenants of £79 6s.

In 1718 the parishioners of St Nicholas's Church decided upon an annual subscription for clothing the pupils. The new clothes were given on 1 May each year, and consisted of footwear and uniform including a coat and breeches for the boys and a gown for the girls. This basic provision was later improved, with further footwear and outer clothing. The uniform was to change little throughout the hundred and fifty years as a church charity school, and was similar to that of the other charity schools.

It seems that from their foundation the four charity schools joined the boys of the grammar school in a weekly sermon on the catechism "who are examined in their turns". If, however, a holy day fell during the week, they would attend that service instead, and during Advent and Lent the lectures were also suspended. There was a rotation of speakers – the Vicar of Newcastle, the Morning Lecturer of All Hallows (viz., All Saints), the Lecturer of St John's and the Lecturer of St Andrew's.

The first additional endowment came via legal documents dated 16 and 17 November, 1722, when Thomas and Elizabeth Bates conveyed for £500 to Thomas Blenkinsop and his heirs "a messuage and tenement with the appurtenances on the west side of a street in Newcastle called The Side, near Kail Cross, and extending from the streets to the walls of the Half Moon or High Castle Moat". Part of the rent of this property was to be paid to the trustees of St Nicholas's Charity School; this amounted to £5 each quarter. It was for "the better support, maintenance and education of the poor children there to be taught."[2]

---

[1] He also endowed St John's Charity School in 1705, though this was not known until after his death. He had been executor to the Allans, and trustee of the first charity school since 1705/6. He died in 1721, and his executors continued as honorary treasurers until 1722.
[2] Further Report of the Commissioners for Inquiring Concerning Charities, 1831-32

Parish Church of St Nicholas. The Allans were buried here, and pupils have attended services here for three centuries. 18th Century view

Further benefactors soon followed. In 1723, Gilbert Campel, an innkeeper, left £20 in his will, and Samuel Nichols, organist at St Nicholas's from 1687 to 1719, left £10, both sums being invested and the interest paid to the trustees. Several years later, Mrs Mary Chisholm, the widow of the Revd John Chisholm, vicar of Wooler (1695-1725) paid £500 to the Corporation of Newcastle to receive the interest herself until her death, when it would "go to the use of this School for ever". Mr Chisholm had himself given church plate, including a silver paten, to Wooler Church in 1722, and his widow was later, in 1763, to give £100 to endow a schoolmaster in Wooler. She died in July, 1769, and presumably her endowment took effect from that date. Mrs Elizabeth Rogers[3] also left £50 by her will dated 15 December, 1733, and that too is likely to have been entrusted to Newcastle Corporation. In 1738 John Hewit or Hewett, a prosperous goldsmith of Newcastle, left £250 to each of the four charity schools, specifically to increase the numbers of pupils. Hewit was also known as Huet, and it was claimed that he was a near relation of the great French scholar, Pierre Daniel Huet.[4]

The second mistress to be appointed, in 1723, was a Mrs Ramsay. The term "Mrs" did not at that time imply she was married: it was simply a politeness. She was succeeded in 1729 by a Mrs Rodham, and she in turn by Mrs Hannah Hall in 1738. She left in 1743 and was followed by Mrs Elliott. They all were almost certainly unmarried.

The subscriptions by members of the congregation of St Nicholas's for clothing the pupils were clearly immensely helpful in keeping them neat and tidy. John Cowling, the treasurer, reported that in 1735 he received the sum of £111 16s 4d from this source. This was considerably more than the income the Schools received for all their purposes. Indeed, in that same year Thomas Swan became tenant of the Wallsend farm, and paid an annual rent of £80. From that the trustees had to set aside money to pay the Dean and Chapter of Durham every fourth year. A cynic might observe that the children were required to attend church on Sunday and Holy Days in full view of the congregation, but their education was less visible.

---

[3]Mrs Elizabeth Rogers, daughter of Benjamin Ellison, married John Rogers at Lanchester in 1684. John died in 1709 and she in April, 1733, when her endowment passed to the Schools. The family wealth came from land, property and mineral rights. We know no particular reason why she left money to the Schools.
[4]Bishop Huet of Avranches (1630-1721), theologian, philosopher, mathematician, astronomer, chemist, anatomist, linguist, classicist: one of the great scholars of the day.

Nevertheless it is recorded that in 1741 the pupils were examined by paid (and independent?) examiners for the first time. The two examiners were paid 6d each for their labours, and it seems that future examiners, even as late as 1776, were paid no more.

It was in houses in The Side, such as these still existing c1890, that the Allans seem to have lived. Similar property was to provide an annuity to endow the Schools in 1722

In 1744 Samuel Mowbray left after thirty-two years as master. After the quick departure of the first two masters, his long reign must have had a steadying influence and contributed to the success of the Schools. We do not know if the mistress who left the year before, Mrs Hall, was related to the new master, Mr Hall. The third member of staff was the singing master. We have noted that it seemed difficult to keep them for any length of time, though James Ainsley, appointed in 1746, served until his death in 1753, and his successor, Thomas Wilkinson, taught until 1760. For the next half-century until 1814, there is no record of payments for a singing master, and other arrangements must have been made, possibly in connexion with St Nicholas's Church.

You may recall that the salaries of the master and the mistress had been fixed by Eleanor Allan's will as "not exceeding" £20 to the master and £10 to the mistress. Mrs Elliott (1743-54) was paid £12 a year, but her successor, Mrs Bulman, received only £8 10s in her first year, raised to £9 thereafter, while the master received £30, a sizeable increase. Whether this reflected the numbers in each School, as it had in 1709, we do not know. Balancing the books cannot have been easy for the trustees.

We saw that in 1735 the income from subscriptions to clothe the pupils was nearly £112, but in 1758 the income had dropped to £18 1s. Each year there was a charity sermon in St Nicholas's, and this brought a small sum. Ralph Jackson, who was an apprentice hostman, recorded in his diary on 12 May, 1751, "In the afternoon I went to St Nicholas to hear Mr Docory Preach the Charity Sermon for the benefit of the Boys of that Parish".

The sermon on 21 May, 1758, preached by the Revd Wilson Bewicke, realised £7 10s 6d. When pupils left the Schools, their employers were paid £2 for each boy and £1 for each girl. The boys largely went as apprentices and the girls into service. One unusual variant on this is recorded for 1760, when a boy named "Valentine Reavley became a schoolmaster, being unfit to be put as an apprentice because of lameness". The £2 was paid to the master, and one must assume that young Valentine therefore taught at the School, if only until he had learned the necessary skills to teach elsewhere. If so, this was a thoughtful Christian resolution of his problem of finding employment, as well as the earliest recorded example of an assistant teacher.

Mrs Bulman died in 1760 and was succeeded by a Mrs Brown. She supplemented her income by making clothes for the girls, but unfortunately she seems to have appropriated some of the cloth for her own use, and was dismissed. The trustees, requiring a replacement quickly, advertised the post publicly in 1766 and Mrs Keenlyside was appointed.

An unusual tenant at Wallsend was Alderman Aubone Surtees, who for many years rented a cottage for £1 a year. He was Mayor of Newcastle in 1761 and 1770 and was thus well acquainted with the Schools as a trustee, since he examined their accounts in both years. He was later to endow the school, but was already a benefactor who gave an annual subscription to the Schools. Other frequent subscribers included Sir Matthew White Ridley, the Revd Mr Lushington, the Revd H. Ridley, Miss Hindmarsh, Mrs Smith, Mr Bell, Mr Williams, Mr Cookson, Mr Lawton and Mr Peareth, who was perhaps the grandfather or uncle of a future benefactress, Mrs Dorothy Duane. Another benefactor was John Fenwick who gave £20 to the Corporation to yield the standard 5%, viz £1, payable to the Schools annually. A like sum was also given to the prisoners in New Gate, both "to be made seven days before Christmas for ever".

The Schools' financial situation seems to have been good at this point and the number of girls rose from twenty to thirty, and Mrs Keenlyside's salary was raised to £16 and later to £20. She stayed for eighteen years – until 1784 – and was clearly appreciated. Meanwhile in 1775, Mr Hall, who had been master for thirty-one years, died in office. Thus the Boys' School had had only two masters in sixty-three years, which must have produced great stability. Since it would have been easy to sack a master who produced poor results, the trustees must have had confidence in the abilities of both men. It is probable that after Hall's death the post of master was held briefly by William Umfraville, later to be keeper of the Poor House before his own death in 1789. Again, needing a new master quickly, the trustees advertised, and appointed Anthony Charlton. They also at about this time decided that children should be admitted between the ages of eight and ten, and must leave on reaching their fourteenth birthday. Whitehead's Directory for 1778 indicates that despite the unsalubrious setting there were by now several schools in the Fleshmarket.

Receipt for £40, being two years' annuity payable by occupier of property in The Side to Allan trustees

Mrs White became mistress in 1784, and the next year Anthony Charlton resigned and Ralph Dees was appointed master. He was the first teacher about whom we have recorded comments. He was a man of energy and scholarship. Earlier, in 1774, the Association of Protestant Schoolmasters in the North of England had been set up under the patronage of the Duke of Northumberland. Its purpose was to provide assistance to indigent schoolmasters, their widows and children, and Ralph Dees was for over thirty years its secretary and prominent in its activities, for which he was paid two guineas (£2 2s) a year.

Corporation Sunday 1771. Pupils were required to attend major services at St Nicholas's; the girls are shown bottom right. Oil painting by Wilson Hepple, c1880, now hanging in the dining hall.

In 1786, the Corporation gave the trustees a site in Manor Chare in the parish or chapelry of All Saints for a new school building. We do not know the reason for the new building, just as we know nothing of the earlier building or indeed buildings. The new school was erected by a Mr Stephenson, for which he was paid £350 and a subsidiary payment of £34 13s 10d. Baillie, writing in 1801, said, "It has a fine front towards the street, well lighted and aired, having more the appearance of the dwelling house of some wealthy family then that of a seminary for charity children. The more credit is due on that account to the worthy patrons of the institution." The building not only included the schoolrooms, probably, as later, one above the other, but also dwelling rooms for the master and the mistress. There is no evidence of how money was raised to pay for such a building: it is highly unlikely that it could have been entirely paid for from income or accumulated capital, and no doubt donations were sought. Nevertheless, within three years the Schools were in deficit.

Mrs White resigned in 1791 and her successor was Mrs Henzell Usher, who was to remain mistress for twenty-six years until her death. In 1791 the interest of £2 10s from the gift of £50 from Alderman Surtees, already a benefactor, was paid by the Corporation for the first time. This was specifically for one child, chosen by the Mayor, to be placed in the Schools. However, the Schools were in financial difficulties, with deficits from 1789 until, in 1793, the trustees were compelled to reduce the number of pupils to thirty boys and thirty girls. Two years later the trustees felt the need to establish clearly who were entitled, by the terms of the original foundation, to be trustees, and they consulted Mr Hopper Williamson, the Recorder, and Sir William Scott, a leading jurist, later Lord Stowell. These gentlemen decided that in addition to the Afternoon Lecturer at All Saints, as previously, the Morning Lecturer should be a trustee. In 1798, a further reduction in numbers to twenty in each School was deemed necessary.

At this difficult moment came a useful bequest from Mrs Dorothy Duane (née Peareth). Mrs Duane (or Delane) was the daughter of Thomas Dawson and Barbara Peareth, and the widow of Matthew Duane. She died at her home in Bedford Row, Middlesex, on 11 April, 1799, aged 77, but her body was brought back to Newcastle for burial in St. George's Porch of St Nicholas's Church beside her husband. Matthew Duane, F.R.S., F.S.A., was a solicitor by profession, but a distinguished numismatist (early Greek coins in particular) and antiquary. He was a trustee of the British Museum, to which he made numerous gifts. By a codicil to her will, dated 24 July, 1798, she left £200 to the trustees of "the free school for girls … The interest to be applied to the extension of the laudable designs of the said charity." This has been said to enable St.

Monument in Newcastle Cathedral to Matthew and Dorothy Duane. 1799

Nicholas's Schools to match the addition to girls' numbers at St Andrew's. It was, however, a strange moment for such a decision - though perhaps it had been made earlier - since for the first time since the foundation girls' numbers exactly matched the boys'. Dorothy Duane is likely to have been well-educated herself, and shared Eleanor Allan's wish to see the girls as well educated as the boys. She is the only benefactor for the one school rather than both. That she also raised a monument to her mother and her aunt indicates a desire to recognise the contribution of women to society. The £10 a year of additional income must have been very helpful, and two years later, in 1801, the number of pupils returned to thirty in each School. Having weathered the storm, the Revd H. Ridley, treasurer since 1786, retired. He had charged £1 a year for his trouble and expense, and then returned it as a subscription. The next year five boys and five girls were added, and two more of each in 1804. The master and the mistress also shared in the returning prosperity, with annual gratuities in addition to their salaries. Irregular attendance was a problem in all charity schools because children were often wanted at home to do jobs. In 1807 it is recorded that one girl was expelled and three others cautioned for this.

In 1807, Ralph Dees resigned to become master of All Saints' Charity School. We do not know the reason for this, but it could have been because the All Saints' School was more prosperous. When Dees died in 1828, after forty-two years at the two schools, he was described as "highly respected … An unassuming and upright man, an excellent penman and a good teacher." He was buried in St John's Churchyard with members of his family; the gravestone no longer exists. His successor at St Nicholas's School, Thomas Charlton, was also an active member of the Association of Protestant Schoolmasters. The following year the trustees gave prizes for the first time; they were for good writing and 6s was spent on them, but we do not know in what form they were given. In 1810, King George III celebrated his golden jubilee, and there were extensive celebrations throughout the country, and "a number of gentlemen" provided a special dinner for the children.

There continued to be an annual service in St Nicholas's Church, when a collection was made for the benefit of their school. The service in 1811 contained a sermon by the curate of St. Andrew's, the Revd Henry Griffith, and the collection realised the highest sum ever raised. Extraordinarily there is a record of the details of this collection:

	£	s	d
3 Twenty Shilling notes	3	0	0
1 Guinea	1	1	0
2 Half guineas	1	1	0
3 Seven shilling pieces (viz, third guineas)	1	1	0
5 Dollars	1	7	6
35 Half crowns	4	7	6
228 Shillings	11	8	0
172 Sixpences	4	6	0
140 Penny pieces		11	8
263 Half pence		10	11$^{1}/_{2}$
	£28	14	7$^{1}/_{2}$

This is a strange array of monetary units and of considerable numismatic interest, for example, a countermarked dollar was current for 4s 9d and a restruck dollar was 5s, but these are valued at 5s 6d[5]

In the same year the Revd John Smith, Vicar of Newcastle, was engaged in a tax battle on behalf of the Schools. He wrote in an account book about a receipt: "Property tax for the year ending April 5th, 1811, on the farm at Wall's End (sic), at length and after the gratuitous officiousness of the Tax Office and the oppressions of the Treasury, recovered for Saint Nicholas' Charity School £14 12s 0d." Again below: "Do Do for the year ending April 5th, 1812, Do Do £14 12s 0d" Two centuries later there is something oddly familiar about this.

[5]Dollars were captured Spanish American 8 reales, reused as British coins either with a small head of George III stamped on top of the Spanish king's head, or re-pressed with a British design covering the original Spanish design. The coins also reflect the twenty years of war against France, and it was not until after peace finally came in 1815 that the long overdue reform of the coinage could be considered and carried out.

Singing was restored as a school subject in 1814, but it seems that the new teacher, a Mr Bolam, was to instruct only on psalms. He was paid £10 a year for this, and in the first year 13s 21/2d was spent on candles for this purpose. He appears not to have attended regularly, and the trustees soon replaced him with a Mr Spark. In the following year new rules were introduced into the girls' school concerning ages of entry and departure. Pupils were henceforth to be admitted between the ages of nine and eleven, and had to leave on their fifteenth birthdays. A further development, applying to both schools, was instituted by the trustees. They resolved that "sand, clay and brushes be provided at the expense of the schools for the use of the schools, and that pens and ink be provided to such children as learn to write". The former materials could only be for instruction in art.

Meanwhile the clothing provided for the children each midsummer is listed as follows. The girls received a dark brown gown, caps, apron, tippets, two pairs of stockings, two pairs of shoes and underclothing. The boys were given a dark grey coat, a waistcoat, a cap, a pair of leather breeches, two shirts and bands, two pairs of stockings and two pairs of shoes. No doubt there were some informal arrangements if a pupil outgrew his or her clothing during the year.

Mrs Henzell Usher, mistress since 1791, died in 1817, aged 57, and her post was advertised. It read:

> Wanted, a Mistress for Saint Nicholas Girls Charity School Newcastle upon Tyne; salary
> £24 per annum; together with a sufficient allowance for coals and with apartments Rent
> and Tax free. No Perquisites whatsoever allowed to the Mistress.
> Women, Members of the established Church, free from the
> Burthen of Children and Care of a Family, not above Forty Years
> of age and of healthy constitution and who can produce as to the
> *above Points* and as to the *General Propriety of their Character*
> UNDENIABLE TESTIMONIALS may apply for further information concerning this
> situation to Mr Charlton, St Nicholas Charity Schools,
> Manor Chare on or before the 27th of July.

The phrase "free from the Burthen of Children and Care of a Family" might have been inspired by Mrs Usher's married state, which the trustees seemed to feel had caused problems. She was already married when she was appointed, and had had a daughter in 1804, which must have created inconvenience to trustees and school. Mrs Margaret Baxter must have satisfied the trustees on all of this, for she was appointed mistress, and remained for over seventeen years.

Although the Schools had been in their premises in Manor Chare only since 1786, their development seems to have been causing overcrowding and restricting growth. In 1819 there were 37 boys and 37 girls. Suddenly an opportunity arose for better things.

Parish church or chapelry of St John. Although it had its own school, children from this parish could also attend the Allan foundation school.

Chapter Three

AT THE CLERGY JUBILEE SCHOOL, 1821-1861

Monument of the Rt Revd Shute Barrington, Prince Bishop of Durham for 35 years until his death, aged 91, in 1826. Sculptor Sir Francis Chantrey. Durham Cathedral

Mitre and coronet of Shute Barrington, penultimate Prince-Bishop, from his monument

Arms of Bishop Shute Barrington, from his monument

In 1819, Bishop Shute Barrington of Durham celebrated the fiftieth anniversary of his elevation to the episcopacy in 1769 as Bishop of Llandaff. He had been translated to Salisbury in 1782 and to Durham in 1791. He was a remarkable man, a vigorous defender of Protestantism and opposed to Roman Catholic political power but one who otherwise sought toleration and was personally hospitable to their bishops and clergy who had fled France at the Revolution. Throughout his life he showed concern for the poor and especially the education of their children, and the clergy of the diocese, which then included Newcastle and Northumberland, decided to mark his jubilee by the erection, in the rapidly growing town of Newcastle, of a school to be known as the Clergy Jubilee School.

The Corporation gave a site on part of the King's Dykes immediately outside the line of the demolished town walls on the east side of the Carliol Croft (Carliol Square), and bought extra land for 100 guineas (£105) from

P.G. Ellison. The site was to accommodate the schoolhouse, two playgrounds and eventually two houses, one for the master and the other for the mistress. The great Newcastle architect John Dobson (1787-1865) was employed to design it and supervise the construction. Work began in July, 1819, and was largely finished in August the following year. Mackenzie (1827) is critical of the schoolhouse: "a plain, unornamental stone building, without even an inscription to explain the cause and purpose of its erection". It had cost the not inconsiderable sum of £2300, but this had proved insufficient "to carry the original purpose of the subscribers into effect".

The building stood empty for some months until the Vicar of Newcastle, the Revd John Smith[1], supported by the other trustees of St Nicholas's Charity School and with the agreement of the trustees of the Clergy Jubilee School, after legal advice, moved the St Nicholas pupils into the new building. He and three other trustees, the Revd Edward Moises, the Revd J. Parkin and the Revd H.G. Griffith, were present on 1 October, 1821, when the school was opened. The trustees paid the trustees of the building a nominal rent of 2s 6d a year, and the Corporation a similar sum for the site; the latter was also paid 5s a year for the sites of the residences to be built for the master and mistress when funds were available. They had not been built a decade later when the Charity Commissioners reported, and the master and mistress continued to live rent free each in part of the old schoolhouse in Manor Chare. At some point thereafter houses were made available in Carliol Square, for the house in Manor Chare was sold by the trustees in 1850. John Brockbank was recorded as living at 15 Carliol Square in 1855, and Miss Reed at 14 Carliol Square. The trustees of the building, viz, the Clergy Jubilee School, had no influence on the workings of the charity schools. Thus the name of the School and the name of the building were, most unusually, different. There were two drawbacks to the new situation: the Schools no longer owned their own premises and the building was located outside the parishes that they served. Both were problems at a later date.

When the Schools moved in, the trustees installed an additional chimney (£50) and spent £300 on furniture and equipment. By 1828 a further £146 was spent in improving the building. Of this the trustees paid £37 out of the funds of the charity, the Revd William Nicholas Darnell (1776-1865)[2] gave 50 guineas (£52 10s), the trustees of Lord Crewe's Charity[3] gave

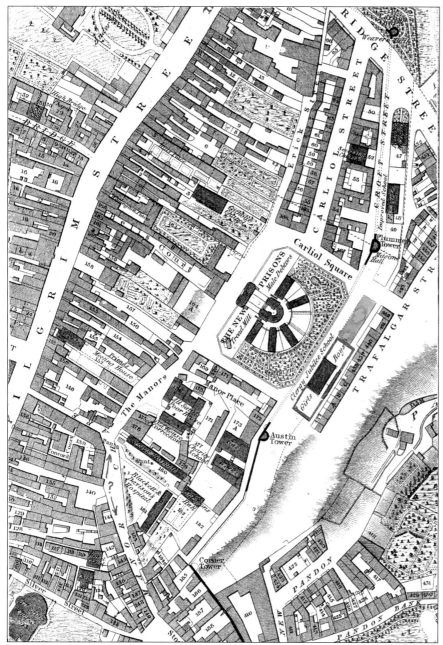

St Nichols's Charity Schools were housed from 1821 to 1861 in the Clergy Jubilee School building in Carliol Square on the site of the ditch of the Town Wall, which had been dismantled between the Austin Tower and the Plummer Tower. (From Thomas Oliver's map, 1831) Green area indicates site rented for future erection of houses for master and mistress. The Schools were in Manor Chase (bottom left) from 1786 to 1821; the exact location is not known

[1] John Smith, vicar from 1804 to 1826, was an experienced schoolmaster, having taught for seventeen years, immediately prior to his Newcastle appointment, at Westminster School, then as now one of the leading schools in the country.

£20, and the Venerable Thomas Singleton, Archdeacon of Northumberland[4], gave £10. The Very Revd Henry Phillpotts, Dean of Chester[5], gave 100 guineas (£105), of which £27 was used in the improvements, £50 was invested through the Corporation of Newcastle and £28 deposited in a local bank. All were men who wished to honour Bishop Barrington.

At the time of the move the trustees made a major change to the constitution of the Schools. Hitherto pupils had been drawn only from the parishes of St Nicholas and St John, but in future pupils could come from any part of the town on payment of one penny a week except for orphans and the children of widows. Mackenzie heartily approved of this payment:

"This is an excellent regulation. The boys attending the Royal Jubilee School and the girls attending the Royal Improved School are educated *gratuitously*. This must tend to blunt the delicate pride of both parents and children, to familiarise the mind to dependence on charitable institutions and to prepare it for the degradation of pauperism. The demanding a small weekly sum from the parents is evidently gratifying to their feelings; for although this school be at some distance from a populous neighbourhood, though the roads to it be broken and miry, though there are very few amusing movements in the school, and though the scholars are not cheered by the approbation of a variety of patrons and visitors, yet the opportunities for admission are now always seized with eagerness." Over the first six months after the move, there were on average 215 boys and 78 girls plus the foundation scholars (40 + 30); see below for numbers only five years later.

St Nicholas's Charity School occupied this building from 1821 to 1861. Architect John Dobson

[2]William Darnell, a Newcastle man, was at the time a canon of Durham and vicar of Norham. Darnell was a theologian and antiquary, and formerly a fellow of Corpus Christi College, Oxford

[3]Baron Crewe of Stene, Bishop of Durham from 1674 to 1722, left valuable estates for charitable purposes, of which this is typical. William Darnell was a trustee.

[4]Thomas Singleton (1783-1842) was tutor at Cambridge to the future 3rd Duke of Northumberland and was later the duke's secretary before starting his ministry.

[5]Henry Phillpotts (1778-1869) was later Bishop of Exeter, but retained his canonry of Durham to the end of his life, regularly taking his turn in residence. He was a man of fierce controversy but great generosity, one of the most remarkable bishops of the century.

Oliver (1844) gives a detailed account of the building. The boys occupied the ground floor, with a schoolroom 70 feet long, 38 feet wide and 22 feet high. Mackenzie had said 80 by 40, with a ceiling "so high as to occasion a very inconvenient echo"; the ceiling was supported by eight iron columns. At the south end was a platform for the master, and a gallery was situated above this. The room was entered from a playground on the north side. The girls' schoolroom was 58 feet long, 38 feet wide and 12 feet high. Unfortunately funds had not allowed for a ceiling and the room was open to the roof, and was "necessarily exposed to too great a variety of temperature". There was a bench or tables round the walls 96 feet long; and the girls sat on moveable forms. They entered from their playground on the south side via a staircase. There were also two small rooms, one described as a committee room.

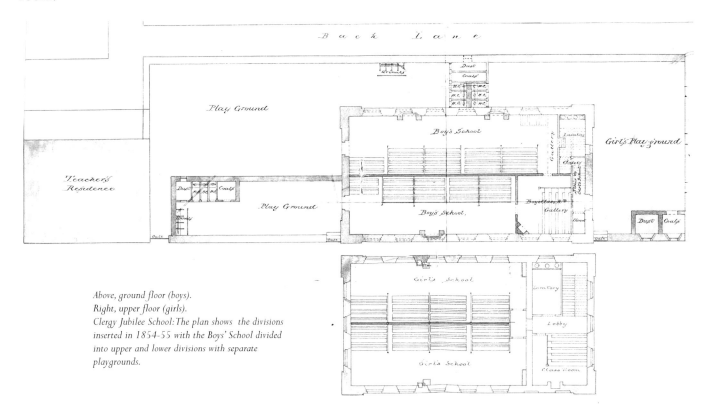

Above, ground floor (boys).
Right, upper floor (girls).
Clergy Jubilee School: The plan shows the divisions inserted in 1854-55 with the Boys' School divided into upper and lower divisions with separate playgrounds.

Mackenzie (1827) took 16 November, 1826, as a sample day, and recorded 425 boys on the books, of whom 32 were reported absent and 14 sick. Over the previous two years about 400 scholars on average attended "which are as many as the schoolroom can accommodate." How this number could indeed have been accommodated, never mind educated, is difficult to understand. Mackenzie praises the master, Mr Thomas Charlton, for "the attention, skill and ability with which he discharges the arduous duties of his office". The girls' school on the same day had 134 pupils on the books, of whom 30 were absent and three sick. Apparently this number of absentees was not uncommon: "their attendance is usually very irregular." No doubt girls were often kept at home to look after younger siblings or to do household chores.

Clearly the master and the mistress could not have taught numbers such as these unaided. Before the move into the Clergy Jubilee School, the master, Thomas Charlton, and the mistress, Mrs Margaret Baxter, went to the Barrington School at Bishop Auckland to learn "the improved system of Dr Bell". Dr Andrew Bell, a Scot and a priest of the Church of England, had devised a scheme while at an orphan school in Madras, India, in which, to overcome the shortage of teachers, the better pupils instructed the less able. He published *An Experiment in Education* in 1797, and within a few years his system was taken up by others. In 1811 he became superintendent of *The National Society for Promoting the Education of the Poor in the Principles of the Established Church* to promote his schemes. Older able pupils were to learn their lessons from the teacher and hand them on to the younger children: this was called 'the monitorial system'. It was to evolve after 1840 into a movement to replace monitors with pupil-teachers. The pupil-teachers were children who were apprenticed for five years from the age of thirteen both to continue their own education and to learn to teach. In the 1840s the monitors or perhaps pupil-teachers of the Boys' School were paid 1/- a week plus £3 7s 2d a year; presumably there were girls doing the same job, and these were no doubt paid at a lower rate.

The boys were taught, "according to Dr Bell's system with some modifications, reading, spelling, writing and arithmetic, and some of the boys in the first class learn book-keeping, the elements of geometry and mensuration[6]. About 250 scholars are at present learning to write on paper[7]. The teachers (i.e. the monitors) who are mostly boys belonging to the free school, are instructed by the master in the mornings and evenings. The vacancies in the old foundation (of forty scholars) are filled up by the trustees from a list of boys whom the master and teachers select, half-yearly, at May and at Christmas, for their good behaviour, rapid progress and regular attendance at school and at church. All the boys appear remarkably healthy and clean; and in warm weather, a hairdresser attends every week to cut their hair, and also occasionally in winter."

Mackenzie reported that the mistress taught writing and arithmetic, but this is surely not all, for it is less than in Dorothy Wild's day. Reading, knitting and sewing must certainly have been done, and both Schools would have had religious instruction from one of the clergy trustees. The trustees indeed visited the schools alternately every week.

Mackenzie regarded the master's £80 salary plus house and coal as "certainly not too much". The Mistress's £40 plus house and coal pass without comment, but clearly she had a much easier job. However, her salary was raised to £50 by 1830. He observed how the income for the Schools fluctuated according to the price of corn, since the rent of the Wallsend farm was determined by that. In 1826 this was £260. The rest of the year's income came from the rent of the property in The Side (£20), interest from £1000 in the "town hutch" (£40) and of £330 "in funds" (£17.10s), Fenwick and Surtees' money (£3 10s), and pennies from boys (£63) and girls, including sale of their work (£20). The total was £424, from which over £80 a year had to be paid to the Dean and Chapter of Durham for the farm lease and £120 to the master and mistress in salaries. That left £224 to cover repairs to the farm buildings, the teachers' residences in Manor Chare and the school building, as well as coal, candles, books, slates, paper, ink, pens, furniture and all the other necessaries of a school – including the hairdresser. In addition the foundation scholars received clothing, and on leaving, three books and further clothing.

The haircutting is an unusual element: we do not know if any similar arrangement was made for the girls, nor do we know the cost since it was never itemised. In 1823 we find "incidental charges, haircutting, chimney sweeping, etc., £1 11s 7d." while two years later for the same services, it was £3 4s 4d. In 1826 coals and haircutting came to £8 15s. One cannot imagine that at such prices hair styling was more than in its infancy. Nevertheless it shows a concern for pupils' welfare that we do not always expect at this date. Other payments recorded at this period are for a man to attend to the school clocks (two were bought new as part of the original equipment, one for each schoolroom) and for another man one guinea a year "for attending the boys in St Nicholas Church", presumably to keep them in good order.

The Revd John Smith died on 22 January, 1826, and the pupils attended his funeral, the girls' dresses trimmed with a crepe rosette and the boys with a similar rosette on the left arm; hats were trimmed with crepe. He was highly regarded in Newcastle, and seems to have cared about the charity school. He left the tidy sum of £75 4s 3$^1/_4$ d to the funds of the foundation. Two years later Ralph Dees died at the age of 72; as we saw above, he had been master of St Nicholas's School and then All Saints' School for a total of forty-two years.

When the Schools opened, it was intended that a bust of Bishop Barrington should stand in the boys' schoolroom, but Mackenzie found it was still in its box and covered in dust. In 1828 it was apparently *painted* by Messrs Richardson of St Nicholas's Churchyard at a cost of 3/-, and presumably erected as intended. We have no idea of its subsequent fate.

Since the early Eighteenth Century there had been annual subscribers to school funds, but these had declined and by 1831 there was only one left, Sir Matthew White Ridley. In that year he gave fourteen guineas, presumably to cover the previous seven years, since he continued to give two guineas per annum for some years afterwards. Another source of income was provided by the girls themselves when their needlework and so on was sold; in

[6]Mackenzie regrets the failure to teach English grammar, the most obvious defect in these new systems.
[7]As distinct from a slate.

one year it yielded £13.

In 1834, Mrs Margaret Baxter, who had been mistress for over seventeen years, fell ill, and was unable to continue her job. She was retired with an annual pension of £15. This is the earliest reference to such an allowance for a retired teacher, though some informal or unrecorded arrangements might well have been made for others. The vacancy was advertised in *The Courant*, and another local paper, and the trustees appointed Mrs Ann Waters. The trustees simultaneously decided to form a ladies' committee "for the purpose of visiting the girls' school". They could not as yet bring themselves to co-opt a woman or two to help them with a decision such as they had just made – that had to wait until the next century – but it seemed at least a tentative step in the right direction. We have, however, no record of what they did. In 1837, Victoria was to become queen, and in 1838 a local woman, Grace Darling, thrilled the country by her heroism – but this was still 1834. The governors also decided that in future no child should be placed on the Foundation whose parents or guardians were not bona fide members of the Church of England. This of course did not exclude such children from the Schools as such.

The Corporation of Newcastle voted the sum of two guineas per annum to the Schools' funds. Exactly what that would buy is demonstrated by a contract the Boys' School had with a tradesman to supply uniforms for foundationers. The blue cloth jacket and waistcoat, together with cord trousers, cost 13s 6d, a matching blue cap "trimmed" was 1s 4d, and a yard-wide blue serge "mantle" or cloak was 2s 3d., viz, 17s 1d. In addition shirts and socks (made by the girls) and boots were needed.

Ann Waters resigned after only one year: perhaps the ladies' committee had visited too often. She was succeeded in January, 1836, by Margaret Hownam, who had been running a small private school for some years in the Carpenters' Tower on the town walls.

John Findley, Head master of St Nicholas's Charity School, 1838-47

In February, 1836, the last Prince Bishop of Durham, William Van Mildert, died, and the Palatinate of Durham came to an end. To us, his great work was the foundation of the University of Durham, endowed out of the revenues of the cathedral and housed in his castle. Many Old Allanians are grateful for his foresight. His successor, the Rt Revd Edward Maltby, MA, DD, FRS, FSA, carried out visitations to parts of his diocese, and from 10 to 13 November was in Newcastle, the largest town. He visited the Schools in the building commemorating Van Mildert's predecessor, and "expressed his entire approbation of them, and directed that a boy who was barefoot should receive shoes and stockings at his expense."

In 1837 Thomas Charlton died and the trustees appointed John Findley on 8 February, 1838. They also directed him and Margaret Hownam to make sure that the rule of the National Society for Promoting Christian Knowledge should be complied with. This rule was that on Sundays each child should attend his or her parish church. This would seem to exclude nonconformists and others, but we do not know how firmly this was actually applied. The work of the Society led to the establishment of many charity schools across the country, as it had in the early Eighteenth Century.

There is little firm evidence of school holidays besides the four weeks' summer holiday, but clearly at the major festivals of Christmas and Easter there were significant breaks. Others, such as occasional days to celebrate national, local and school events, would certainly have taken place. One such was the coronation of Queen Victoria on 28 June, 1838, which aroused great public rejoicing throughout the country. The children of St Nicholas's Charity School were treated to a celebratory meal. "The Bishop of Durham stood on one side near me," wrote the Queen in her diary that evening; some of the children no doubt recalled the kindly Dr Maltby who had visited their school some eighteen months earlier.

There are occasional glimpses of a world not so different from our own: one poor boy broke some windows in 1839, and the trustees sent father a bill for 5s – no mean sum in those days. The balance of subscriptions from the Bishop Barrington jubilee was received, but it is not clear to whom it was paid. The sum properly belonged to the Clergy Jubilee Trust, not to the St. Nicholas's Charity School Trust. The latter had already carried out work at its own expense, and was to do so again. Meanwhile the trustees maintained investment in $3^1/_2$ % stocks, holding them to the value of almost £820, yielding nearly £29 per annum for school funds. We do not know exactly how the buildings were cleaned, but there is record of payment to boys of 13/- for sweeping; whether this was inside or in the playgrounds, or both, we have no evidence.

A significant development in the Girls' School in 1839 was the creation of a small library; some books were supplied by SPCK in London and were probably of an improving nature. Still, nothing else was available at that date, and it was at least a start. Meanwhile the number of girls on the Foundation, which had fallen to only thirteen, was restored to the more appropriate level of thirty.

At this point John Findley resigned. There is no reason known for this, since the trustees, while accepting his resignation and writing to the London Central School for a replacement, offered that he should stay in office until after Christmas if he wished and expressed their "entire satisfaction at the undeviating attention and ability of Mr Findley". However, Findley withdrew his resignation and they re-appointed him. Shortly afterwards he was given an allowance "because he had given up housekeeping and gone into lodgings".

The success of the coronation meal was perhaps the inspiration behind the institution of an annual treat in the summer of 1841. The pupils were taken behind one of Mr Stephenson's steam locomotives to pleasant and interesting venues – Tynemouth, Durham and Alnwick amongst them. They were fed and played games and no doubt looked at the historic sights. Later a Christmas treat was also provided, with buns (£2 12s 4d), oranges (£1 2s), ginger beer (£1 3s 5d), wax tapers (8s 9d), sundries (£1 5s) and music (2s) – a total of £6 13s 6d. In another year we learn the quantities involved: 600 buns, a box of oranges and 192 bottles of ginger beer. These are not spectacular occasions but no doubt they were enjoyed and were steps on the way to seeing the Schools as communities and not merely educational machines. Mr Gradgrind and Mr M'Choakumchild would have been much distressed.

In 1844 Margaret Howman died and was replaced by Mrs Findley. It seems obvious that she was John Findley's wife, particularly as no expense is noted for advertising the post, but there is no proof of this. She does seem to have been married, however, since both her predecessor and successor were described at "Miss"; the old convention has changed. At this time John Findley had an assistant, John Stokoe. The assistant (pupil) teachers were paid 1/- a week, but Stokoe was clearly an old pupil and was paid 4/- a week. He must have been quickly valued, since his pay was raised several times until it became 7/- within a few months. He was certainly needed.

In 1845 *The Newcastle Chronicle* recorded that the numbers in the School had risen to 370 boys and 111 girls, and only five years later they had grown to the extraordinary figure of 460 boys and 200 girls. How 660 pupils were accommodated in two schoolrooms 70 (58) feet by 38 feet, in particular the boys, is hard to comprehend. One imagines a level of discipline that would deeply shock the liberal-minded of the present day.

About 1844, the Schools bought a piano, and the office of singing master to both Schools was revived after a gap of half a century. The man chosen was William J.Ions, later Dr Ions, organist of St Nicholas's Church, 1834-57. His initial salary was only £5, but was gradually raised to £13, and an assistant singing master, Mr A. Wilson, was appointed in 1855. Later, the Schools also acquired an organ, but we know no details of it. Likewise we do not know if the curriculum was wider than psalm-singing, which is all it was in the previous century. Hymns are certainly a possibility, but secular songs are less likely.

In 1846, Mrs Findley left (a baby, perhaps?) and the next year John Findley finally resigned too. Rather curiously, but also rather movingly, seven years later he was presented by former pupils with a gold watch and silver chain, together with an address on parchment signed by the donors. Perhaps it marked some special event, or simply the boys had to wait until they had the money to pay for the present. Even then, the silver chain suggests they had insufficient money to make it a matching set. Mrs Findley was succeeded by Elizabeth Jeffreys Reed, who was born at Alnwick in 1818, and was thus twenty-eight years old. Findley was succeeded by Michael Wilson.

In 1851, the situation in Britain with regard to education for children between five and fifteen was very unsatisfactory: only half were receiving any education. As Middlebrook shows, in Newcastle the figure was about 43%. Of 18,520 children, only 7,853 were attending school. At this point the formidable figure of the Revd Clement Moody, Vicar of Newcastle 1853-71, stepped in with a proposal to construct ten new schools to accommodate 6000 pupils at an estimated cost of £20,000. It was known as the Ten School Scheme, and was approved and a governing committee was set up to achieve the target. In fact only two schools were built but St Nicholas's received a grant of £850. It is not clear how this windfall was used.

Wilson left in 1851 after only four years but the trustees presented him with a gift of £15 in recognition of his services. They appointed John Brockbank to succeed him, and also an assistant master, the latter at £10. Just over £5 was approved for an assistant mistress, but in fact within a short time there were two, Miss Pringle and Miss Laing. Since there were 210 girls, this was clearly necessary. Brockbank retired in 1854, again after only four years; this time the trustees' gift fell to £5.

Because of the size of the Boys' School (350 boys), the trustees decided to create an upper school and a lower school (as in the Royal Grammar School from 1823). William Henry Thorn was master of the upper school and Holland Eckersley of the lower. There were several assistant teachers to cope with the numbers. Henry Callard was well qualified and obviously competent: he had a teaching certificate (I.ii), and went on to be head master of St Nicholas's National School in Castle Garth. J. Wait taught drawing and a Mr Bliss taught singing. J. Bolam, at first a pupil teacher, became an assistant, and there was also a Miss M. Jopling. This decision was not a success, and Thorn moved to become master of Trinity House Navigation School. He was replaced by George Lake as master of the whole school and the trustees considered Eckersley's situation. There is no minute of their decision, but he clearly left. Eckersley was a scientist and he later took a science degree at London University with a view to teaching for the Kensington examinations. He was also ordained and became a head master in Ulverston. Perhaps the trustees should have appointed him instead of Lake.

In 1857, for the first time a salaried secretary is appointed, George Thirkeld Gibson, who for some years had audited the Schools' accounts. He was paid £10 per annum, and had his office at St Nicholas's Church.

The Charity Commissioners relate the conditions of entry: "The boys were admitted upon application to the master, with a recommendation from one of the trustees; they are required to be of the age of six years, and they are allowed to remain in the school till they attain the age of fourteen; each boy pays one penny a week. Forty of these boys are completely clothed (viz, by the trustees); of these one is appointed by the Mayor in respect of Aubone Surtees' benefaction, and one by Sir M. W. Ridley, on account of his subscription (two guineas a year; he was the last remaining subscriber). The others are appointed by the Vicar of Newcastle and the other trustees, in rotation, and are chosen according to merit, it being required that they should have been in the school at least two years. These are called free boys, and are excused from payment of the weekly pence.

"The girls are admitted in the same manner as the boys, and forty of them are appointed by the trustees to the freedom, and are clothed, the same regulations being observed as with respect to the selection of the boys." This selection, made after at least six terms, ensured fairness, and the system lasted into the next century. When a free girl left to go into service, she was given clothing to the value of £1 and copies of *The Bible*, *The Prayer Book* and *The Whole Duty of Man*. Free boys who were bound apprentices received clothing worth £2 and the same books. There were also prizes, and one such of which we have evidence is a cookery book of 1863, given to a girl soon after publication. It was a curious compilation of nearly four hundred recipes which "have been taught upwards of fifty years, with great reputation". The recipes were not only for food but also for medical purposes.

One is "a receipt for the bite of a mad dog, taken from the church of Calthorp in Lincolnshire, where almost the whole parish were bit, and they who used it recovered and inserted it in the London Magazine, 1746". It may have been Mrs Beeton's celebrated *The Book of Household Management* which had been originally published only two years earlier, and which is also much more than a cookery book.

An article by R Rallison in *The Evening Chronicle* in 1935 observed that "all records seem to have disappeared for the years 1830-60, and the history of what is now Dame Allan's is difficult to trace." Mr Rallison claimed that the future Dame Allan's moved a third time between 1827 and 1833, back to the old premises in Manor Chare, latterly the dwelling of the master and mistress. This is not so. Middlebrook says that it happened about 1860 and is quite right. At some point c.1850-55 it was resolved to transmute the Allan foundation into a trades school. In reality it was that already: it prepared children for work by equipping them with a sound basic education so that they would be good employees, literate and numerate. St Nicholas's Church had opened a National School, which was sometimes known as Castle Garth (National) School because of its location in Castle Street between the castle keep and Queen Street. It was the site of Castle Garth Chapel, the oldest dissenting meeting house in the town, and acquired for a Sunday School and rebuilt by St Nicholas's about 1835. It is clear from St Nicholas's service book that collections were frequently donated to that school and not to its former charity school, located as it was outside the parish. Kelly's Directory for 1858 describes the building in Carliol Square as "Clergy Jubilee Trades' School". The Allan foundation schools were legally only tenants of the Clergy Jubilee School Trust, and they were in danger of being swamped, with the original connexion with St Nicholas's and with Eleanor Allan being lost.

In January, 1860, the Charity Commissioners received an application to convert the Clergy Jubilee School to a parochial school for All Saints' parish, though indicating that the St Nicholas pupils should remain "until the Trustees of St Nicholas's Charity can erect a new school of their own". There were 170 boys and 95 girls.

The Charity Commission file in the National Archives (November 1860) observes that the building had been used "for the purposes of a Trades school and a Girls' school in which certain children educated out of the funds of a charity known as Allan's charity for boys and girls of the parishes of St Nicholas and St John have until lately been taught, but for these children a new arrangement has now been made". Under a scheme approved by Newcastle County Court on 20 December, 1860, the Clergy Jubilee School building was made into a National School for All Saints' parish, the education of Allan's Charity pupils to be continued as a temporary arrangement only. The Commissioners were quite clear that for the trustees of Allan's charity "the proper course appears to be to acquire a site in some central position in one of the parishes interested and to erect suitable buildings therein." The income of the charity, less expenditure, was about £200 per annum. In addition it owned the two teachers' houses and had a balance of £398. The commissioners recommended that the £1150 Corporation Bonds, yielding 4%, be sold and invested in the Funds; that the Wallsend estate be enfranchised, viz., become freehold, so that it could be let at a higher rate[8]; and that the sale of the shops and teachers' houses "may at some future time become expedient". The fluctuation of both income and expenditure was observed to be a problem and the accounts from 1854 to 1860 which survive in the National Archives, show this clearly.

In the summer of 1861, George Lake left. We do not know the reason for this, but he might well have tired of the struggle to keep the Allan Foundation intact.

[8]This was done in 1867

Chapter Four

ROSEMARY LANE AND HANOVER SQUARE:
CONTROVERSY, CHALLENGE AND CHANGE,
1861 - 1877

The years 1861 to 1883 marked a time of great upheaval for the schools. It was to prove a period of controversy, challenge and change. The controversy centred on the trust's finances with allegations of mismanagement and misspending. The challenge came from the unsatisfactory buildings the schools had been removed to in 1861. Finally, in 1877 and after much debate, there came a great change in the history of the schools: their reconstitution as future grammar schools and the consequent search for new premises. This chapter will deal with these three struggles.

Having left the Clergy Jubilee School buildings in October, 1861, the schools were opened in Rosemary Lane but controversy was already in the air. In July, the schools had reopened with a certificated master at the helm, William S Norris. He left after only three months as the school moved to Rosemary Lane. One can assume that he recognised these buildings as unsatisfactory and a temporary measure from the start. His successor was John Stubbs. He was not a certificated master, but was appointed to "raise the tone" of the schools, no doubt a necessity in the dismal buildings.

At this time the mistress remained Miss Elizabeth Read. She seems to have been a redoubtable figure and challenged the management of the schools as these changes were being planned. The trustees had intended to appoint a certificated mistress in 1861 but she wrote a letter protesting that the trustees were attempting to deprive her of her income and that she had to maintain her 81-year-old mother. She had already written to her councillor in 1860, complaining of mismanagement of the charity on the part of the Vicar of Newcastle, the Revd Clement Moody, and seeking the support of the Corporation. The Mayor undertook to investigate as a trustee but nothing is known to have come of this. Her tenacity bore fruit: she did not lose her house, 14 Carliol Square, and it continued to house her successor as mistress of the Girls' School. She had done well to keep it, as the master of the Boys' School had no house provided after 1861.

On 2 August, 1861, the Charity Commissioners wrote to the Mayor and other trustees about what they regarded as the unsatisfactory position of the Trust. When the schools were moved to the Clergy Jubilee School building, the old site in Manor Chare had eventually been sold in 1850 to the Newcastle and Berwick Railway Company for £600. This sum, together with accumulations of funds, had been used to buy £818 16s 5d stock. While the Schools occupied the new building, £450 was spent on alterations "to adapt it to the purpose of a trade school which was then established and subsequently maintained out of the funds of Allan's Charity". The Commissioners regarded this as an improper use of these funds since it was on premises the trustees did not own and was not for the benefit of the parishes of St Nicholas and St John, contrary to the wishes of the founder.

One of the trustees, the Revd John Reed, lecturer at St Nicholas's, who had already in November, 1860 registered his disapproval of Trust funds being spent on the building, wrote to the commissioners again in January, 1862, to ask for an enquiry into the management of Trust funds, claiming that for several years there had been no certified examination of the accounts; that between 1853 and 1860 considerable capital had been spent; that the number of foundation scholars "has been very materially reduced" and that the Clergy Jubilee School had refused to release "valuable presses (viz., cupboards) for the children's clothing". He felt that the provision of houses for the Master and the Mistress was not a proper use of the £600 raised by the sale of the Manors property.

Accommodation was provided throughout the time at the Clergy Jubilee School and two houses adjoining the school were purchased for this purpose in 1858 but lay outside the parishes that were to benefit from the trust. Further, that between 1855 and 1858 there were extensive alterations to the boys' school[1], the cost of which had totalled £517 3s 2d, of which £400 had been covered by a Privy Council grant but the rest, £117 3s 2d, had been "lost by the Trust". He also felt that capital – over £77 – had been unwisely spent on "Amusements" between 1853 and 1861; these amusements included trips to Tynemouth and Alnwick, "an Xmas tree" in 1853 and "Xmas Treat New Town Hall". He also complained about £26 being paid on "unnecessary subscriptions" to various bodies, including one to induce children to stay at school after the age of fourteen.

In their reply, the Commissioners agreed that "the past administration of the charity had been most improvident and the sale of the stock in 1859 (to build the two houses) as far as it represented the capital endowment of the charity was wholly unauthorised and improper". However, since they felt the trustees had acted in good faith, they proposed to take no further action.

The Revd Clement Moody, presumably implicated in this "mismanagement", clearly had a vision for education in Newcastle and was the originator of the Ten School Scheme for Newcastle. Although this scheme only built two new schools[2], it had expended £850 upon St Nicholas Charity School in the Clergy Jubilee building in 1851. Moody must have seen these two charities – he was trustee of both the Allan Charity and the Clergy Jubilee School Building – as part of his wider plans for the town. As such his actions were made in good faith, as the Charity Commission concluded, but not within the rules. He was no stranger to controversy, having caused a stir with his appointment to the Mastership of the Hospital of St Mary the Virgin and Chaplain of St Thomas's Haymarket in 1856. He managed to alienate the congregation there but enjoyed a high status within the town.

By way of an epilogue to this controversy, the Council Minute books of 1866 reveal an interesting exchange about the Clergy Jubilee School. A wall belonging to the school was falling down and the mayor, as a trustee, sought funds for its repair as the school, he informed the councillors, "haven't a rap". One councillor, Mr Gregson, replied that the school was in possession of funds that did not belong to them having robbed Dame Allen's School [sic]. To great laughter he pronounced that "There had been robbery by some person." This shows that the controversy surrounding the school funds was well known in civic circles. Interestingly the council put £50 to repair the wall and the wall still collapsed later in the year.

As the controversy over funds was worked out among the trustees and officialdom, the challenges of accommodation must have been far more pressing in the day-to-day running of the schools. Shortly after October 1861, the children of the Allan foundation were moved to "rooms, etc., in a situation not the most healthy", as the Vicar of Newcastle termed it. These rooms were at 11 Rosemary Lane, a narrow street between St John's Church and Pudding Chare, a site now occupied by the *Evening Chronicle* building. The building belonged to St John's Church, and was used as a Sunday School; the passage was floored with gravestones from St John's churchyard. The rent was £20 per annum.

The redoubtable Miss Read left in 1867 at the age of 49. She was to marry Lawson Jackson, a man three years her junior, the following year and died in 1881. The Assistant Mistress, Mrs Jane Anderson, succeeded her.

It was a matter of urgency to find better accommodation. With the acquisition of the freehold of the Wallsend estate, the trustees were in a better position to raise capital, in particular by disposing of some of the estate. In December, 1867, the Revd Clement Moody sought permission of the Charity Commission to sell some land "which as farming land the part they would like to sell is almost valueless on account of the smoke from the manufactories adjoining but as building ground it would be much sought after" (13.12.1867). The proposal was to sell thirty-five acres of the Wallsend property in two lots and 645 square yards of land in Carliol Square, with the master's and mistress's houses, a warehouse and yard. Within days the Charity Commissioners agreed to the sales, with reserve prices of £5085 5s for Lot 1 at Wallsend and £6653 6s 9d for Lot 2, and £980 for the Carliol Square property. Lot 1 sold at the reserve price within a month, the Carliol Square property in January to Newcastle Corporation, also at reserve price, and in April 1869, Lot 2 also sold at reserve price. The proceeds

[1]The division of the original single schoolroom into separate classrooms in accordance with the rules of the Education Department.
[2]St Andrew's in Leazes Lane and All Saints', Shieldfield.

William Walton. Foundation scholar in uniform. 1867. St Nicholas's Charity School. (Tinted Photograph)

were paid in to Official Trustees of Charitable Funds Account at the Bank of England and invested in 3% annuities. With the increase of funds, the school even chose to decline the annual gift of ten guineas from the corporation of Newcastle, thanking them "most cordially for their uninterrupted kindness and consideration".

According to a petition from the trustees to the Charity Commission of 2 May, 1868, the release of such funds allowed "for the erection of large and commodious schools for boys and girls, playgrounds, conveniences and residences for the Master and Mistress". The Trust's solicitors, Ingledew and Daggett, wrote to the Commission on 19 August, 1870, with regard to an offer from St Nicholas's Church to sell for £800 "a piece of land with the houses and buildings thereon in a place called the Long Stairs formerly used as the workhouse of the parish, and we are instructed by the Trustees to ask the sanction of the Charity Commissioners to the purchase to enable the Trustees to build Schools for the Charity". However, under the terms of the 1869 Endowed Schools Act, the responsibility had passed to the Endowed Schools Commission, and no longer of the Charity Commissioners. The trustees thereupon supplied the Endowed Schools Commission with a statement of purpose and endowments. This useful document shows us the Schools at a difficult moment in their history.

In 1871, the Trust's annual income from land, rent charge, interest and dividends was £691 16s 0d. Of this the master received £64 per annum plus about £22 in weekly pence (i.e. school fees), the mistress £41 12s, and the music master £5. The statement describes the Schools thus:

> Boys and girls are admitted on the foundation when eight years of age and remain at school until they are respectively fourteen and fifteen years of age. They are provided every year with a suit of warm clothing and with under garments, stockings and two pairs of shoes each and cloaks for the girls and capes for the boys. The children on the endowment, of which there are now 34 boys and 24 girls, attend divine service at the parish church of St. Nicholas twice every Sunday under the superintendence of the master and mistress, and they chaunt and sing the afternoon service every Sunday and they do the same twice in every week during the seasons of Advent and Lent. Children not on the Endowment, of which there are now at the School 56 boys and 58 girls, are the children of the working classes and are admitted to the School on payment of a small weekly rate of School Pence at an earlier age then eight so that the Master and Mistress may select from them the best, most orderly and most docile for recommendation to the Trustees to be placed on the endowment. The rate of School Pence is for boys 3d and 4d per week and for girls 2d and 3d per week. The boys and girls have separate school rooms with separate entrances. The educational course pursued under the Master and Mistress, assisted by Monitors and Monitresses, includes moral and religious instruction, reading, writing, arithmetic, geography, history, grammar and music. The girls are also taught knitting and sewing.

The new commissioners found that in most respects the Schools were "on par with an ordinary elementary school", but that "considerable changes will have to be made in order to render the School as conducive to the education of boys and girls as it ought to be and in view of the provisions now made by law". An Assistant Commissioner, Charles Stanton, investigated the position of Allan's charity in May, 1872, and the next month the trustees enquired if any progress had been made on their request for funds to be released for the Long Stairs project, reminding the commissioners of the "very bad neighbourhood and the dilapidated state" of the current building. On 31 March, 1873, the Revd Henry Martin[3], the Vicar of Newcastle, wrote again to the Endowed Schools Commissioners complaining that "the Schoolwork is being carried out in buildings very ill-suited to the purpose, small, ill-ventilated and old, accommodating fifty children of each sex". It is not clear what had happened to the Long Stairs proposal, since the Vicar now put forward a new scheme. "An offer has been made to us by an owner of property in the Parish of St Nicholas to rear a suitable building capable of accommodating 300 children (150 of each sex) provided we the Trustees will rent it at a fair annual rent... It is proposed that these 300 children should have a free education similar to that provided in public elementary schools and that the management should remain vested as at present... If the Commissioners do not view this proposal with favour,

[3]The Revd Henry Martin, MA, had become Vicar of Newcastle in 1871. He was additionally Rural Dean of Newcastle upon Tyne from 1872 and Honorary Canon of Durham from 1874.

will they authorise us to purchase the site and build for ourselves?"

This was a radical new proposal which could have fundamentally altered the nature and purpose of Allan's charity since it proposed that the funds be used almost to double the number of pupils but provide them with a free education that did not go beyond elementary level. If it had succeeded, it is almost certain that there would not be a Dame Allan's today.

Stanton's report, in two parts, April and May 1873, is very revealing in several ways – the present situation of the Schools, the attitudes of the trustees and the variety of views about the Schools' future structure. He found the Schools had 150 children, of whom 58 were free scholars and 92 paid 2d a week. 64 received clothing, which was made by the girls. The buildings were inadequate and lacked a playground, though they were regarded as just "efficient" by H.M. Inspector. Despite the challenges posed by accommodation, the instruction was also efficient. He also noted that the master and mistress selected "the best, most orderly and most docile pupils" to become foundation scholars. The trustees wished to build accommodation for 300 children, but they did not want to accept any public grant of money "which they said a vote of the House of Commons might at any time abolish". (St John's and St Andrew's National Schools already received a government grant). The State's role in the provision of elementary education grew by leaps and bounds after the passage of the 1870 Elementary Education Act, but many local bodies remained suspicious and fearful for their independence. Initially opposed to government inspection, the trustees accepted it by May. Interestingly they "thought that the general proposals of the Commissioners favoured only the clever children and neglected the stupid, to whom more attention should be given than to the former". This sounds very high-minded, but the report continues: "The Mayor was especially afraid that the children would be overeducated and said it was almost impossible even now to get domestic servants in Newcastle, which he attributed to this cause." Was the primary purpose of the Schools therefore, to produce a docile servant class with a minimal level of education to allow them to do their jobs properly? Other trustees clearly thought differently. Henry Martin, the Vicar of Newcastle, favoured the enhancement of educational opportunities with an upper department for superior instruction both for boys and girls; indeed he felt strongly all elementary schools should have such provision. It would seem that the vicar not the mayor was in tune with the wishes of the foundress. The trustees pointed out that since the girls made clothing for the free scholars, the Girls' School was in some sense "an industrial school", i.e., one that taught a useful trade.

Charles Stanton summed up the trustees' views thus: "We are a Church of England foundation and don't want a conscience clause. We want authority to establish ourselves in better buildings, but otherwise we wish to be let entirely alone. We don't want a government grant which may suddenly be withheld or give the government such power of interference that they might forbid any religion to be taught."

At some point after 1875, the conditions at Rosemary Lane were considered too bad for the pupils to remain, and a lease was taken out on premises in Hanover Square. One pupil, O.F. Wilson, later said it was in Clavering Place, but since the latter runs into the former, the confusion is understandable. It was in this accommodation that St Nicholas's Charity Schools were to end their days, and the name Allan's Endowed Schools came into being.

The challenges caused by the lack of adequate accommodation were great but the discussions prompted by the need for new buildings led to a deeper discussion of the aims of the foundation. It was at this point that there came a major alteration of direction leading to one of the greatest changes in the Schools' history. We do not know if it originated with the trustees, with the town council or with the Endowed Schools Commission, but the last seems the most likely. The new intention was that the Schools of the Allan Charity should cease to be elementary schools and evolve into grammar schools. It seems likely that with the provision of more public elementary schools, funded by ratepayers, there was simply no need to create a further 200 places at the Church's expense, whereas there was a clear local need for more church school provision at a higher level. The earlier scheme for a trade school, described by the Endowed Schools Commission as "a school of secondary instruction for older boys", had at least shown that there was some need for secondary provision, and now the trustees started to think more ambitiously. There may well have been another factor – the lack of a Church of England grammar school. The Royal Grammar School was not a church school, and the School of Science and Art, later Rutherford Grammar School, was founded in 1877 by Dr John Rutherford, a prominent evangelical. Moreover, the Roman Catholics, encouraged by the conversion of their central parish church of St Mary into a cathedral in

1860, also felt the need for secondary school provision, and in 1881 St Cuthbert's School was to open in Westmorland Road.

In May 1874, the Endowed Schools Commission wrote to Henry Martin recommending a new structure. The Boys' School should have a lower school, essentially public elementary with fees of 4d to 9d a week and £20 p.a. should be used by the governors towards the fees of poor boys. There should also be a technical school with "instruction in English, Mathematics, Drawing (with special reference to Mechanics and Engineering) and such other branches of practical and experimental science as the Governors may direct. The master was to have a London B.Sc or certificate of proficiency, and there were to be thirty foundationers, exempt from fees and granted £3 per annum, those from elementary schools being based on ability. The fees for paying scholars should be £2 to £4 per annum. The governors were invited to establish exhibitions tenable at Newcastle Science College or its equivalent for their boys. A similar provision was to be made for the girls, with a public elementary lower school and an upper school "to provide education of a more advanced but at the same time of a practical character with some provision for industrial training". The fee arrangements were similar to those for the boys.

The trustees replied, disagreeing about fees (too high) and other matters, but accepting the pattern of upper and lower schools, and the idea of exhibitions for promising pupils, with £30 a year for boys and £20 for girls. The reply came promptly that the powers of the Endowed Schools Commission were to be returned to the Charity Commission as the Endowed Schools Department. The secretary to the trustees wrote several times in the second half of 1875 to modify the proposals for a technical school. First, they felt that elementary Latin should be included in the curriculum but not a modern language, and that religious instruction should be in accordance with the doctrines of the Church of England. Importantly, all pupils should be admitted as non-foundationers "and then after examinations and reference to acquirements" be eligible for foundation status.[4] They required that all lay members of the managing body should be members of the Church of England.

The trustees a few weeks later affirmed that they "are prepared to adopt the Educational Scheme in its essential features provided it meets with the approval of their fellow townsmen as likely to supply a general want". Now a new problem arose: the constitution of the governing body. The Commissioners indicated they wished representatives of the College of Physical Science to be governors, but the trustees were insistent that there should be no more than ten and that five of them should be clergy. Given the chairman's casting vote, the Church would thus retain control.

Moreover not all their "fellow townsmen" did agree with the new scheme. Objections were swiftly lodged by the Board of Guardians of the Newcastle upon Tyne Union, the School Board of Newcastle upon Tyne and the Executive Committee of Newcastle Mechanics Institution, who all said much the same. Their primary aim was to use the Allan endowments to expand and subsidise the provision of elementary education in the city. This would reduce the financial burden on the ratepayers that they represented. "The funds of the said Charity will be diverted from their original purpose, viz., that of providing a suitable education for poor and destitute children, and will, to a large extent, be applied to provide a superior education for the children of well-to-do parents," complained the School Board. The other two bodies condemned "establishing a middle class school", while many people cannot afford to send their children to school "not only for want of school fees but for want of decent and necessary clothing". On the face of it, the three bodies seem to have a strong case, but the Charity Commissioners in three letters, all posted on 14 June 1876, pointed out various misunderstandings both of Eleanor Allan's original endowment and of the new scheme. The former made no reference to clothing or maintenance: it was purely an educational charity. Moreover, Clause 57 of the new scheme "provides that gratuitous education of a superior kind shall be given to 60 poor children being the number specified in that deed (viz., Eleanor Allan's will). Clause 48, which defines the instruction, makes special provision enabling those scholars to receive such elementary scientific instruction as is likely to qualify them for mechanic trades, an object in which the foundress appears to have taken special interest"[5]. The endowments were to cover the education of the sixty children "while the advantages of the School are open to others on payment of a fee representing the cost of the education given". The trustees had persuaded the Endowed Schools Department to

[4] It is interesting that this eminently sensible system was adopted by the Universities of Oxford and Cambridge over a century later.
[5] It would be very interesting to know more about this claim and the evidence on which it is based. Surely the commissioners did not make it up to serve their case.

lower the minimum fee from £3 p.a. to £2, but the department pointed out that there was a danger that this might not cover costs. It did, however, give the future governors more flexibility. The Newcastle School Board had also urged lower fees, but they had likewise been told that the Schools' endowment income would not cover new buildings, sixty scholarships, the proposed exhibitions to higher education and subsidise fee-payers. Two provisions in the scheme were altered to satisfy the trustees. The first was that the acceptance of a representative as a governor from any body unconnected with the town and so not responsible to its inhabitants, such as would be one from Durham University or from the College of Physical Science, would excite a very great opposition. The department suggested the two from the College be dropped and replaced by three nominated by the Town Council. They also agreed that the proposed limit of £5000 on the cost of the new building be dropped.

The Newcastle School Board clearly wished to assert itself, and not only in the matter of fees. The board had indicated that it felt the new schools should be "a connecting link between the public elementary schools and the higher schools of the borough". With this the commissioners largely agreed, but they "regard the suggestion that the School should be a mixed school for boys and girls between the ages of ten and seventeen as ill-advised and impracticable." They also rejected the suggestions that the charity's funds be used to pay fees in public elementary schools and pointed out that the proposal that each able free scholar should be "entitled to an exhibition of £20 yearly seems to be made in forgetfulness of the conditions and cost of a University education". The School Board proposed that the headmaster should be paid £250pa and the headmistress £100, and that some governors should be elected by the managers of public elementary schools. It is difficult to know whether they were keener to acquire the Schools' assets or simply seize control. It is evident why the trustees were determined to retain control of these church schools: other interests were keen to grab what they could. The commissioners rejected both proposals.

The Board of Guardians of the Newcastle Union (Poor Law Guardians), in a submission on 26 July, 1876, to the Lords of the Committee of the Council on Education, raised other objections. The Guardians argued that if all scholarships were not given on entry, poor parents would be unable to pay the fees – higher than in public elementary schools – for the first year or more. Their suggestion was that at least a hundred children should have their fees at elementary schools paid by the Allan governors and at ten years of age they should be examined and the most promising transferred to Allan's Endowed School on scholarships. The sting in the tail was that those not chosen were to continue their education at public elementary school *and have their fees paid by the Allan governors.* They also said that the Schools should have accommodation for no fewer than 500 children. Mr Fitch of the Charity Commission rejected these proposals on several grounds, especially as financially impractical. In January, 1877, the Charity Commission argued that "in framing the scheme the object of the Commissioners was to make the Allan foundation chiefly available for assisting meritorious poor scholars to obtain education higher than elementary by means of scholarships and exhibitions". To achieve this "other classes using the schools must pay fees representing approximately at least the actual cost of the education given." The new scheme was approved by the trustees and by the Town Council, and on 22 March, 1877, it was approved by the Lord President.

In May, the Poor Law Guardians wrote again to the Lords of the Committee pointing out that the curriculum proposed was very similar to that in the elementary schools and increasingly the subjects would be studied in the higher standards in those schools. "(We) earnestly urge the importance of making Allan's Endowed School a truly secondary school and of locating it in that part of the borough where it will be of greatest utility... A Technical School in the eastern part of the borough where the subjects of instruction and the course of study will be such as to form a connecting link between the Public Elementary Schools in that district and Higher Education." This is an interesting volteface by the Guardians – and a far-sighted view of the developing situation of the School.

Minor opposition to the scheme came from a completely different quarter, the head master and the head mistress. John Stubbs, who had been appointed in 1861, complained in a letter to the commission dated 22 November, 1875, that the governors had promised him at that time a move to better premises and support in raising "the tone and status of the school", and had considered it unnecessary for him to hold a certificate[6].

[6]The proposed scheme required that both master and mistress held teaching certificates. He felt his position had been "entirely ignored" in the proposals, and that "it might be difficult at my time of life to obtain a certificate". Jane Anderson wrote on the same day requesting "due and ample compensation", since she had given up a flourishing business, first to assist Miss Read, and, when she left, to become head mistress. Both had already written to the Education Department objecting to the scheme; it would leave both without a job.

On 11 July, 1877, the final scheme was ratified in Council by Queen Victoria. It is now necessary to look in detail at this scheme. First, Eleanor Allan's Charity was henceforth to be known as Allan's Endowed Schools, with eleven governors in place of the trustees. These were the five ex-officio members of the Mayor and the four vicars, three representatives of Newcastle Council and three co-optative members: initially the Revd John Reed the lecturer or afternoon preacher of St Nicholas's, who had played such a large part in preserving the Allan foundation from poachers, and two lay Anglicans. When Mr Reed left his post at St Nicholas's, a third Anglican layman should be chosen. There was some consternation among council members when three nonconformists were chosen as their representatives on the governing body as this went against the spirit of the new constitution; nonetheless all three were appointed. Both head teachers were required to be members of the Church of England. The Head Master was to have an official residence, but there was no similar provision for the Head Mistress. Boys were to be educated from seven to fifteen and girls seven to sixteen, and buildings should be acquired to house at least 150 boys and 100 girls, with the possibility for "convenient extension".

There were to be thirty Foundation Scholars of the First Class (twenty boys and ten girls) and thirty of the Second Class (twenty boys and ten girls); the former were exempt from tuition fees and also received £3 a year maintenance; the latter were only exempt from fees. The remaining scholars were to pay between £2 and £5 a year, the actual rate being determined from time to time by the governors. No pupil was to be admitted unless he or she had passed an entrance examination. There was a conscience clause whereby a parent could request that his child be exempt from acts of worship and religious instruction without prejudice of any kind. Such instruction would be in accordance with the doctrine of the Church of England.

The curriculum to be followed was to be extended to include "Latin or some foreign language" as well as science subjects for the boys and natural science, domestic economy, the laws of health and needlework for the girls. Special regard was to be given for the boys in "technical instruction and instruction in practical science". This went beyond the scientific curriculum pursued as a trade school in the Clergy Jubilee building and had a greater emphasis placed upon all aspects of academic scholarship. Since there were no women on the governing body, a Ladies Committee, up to five in number, was to help with "superintending the internal management of the Girls' School". The governors could refer any matter to this committee "for investigation and determination". It was at last a nod in the right direction and may indicate that the Ladies Committee set up in 1834 had survived.

Exhibitions for three years for study in higher education were to be available to a total of £50 for boys and £30 for girls per annum. Provision was also to be made for pupils who "showed special promise and aptitude for teaching" to remain as pupil teachers, being instructed by the head and other teachers, and giving assistance in the Schools. The governors were to remunerate both the pupil teacher and the head teacher. This reconstitution, with amendments in 1895, 1899 and 1901, lasted until 1921 in much the same form.

The trustees asked the Charity Commission for permission to maintain the existing schools until the new ones were built, but this request was turned down. The schools were to continue only until 11 November, 1878, when the lease was to expire, and pupils were to be transferred to other schools, the foundation scholars having their fees paid by the Foundation. The trustees, now described as governors, did not give up. As late as October they were pointing out that the schools could be kept going at moderate cost and "it would be inexpedient to have to open the proposed new schools without the immediate presence of scholars". It seems that the governors were overruled, despite the good sense of what they said. The Schools appear to have continued until the end of term, and the pupils were then transferred to the other schools. John Stubbs and Jane Anderson were paid off at the end of January with £300 and £125 respectively; they do not seem to have been considered for future employment.

O.F. Wilson (1875-81) recalled that when his brother left the School in 1875, he, aged seven, was offered a free place by the Master, John Stubbs, at the School in Rosemary Lane. The Master gave him the uniform: coat and waistcoat of dark blue serge, the coat bound with yellow cord and the waistcoat with brass buttons, light corduroy trousers, a grey cape, a pair of boots, two pairs of shoes, and stockings and white shirts made by the girls. To accommodate the changes in the structure of the Schools, pupils living nearest St John's School in Sunderland Street were transferred there, and others near St Nicholas's National School in Castle Garth had to go there to complete their education. Wilson was the last scholar of the old foundation to be enrolled, and when he left St John's School in 1881, he was given copies of *The Bible*, *The Book of Common Prayer* and *The Whole Duty of Man* in accordance with practice. These were the last so to be given. He and the other scholars continued to wear the uniform and to have their fees paid by the Allan Foundation.

The Girls' School possesses two copies of a photograph of girls in the traditional costume of the foundation scholars. One bears on the back this inscription:

> Three scholars of Dame Allan's Charity School, St Nicholas, Newcastle upon Tyne, photographed from life by A. J. Robinson (amateur photographer). June 1877. After the celebrated picture by Henry Barraud[7] "Lord have mercy upon us" Copied May 1914. Sarah Elizabeth Watson – Polly Bell – Elizabeth Hill.

The date and the hybrid name of the School are significant: the Schools were in transition from charity school to grammar school.

Foundation Scholars in their uniform in 1877

---

[7]Henry Barraud (1811-74) was noted for similar pictures and London scenes. The photographer no doubt knew the engraving or autotyping of this picture; much of his work was so reproduced. The heavy wooden frame of one of them is inscribed "Dame Allan Charity Scholars St Nicholas, Newcastle". These costumes were copied for the 1955 celebrations and are known as "pollybells". They provide a connexion between the two phases of the Allan foundation.

The next problem was to determine the location of the new schools. The first site that was considered was on the Elswick Park estate. "It is in a healthy and respectable locality, in the immediate vicinity of a large population of the upper working class and the lower middle, and is within twenty minutes' walk of the centre of the town. There is also ample vehicular accommodation plying at all hours of the day." The site, however, was of only 1500 square yards. It was available for £1625, and the estimated cost of the building was £4000. The Newcastle School and Charities Committee looked further into the matter and published a printed report rejecting not so much the site itself as its location. "It is unsuitable, being almost at the extreme west of the Borough, and too remote from the districts most in need of the class of education contemplated by the scheme. Your Committee have ascertained that middle-class education is provided for 1 in 28 in that portion of the Borough lying west of Westgate Road; in the Central District, or between Westgate Road and Northumberland Street it is only 1 in 144; and in that portion lying east of Northumberland Street it is 1 in $54^1/_2$. They urge that another site at the north-west of the Cricket Field is well adapted for the erection of schools, the situation is open, and being near the boundary of the Central and Eastern Districts would be of easy access to that portion of the population most scantily supplied with middle-class education." It is interesting to observe a body which regards the new schools as intended for "middle-class education". By this one understands that it was education for future middle-class citizens, whatever their parentage, the generous provision of scholarships making it possible for at least the better-off working class parents to send their children to the Schools.

The whole Elswick Park estate was then acquired by the Corporation for a public park, and that left the Cricket Field site as the only candidate. Some of the governors were ill pleased by this development and indicated that other sites should at least be considered. One such was the Spring Gardens Engine Works site in Bath Lane. Mr Durnford, the Assistant Commissioner, recommended that the Cricket Field site most strongly: "Nothing could be better than this so far as the actual place and facilities it affords for buildings are concerned. It is a fine open space surrounded by houses of a substantial character and approached by broad and cleanly thoroughfares." The mayor and the councillor governors agreed with this, but the clergy governors preferred the Bath Lane site, despite its higher price, its less pleasant surroundings and denser population, claiming that the other site was too remote from the homes of likely pupils. It is likely that the Vicar of Newcastle and the other clergy felt they were being pushed around both by the Charity Commissioners and even more by the Corporation. It seemed that the Cricket Ground site was the property of the St Mary Magdalene Hospital of which the Corporation were governors. The Allan governors decided to buy the Bath Lane site, but agreed to postpone a decision until the Charity Commissioner's inspector, Mr Good, had reported on both sites.

He wrote of the Cricket Field site: "Beside being in a high, open, airy and healthy spot approachable by good streets and roads, it is capable of being easily enlarged to any reasonable extent[8], and being Charity land, probably without cost to the Governors[9], and it is likely to be made more accessible by the formation of certain projected roads and streets." He recommended acceptance of this site and rejection of the other, which he found to be in "a low and disreputable neighbourhood, too near to the military barracks and industry". Moreover, it would cost £2000 for only 1000 square yards. On 23 December, 1879, the Commission stated in a letter that they approved of the site at the Cricket Field. The following May the governors indicated that they wished to purchase 1749 square yards of the north-west portion of the Northumberland Cricket Field at a cost of £918 3s 6d plus £18 costs.

The next consideration was the building itself. The well-known local architect, R. J. Johnson[10], drew up plans for a building to accommodate "about 100 girls and fully 180[11] boys" at an estimated cost of about £4000. The governors and the Newcastle Corporation Schools and Charities Committee approved the plans, and they were accepted by the Charity Commissioners. Earlier the Commission had urged the governors to invite donations from local people towards the cost of the new building, but the governors had not accepted this. Perhaps they soon had reason to regret this, since it was found impossible to get tenders for the work at the estimated cost. Plans were revised, but the tender they accepted from S.B. Burton was for £5397, though this did allow for

8 An advantage carelessly thrown away. See below.
9 In fact the Corporation failed to give the site: in 1786 it had been more generous.
10 R. J. Johnson (1832-92) was the architect of numerous churches, notably Summerhill St Matthew, Gosforth All Saints and Wylam St Oswin. He designed Newcastle Cathedral fittings, the Armstrong Building at the university and restored the Black Gate. At his death *The Builder* described him as among the best architects in England to have worked exclusively in the provinces.
11 Later revised to 150 boys.

increased accommodation (about 30 places) for girls. Further changes raised the cost to £5527. The Commissioners pointed out that this figure was almost twice the cost of a similar elementary school in London, and urged architectural simplification to save money. This the governors rejected, arguing that the site demanded a building of some distinction, and that changes would seriously impair the character of the building while the saving would be insignificant. Indeed the architect was soon requesting a further £100 to improve the design of the upper part of the turrets.

The ceremony of laying the foundation stone took place on Tuesday, 31 October, 1882. In fact the building was well advanced. According to the report in *The Northern Daily Express* the next day, the weather was fine and pleasant, and the ceremony was performed by the Revd Canon Martin, Vicar of Newcastle and Chairman of Governors, who was about to leave to become Archdeacon of Lindisfarne. The Mayor of Newcastle, Alderman Angus, presiding over the event, gave a full account of the scheme for the Schools, and then handed an engraved silver trowel to the Vicar who laid the stone. Buried beneath it was a time capsule (a bottle) containing current coins, a copy of the Express and other newspapers and a parchment recording the event. Others present were the Bishop of Newcastle, Dr Wilberforce[12], the Sheriff J. G. Gibson, six aldermen and councillors, the Town Clerk, seven clergymen, the head master of the Grammar School, the architect, the builder and many local people.

And so the schools had endured the controversies and challenges of the 1860s and 1870s and emerged transformed. In this time they had fallen back from the thriving trade school, partly secondary in character, of their sojourn in the Clergy Jubilee building. Nonetheless they had continued to provide a sound education in accordance with Eleanor Allan's wishes and this success, as well as the benefits of that original endowment, had allowed them to be reconstituted by The Queen in Council as grammar schools in the making.

The changing face of Newcastle: Eldon Square (1825-31). Soon the elegant streets in Tyneside Classical style would transform the town centre.

[12]Ernest Roland Wilberforce, first Bishop of Newcastle 1882-96, son of Samuel Wilberforce, Bishop of Winchester, and grandson of William Wilberforce, the slave emancipator.

Chapter Five

ALLAN'S ENDOWED SCHOOLS IN COLLEGE STREET:

ESTABLISHING THE RECONSTITUTED SCHOOLS 1883 – 1892

The College Street school is a handsome listed building, though at the time of writing in a sadly dilapidated state, requiring restoration and occupation. Sir Nicholas Pevsner describes it thus: "In Norman Shaw style, both his Chelsea and his Queen's Gate varieties. A charming building, far more than the sum of its parts, with fat Tuscan columns flanking the entrance under an Ipswich oriel, between ogee-hipped towers, thick-framed sash windows, and, in front, fine entrance piers, repeated at the smaller entrance (viz, to the master's house) on Northumberland Road, and linked by iron railings." Mercifully these railings – also listed - survived the 1940 desire to convert all such into Spitfires. The gateway has two intertwined As.

The girls occupied the ground floor and the boys the upper floor. The main entrance was used by visitors, the two staffs and sixth formers of both schools. There were entrances from the two playgrounds, which were separated by a high wall. In the Boys' School there were six classrooms; in the Girls' five: two of these were separated from each other by a wood and glass screen that could be slid open for school prayers and other assemblies.

In the Boys' School there were a "chemical laboratory" and a "physical laboratory". These were in line with the rise in interest in science teaching. The Science and Art Department at South Kensington in London, itself a product of the Great Exhibition of 1851, was promoting such developments in schools, with substantial grants. At Bath Lane Elementary School a room had been adapted as a chemistry laboratory in 1877 for the use of the new Science and Art School, later Rutherford Grammar School. In 1879 the new buildings included "a small but well-equipped laboratory". At the Royal Grammar School it was reported as late as 1888 that the development of science was impeded by the lack of "properly appointed laboratories". The physical laboratory at College Street may well have been the first purpose-built one in a Newcastle school. The chemical laboratory had at least twelve benches, and possessed "fume closets". It is clear that boys carried out some experiments themselves, and there are frequent references to enthusiastic pupils: "some boys stayed late doing experiments in magnetism and electricity." In the Boys' School there was a board room for the use of the governors, but in August, 1889, it had to be made into a classroom. The buildings were centrally heated, and lighted by gas.

Outside there were toilets in both yards, and somewhere adjacent to the girls' yard was an area referred to as "girls' school paddock". The paddock is referred to in the same terms in 1892. This additional land does not appear to have been used for anything, but may have been acquired with a view either to expansion or to the erection of a head mistress's house to match the head master's. In July, 1900, the land was sold to Joseph Duffy for £1546 11s 3d, perhaps because it was already felt that the site was too cramped for development, and lacked playing fields.

The head master's house stands at right angles to the schools, facing Northumberland Road, then known as Bath Road. It too is a handsome building of two storeys plus dormer-lit attic rooms. *The Northern Daily Express* describes it in 1882 as "commodious". There were two sitting rooms, six bedrooms and kitchen accommodation, but the rooms were not very spacious. There appears to have been direct access to the first floor of the Schools from the half-landing of the house, now sealed. In the rather Flemish west gable is an elaborate niche containing

The Schools, College Street to left and Northumberland Road (formerly Bath Street) to right. Head Master's house to right, with Eleanor Allan's statue in niche on gable. 1883

a stone statue of Eleanor Allan as she may have looked. It is by an unknown sculptor, who shows her in distinctly medieval clothing and holding a closed book in her left hand. It is life-size, and was cleaned in 2004 by the University of Northumbria which now occupies the building (see cover). The founder's statue no doubt emphasised that the Schools were now known as Allan's Endowed Schools.

The governors were meantime looking for heads for the Schools. Although not laid down in the 1877 scheme, it was clearly understood that the Schools should have graduate or certificated head teachers, and it is specified that "in order to obtain the best candidates the governors shall... give public notice of the vacancy and invite applicants by advertisements in newspapers" and similar means. Such applicants would have to be practising members of the Church of England. Their first appointment was Thomas Merrick, aged 35, who was certificated by the Education Department in Science with some distinction at Battersea Training College. He became tutor and lecturer in mathematics at Culham Training College for three years, and then from August 1876 to March 1883 he was assistant master at Newcastle Royal Grammar School. The governors appointed him early in order to prepare for the opening on 5 August. His salary was a fixed £100 plus 25/- for each pupil.

The head mistress was Mrs Catherine Landells, who was born Catherine Jackson in 1842 at Bishop Auckland. She was a certificated teacher and had been mistress of St John's National School in Sunderland Street, one of the schools to which the Allan Foundation pupils had been sent on the closure of their school in December, 1878. She was thus known to at least some of the governors, and must have been regarded as a suitable person to be the new head mistress. In 1882, at the age of forty, she had married another certificated teacher, James Landells, living in Westgate Road. It is possible that St John's School had required her resignation on marriage, and that Allan's Endowed School had a more enlightened philosophy and seized the chance to appoint a mature and qualified head. Certainly the choice of a married woman was unusual though not unprecedented in the Foundation but she had no children and was unlikely to have any. Since the new building plans made no allowance for a mistress's house, this appointment solved the problem without further expense. Her salary was £60 plus £1 for each girl. She too was appointed early (Easter?) to prepare for the opening.

Of the assistant staff, five masters and four mistresses, we know the names of only three: John Young, who left the next year, M. Vuez, the visiting French master, and the second master, Alexander Begg Noble, who accompanied Merrick from the Royal Grammar School. He had been trained in Glasgow and taught in Inverurie and Fraserburgh before moving to the RGS in 1880. His qualifications (certificates from the Department of Science and Art) were in "Magnetism and Electricity, Physiography, Freehand, Model Geometry and Perspective". He was 29 and was paid £150. By 1890, only he and Merrick survived of the original staff of the two Schools.

All the Schools lacked now, in the summer of 1883, were pupils. It may be remembered that the governors had wished to maintain the old charity schools until the new schools opened so that pupils would be immediately available, but that the Charity Commission had refused. Merrick conducted examinations and in June twenty boys at public elementary schools accepted places for the autumn term as Foundation Scholars. The remainder would be feepayers. In fact the governors need not have worried since the Schools were almost fully subscribed before they opened, and were full by January. A few pupils might have been formerly at Rosemary Lane/Hanover Square, either as Foundation Scholars or feepayers, but four and a half years had elapsed since the old schools closed, and only a small number of older children could possibly have done so. The surviving records do not give the names of these first students, apart from the Scholars, but we know that they included William Potter, whose academic record would suggest that the calibre of at least some of the intake was high.[1]

The education to be given in the Schools was to follow this pattern:

All pupils
Religious Instruction
Reading, writing and arithmetic
Geography and history
English grammar, composition and literature
Latin or some foreign language
Drawing and vocal music

Boys
Algebra and geometry
Practical mechanics
Chemistry in its application to the
arts and manufacture

Girls
Some branch of natural science
Domestic economy and the laws of health
Needlework
Other subjects as prescribed by governors

In those early days of the reconstituted Schools, it would appear that two men were involved with the teaching of the girls. Canon Arthur Lloyd, Vicar of Newcastle and governor, taught scripture to both boys and girls and Thomas Merrick taught science, until a teacher with science expertise, Miss Agnes Hawthorn, was appointed as Third Mistress in April, 1886.

In March 1886, Catherine Landells, now 44, resigned. Her husband James became Master of the Royal Victoria Blind Asylum in Northumberland Street. We do not know what prompted her resignation, but her husband was already over sixty and certainly required assistance in his new post. Mrs Landells' sister, Anne Aisbitt, joined them at the Blind Asylum as matron and her nephew, Richard Aisbitt, was a pupil teacher there. The Landells did not have children of their own, but adopted a girl around this time. She had established the Girls' School firmly and was the last married head mistress. She was succeeded by Emma Maria Mousley, a Londoner, who was only 26. Having started as a pupil teacher at the age of fourteen, she had trained at Bristol College and was head mistress of Aylesbury Girls' School at 21. Such evidence as we have points to her considerable success during her eight years in College Street.

---

[1] William Potter later went on to attend Fitzwilliam College, Cambridge, before becoming Headmaster of the Roan School, Greenwich, and author of a number of mathematical textbooks.

BOYS' SCHOOL.

The course of Instruction comprises :—

1.* RELIGIOUS KNOWLEDGE.

    Old and New Testament History.   Book of Common Prayer.

2. READING, WRITING, AND ARITHMETIC.

    Reading and Recitation. Plain Hand-writing, making a *fair copy* of a somewhat illegible manuscript, Short-hand. Arithmetic, Theoretical and Practical. Civil Service Questions.

3. GEOGRAPHY AND HISTORY.

    The Physical and Political Geography of the chief Countries of the World, Mapping. History of England.

4. ENGLISH GRAMMAR, COMPOSITION, AND LITERATURE.

    Parsing, Analysis of Sentences, Prosody, the study of a selected portion of the works of Shakespeare, Milton, or of some other standard Author. Original Composition. Historical English Grammar.

5. FRENCH.

    Grammar. Study of a selected work of a standard Author. Commercial Correspondence.

6. ALGEBRA, GEOMETRY, MENSURATION, PLANE TRIGONOMETRY.

    Algebra to the Binomial Theorem. Series. Geometry, Euclid's Elements. Syllabus of the Association for the Improvement of Geometrical Teaching. Problems. Mensuration of Surfaces and Solids. Use of the Slide Rule. Plane Trigonometry. Solution of Triangles. Use of Mathematical Tables. De Moivre's Theorem.

7. THEORETICAL MECHANICS.

    Statics, Dynamics, Hydrostatics, Pneumatics.

8. PRACTICAL MECHANICS; MAGNETISM AND ELECTRICITY; SOUND, LIGHT AND HEAT.

9. CHEMISTRY, IN ITS APPLICATION TO THE ARTS AND MANUFACTURES.

    Laboratories are being fitted up with working Benches, Apparatus, and Chemicals, for the performance, by each Pupil, of Quantitative Experiments in the Subjects of Group 8, and Qualitative and Quantitative Experiments in Subject 9.

10. DRAWING.

    Freehand, Model, Geometrical and Perspective Drawing ; Solid Geometry and Machine Drawing, for which Models and Specimens are provided.

11. VOCAL MUSIC.

    Singing from Notes.

    Latin or German may be added to the above Course.

SCHOOL HOURS.—JUNIOR CLASSES, 9—12 a.m., 2—4 p.m.

       „   SENIOR CLASSES, 9 a.m.,—12·30 p.m., 2—4·30 p.m.

       „   PRACTICAL PHYSICS AND CHEMISTRY, 2—5 p.m.

VACATIONS.—Christmas, three weeks ; Easter, one week ; Midsummer, six weeks.

FEES FOR TUITION.—For Boys 7—11 years of age, 3 Guineas per annum.

       „   For Boys 11—15 years of age, 4 Guineas per annum.

    Latin or German, 5s. per Quarter extra.

    The Fees in each case to be paid Quarterly, in advance.

PRACTICAL CHEMISTRY.—Beginners 2s. 6d. each, Advanced Scholars, 5s. each, per Quarter, for Chemicals.

CAUTION MONEY, for the safe custody of Apparatus, 5s. each, which will be returned if the Apparatus be given up intact.

NOTICE OF REMOVAL.—Three months' notice must be given previous to the removal of a Pupil.

    For particulars as to Scholarships at the School, and Exhibitions, see the enclosed extracts from the Scheme.

    Pupils can be entered on Mondays and Wednesdays, from 5—6 p.m., at the School.

    The School will be opened on Tuesday, August 7th, 1883.

THOMAS MERRICK, LONDON UNIVERSITY,

HEAD MASTER.

Monday, April 23rd, 1883.

_____

   * Any Pupil may be withdrawn from the Religious Observances and Instruction, by a written notice addressed to the Head Master.

Prospectus for Allan's Endowed Boys' School, April 1883, for first academic year beginning in the autumn

GIRLS' SCHOOL.

Subjects of Instruction :—

1.* RELIGIOUS KNOWLEDGE.

Old and New Testament History. Book of Common Prayer.

2. READING, WRITING, AND ARITHMETIC.

Reading and Elocution. Plain and Ornamental Writing. Short-hand. Theoretical and Practical Arithmetic. Book-keeping.

3. GEOGRAPHY AND HISTORY.

Political Geography and Physiography. Mapping. English and General European History.

4. ENGLISH GRAMMAR, COMPOSITION, AND LITERATURE.

Historical English Grammar. Source and Growth of the English Language. Syntax. Philology. Composition. Reproductions. Essays and Letters. History of English Authors ; and Study of a selected Work of a Standard Author.

5. FRENCH.

Grammar, Conversation, and Literature.

6. ELEMENTARY MATHEMATICS.

Algebra. Euclid's Elements of Geometry. Mensuration.

7. ELEMENTARY NATURAL PHILOSOPHY AND CHEMISTRY (taught by the Head Master.)

8. DRAWING.

Freehand, Model, Geometry, Perspective, and Sketching in Water-colours, &c.

9. VOCAL MUSIC.

Singing from Notes. Old Notation.

10. DOMESTIC ECONOMY AND THE LAWS OF HEALTH.

Nature and Uses of Food. Cooking. Condiments. Beverages. The Dwelling. Situation. Water Supply. Ventilation. Heat. Light. Furniture. Clothing and Washing. Domestic Medicine and Nursing. Expenditure.

11. NEEDLEWORK.

Plain and Fancy. Cutting Out.

SCHOOL HOURS.—JUNIOR CLASSES, 9—12 a.m., 2—4 p.m.

    ,,   SENIOR CLASSES, 9 a.m.,—12·30 p.m., 2—4·30 p.m.

VACATIONS.—Christmas, three weeks ; Easter, one week ; Midsummer, six weeks.

FEES FOR TUITION.—For Girls 7—11 years of age, 3 Guineas per annum.

    ,,   For Girls 11—16 years of age, 4 Guineas per annum.

    The Fees in each case to be paid Quarterly, in advance.

NOTICE OF REMOVAL.·—·Three months' notice must be given previous to the removal of a Pupil.

For particulars as to Scholarships and Exhibitions, see the enclosed extracts from the Scheme.

Pupils may be entered on Tuesdays and Thursdays, from 4—5 p.m., at the School.

The School will be opened on Tuesday, August 7th, 1883.

                                C. LANDELLS, HEAD MISTRESS.

Monday, April 23rd, 1883.

---

* Any Pupil may be withdrawn from the Religious Observances and Instruction, by a written notice addressed to the Head Mistress.

Prospectus for Allan's Endowed Girls' School, April 1883, for first academic year beginning in the autumn

Amongst surviving documents in the National Archives is one that lists Foundation Scholars, with their parents' occupation and their own careers, from 1883 to 1889. The range of occupations is wide: clerk to the governors, inland revenue officer, master mariner, dentist, chartered accountant, architect, master of jail, schoolmaster, cab proprietor, coach painter, wharfman, innkeeper and musician, bricklayer, shooting gallery owner, shoemaker, draper, farmer, dressmaker (mother), labourer and many more. Some boys go on to work with their fathers: chartered accountant/accountant apprentice, or foreman in leather factory/apprentice in leather work. A builder's son went to the College of Medicine, and an innkeeper's son won an open exhibition to the College of Science, as did a farmer's son. One boy wisely decided that his dad's job was not a good idea. Father was a sergeant-major who in 1854 was in the Charge of the Light Brigade in the Crimean War, "One of the Six-Hundred" of whom 40% were casualties. Young Forbes became a watchmaker.

The first printed report on the Schools came in August 1889, when the Revd T J Sanderson presented it to the secretary of the Syndicate appointed by the University of Cambridge to provide for the examination of schools. The examinations were those held in June, and he reported that "both schools appear to me to have reached a fair average standard" but recommended smaller classes with more teachers and classrooms. Sanderson reported the next summer in similar terms. Already, after a mere six years, the building's inadequacy is criticised.

On the boys the reports were very favourable in mathematical and scientific subjects, very good in drawing, good in Latin, fair in English and weak in French. On the girls the reports were more favourable all round than those on the boys. "The rapid and continuing success of the Schools is very creditable to the teaching staff, especially to the Girls' School." Sanderson observed that entrance scholarships were in the first instance open to pupils of Anglican elementary schools, and thereafter to any denomination. There was strong competition for places: the most recent admission was of three pupils from thirty candidates, two from Elswick Road School and one from Byker Board School. He observed that almost every girl who had held a scholarship went on to be an elementary school teacher. Merrick argued that the boys, should, like the girls, have a leaving age of sixteen, and the governors agreed with him. This Sanderson supported, but the request was not submitted until December, 1898, and approved by the Board the next June. The blame for the delay must lie with the governors.

The prospectus for the Schools for October, 1890, lists the governing body of twelve men. The three representative governors call for comment. Councillor Sutton and Alderman Gibson, representing the Town Council, were nonconformist laymen, and the Revd Dr. J. Collingwood Bruce, (a distinguished local antiquary and head master), representing (it seems) both the council and Armstrong College, was a nonconformist minister. Their presence produced hostile comment from outside and council minutes record this.

The prospectus offered thirty first class Foundation Scholarships which remitted tuition fees and also gave "a yearly payment of £3 each, to be applied at the discretion of the governors in the purchase of books, in making deposits at a savings bank, or otherwise for the benefit of the holder". In addition there were thirty second class Foundation Scholarships giving exemption from fees. In both cases, twenty were for boys and ten for girls. A full list of pupils, their parents' occupations and their addresses survives. There is a wide range of occupations, including clerks, drapers, provision merchants, master mariners, platers, plumbers, cab driver, ostler, labourer, charwoman, schoolmaster, Methodist minister, genealogist and antiquarian, and "gentleman". Clearly the fears that it would become an entirely middle class school had not been realised, but neither was it working class. The composition of the girls' classes were thus: Class I – 27; Class II – 40; Class III, Div I – 32; Class III Div ii – 23. For the boys, Class I was 8; Class II – 27; Class III – 40; Class IV – 24; Class V – 25; Class VI – 21. The staff are also listed and are in strict order, viz., second, third, fourth, fifth master/mistress; a new teacher would be appointed to be third master/mistress, though some account was no doubt paid to special skills in which he or she had gained subject certificates.

On 23 December, 1890, there came a report on the Schools by A. F. Leach to the Charity Commissioners. His comments are unsparing of the governors and of the new building. "I must say that I have never come across a case in which fairly successful schools have been less assisted by their governing body." The governors had expressed dissatisfaction with Merrick: their main objection was that "he was not sufficiently obsequious and withstood some of their proceedings. It appears to me that they have no just ground of complaint." One cannot help but feel that he had higher ambitions for the Schools than they had, despite the fact that many of them were graduates and he was not. Their poor judgement is further borne out by Leach's comments on the buildings. He liked the site opposite Durham Medical School but observed there was no room for expansion. "The governors apparently relied on their late clerk and while he slept the ground has been bought up and built on all round. Consequently there is only a dirty little yard for a playground and urgent need for extension of buildings and there is no way of extending either[2]. The school buildings are very pleasing to look at outside, of a solid and handsome Queen Anne style, but they are about as badly designed for school purposes as could well be imagined. It is really sad that an expenditure of £6000 should have produced no better result and that no greater regard should have been had to the accumulated experience of school building now available." He found the interior so dark that in the Girls' School "gas was burning in broad daylight and the stuffiness was disgusting". He was also unimpressed by the head master's house, and found that Merrick was keen to convert it into further classrooms and to build on the playground. Since nothing of the sort happened, the governors clearly took no notice.

Decorated iron work, incorporating two "A's" at main entrance to College Street building. 1883

Leach observed that the two Schools "are independent institutions, the head master being co-ordinate with, not superior to, the head mistress", but noted that arrangements were being made for "girls to attend some of the science classes", viz, in the boys' laboratories. He noticed, too, that the pupils were lower middle class, with the girls "somewhat higher class than the boys, and a quarter of them nonconformist. Only 56 of the 307 pupils came from outside Newcastle. The governors, against the wishes of Merrick, sought to limit scholarships to children of parents with not more than £150 a year and exhibitions to those under £500 a year, but the Board of Education refused to sanction these limits.

A remarkable insight into the workings of the Boys' School is given by the logbook kept by Thomas Merrick from 1 March, 1886, to 21 December, 1892. By the Department's New Code of 1882, schools were required to keep such a record of "the introduction of new books, apparatus, or courses of instruction, any plan of lessons approved by the inspector, the visits of managers, absence, illness, or failure of duty by any of the school staff, or any special circumstances affecting the school, that may, for the sake of future reference or for any other reason, deserve to be recorded". In fact Thomas Merrick chose to ignore parts of this, and to add whatever he thought appropriate. Of course, events are seen only through his eyes, and perhaps colleagues, parents and pupils often saw things differently. Plus ça change ...

The first thing that strikes a reader is that he was on duty twenty-four hours a day, seven days a week, and fifty-two weeks a year – the price of living on the premises and being virtual caretaker.

> "Whit Monday: wound clocks and looked at W.C.s about 9.00am"
> Saturday, Sept 15, 1888. Came into school and worked off and on until 12 midnight.
> Lowes IH and Robinson RM (pupil teachers) at lessons this morning. Harbottle EB and
> Hay Alex here helping me to repair lockers for Examination next week.
> Sent for coal and coke …. Received and paid for 300 bundles of sticks.
> Received oiler, oil and oil can for oiling the girls' swings.
> Paid 6d for clearing snow from one of the girls' W.C.s and for helping to carry bucketfuls
> of hot water to cleanse the soil pipe. WC cisterns all frozen; spent greater part of
> afternoon attending to them.
> Boxing Day, 1890: sent out notice for fees. Saw Clerk re cash.

---

[2] The fault went back to the original purchase of land. The governors should have bought a much larger area to the east and north of the site. St James Congregational Church was built in 1882-84, blocking all development to the east before the Schools were even built. It is difficult to understand the claim by the Charity Commission that the building would be capable of being enlarged, when it clearly wasn't. Why did the Commission not reject the proposed site as too small? The Commissioners were at least as much at fault as the governors and their clerk: they all slept.

> Saturday 27 Dec. Sat for fees 9-11a.m. and got Percy's only. Crow's came at night by post[3]
> Paid into Bank 27£ for the Governors. Gold £24. Silver 18/- Cheque £2 2.0 Sent Mr Willoughby 5/- for bandboys as a remembrance of playing at our sports.
> Turned off water from Chem Lab to prevent water leaking from an old soldered patch on that part of the pipe lying across the cistern in Girls' lavatory at 8.20pm

He had repeated battles with burst pipes, water and gas taps left on, doors left unlocked, snowfalls, broken locks. He had no caretaker and his cleaner was not entirely reliable, though she did suffer from genuine ill-health. She died only a few days after her last appearance in school; the Schools not only gave a wreath but contributed to her funeral expenses.

Parents appear in the log book quite regularly, and Merrick was sometimes quite exasperated by them.

> Mrs Henry hindered me from 12 to nearly half past.
> Received a note from Mr Chubb asking governors to cancel his debt for Sidney Chubb's school fees.
> Mrs Forster called and said there was nothing but favouritism in the school. Her boy had never got a 6d prize ever. I challenged her to look through the marks. She declined but agreed for Mr Forster to call on Wednesday next (he didn't!)
> Mrs McAllum called: she thought I had spoken to D. Roy about his boots and ears before the whole school. Mrs Ritson called to enquire about her youngest son's character. She had been mis-informed that he had been caned twice every day.

Other parents also complained about their sons being punished, by slapping, caning or detention.

> Received a letter of complaint from Mr Robson about my having caned his son.

Since we do not have the caning book, also a government requirement, we do not know how often Merrick resorted to this. He does mention some occasions when he used the cane, and observed his first use of the tawse. Other masters were not allowed to use corporal punishment; if they felt it to be deserved, they would make an entry in the book for the head master to take action. Some of the complaints by boys and parents were concerned with assistant masters striking pupils.

> Mrs Boag called at 2pm and complained about Mr Goodacre hitting her son on the head and wished to withdraw him, and I gave her leave to do so at once. 'The boy says Mr Goodacre hit him on the head with his hand and with a book, and in consequence he was afraid to come to school. ... He begged his mother to allow him to go somewhere else, said his mother in his presence, and he affirmed it was true ... Mr Goodacre denied the statement.

Mr Goodacre was in poor health at the time and had to take a Mediterranean cruise to convalesce. On his return, the boys clapped him. This, together with Merrick's alacrity in agreeing to young Boag's withdrawal, suggests where the real fault lay.

Some parents understood their sons very well. "Mrs Ferrow brought her son to school. He said he could not keep up in his Latin class; she said he played too long at nights."

Members of staff are frequently the subject of entries. At the beginning of each term Merrick recorded the names of the assistant masters. On 30 July, 1886, he recorded five colleagues: Mr A. B. Noble, Mr A. Goodacre, Mr N.H.M. Martin, Mr Nesbit and Signor C. S. Catoni. In addition he had two pupil teachers, Jamieson and Robinson. Over the course of the next six years that was the usual staff complement, apart from the addition of a "manual instructor" in November, 1891. In addition, the Vicar of Newcastle, Canon Lloyd, gave lessons. This

[3] Yes, a hundred years ago post *was* delivered in the evening on Saturdays, even on 27 December.

was for 186 boys. The head master taught and examined classes, but was frequently called away to meet visitors, from governors to plumbers. The little evidence we have suggests that pupil teachers may also have been present in the girls' school; for example Emma Nash joined the staff in April, 1890, aged 20, after two years as a governess. Her successor, in 1894, was the sixteen-year-old Jane Malkin.

The small staff meant that illness among them created considerable problems, and all seem to have been versatile in what they could teach. Merrick's own speciality was chemistry, about which he was clearly very enthusiastic. However, he records, without comment: "Query from the Department of Science and Art as to my qualifications for teaching certain subjects." On 23 March, 1891, there was a governors' meeting to which the head master might well be summoned, and that day four of the five members of staff were ill. Unfortunately, we do not know how the School coped – a surprising omission from the log book. If it were known that a member of staff would be away for some time, a supply teacher might be employed. One such was a former pupil teacher of the school.

Portrait believed to be Thomas Merrick, Head Master 1883-93

It was a matter of honour that a school of standing should have modern languages taught by a foreigner, ideally by a native speaker. The original French master was M. Vuez, but in April 1886 he died. During his illness and for a while afterwards, French was taught by Dr Schünemann. His successor was Signor Catoni, who demanded £55 a year to teach French. Merrick sought the advice of Professor Garnett, but "Catoni was the only man in the field." Still, it looked all right in the prospectus. The boys, however, did not accept him very easily, and Merrick records: "Punished several boys of Class V for misconduct in S. Catoni's lesson and kept in Class III for levity with S. Catoni". He seems to have been an odd man. Merrick records: "Signor Catoni called on Friday last, and informed me that Mr J. H. Martin had been to his house intriguing against me, and advised me to get rid of him."[4] Nevertheless Catoni stayed for four years and was briefly succeeded by Basil Porter, who was paid £90 in 1890, which made Catoni's demands appear very modest. He held the Intermediate Certificate of Melbourne University. His successor was Thorvald Demant, a Dane – the fifth nationality to teach French in five years. By 1895 Louis H Burvenich was languages master, and was in turn succeeded by G. H. Milner, B. A. (Durham) in 1895. We know less of the Girls' School staff. In 1890, Miss Mouseley was assisted by five mistresses. Her second mistress was Mary Heylin, trained in Edinburgh, who had been appointed very shortly after the opening of the new buildings. None of the staff held degrees – unsurprising as most universities were still refusing to admit women to degrees. Assistant teachers did hold the relevant qualifications expected at the time; Agnes Hawthorn (Edinburgh) and Maggie Ross (Moray House, Edinburgh) but Emma Nash was unqualified except perhaps as student teacher. All the qualified teachers were paid £75 per annum.

Alex Begg Noble was second master and was to continue in that post until 1898 – fifteen years. He seems to have been quietly effective, and figures little in the log book. Arthur Goodacre was appointed in 1886 at the age of 23. He had already been an assistant master for four years but somehow by 1890 he graduated B. A. of the Royal University of Ireland, and was thus the first graduate on the staff. He was to stay until 1923 – thirty-seven years, twenty-five of those as second master. By 1890, Catoni had been replaced by Porter, and Martin and Nesbit by Charles J. Robinson and George Price Dodds. Both had qualifications in science and mathematics, so

4 Catoni may have been correct - Merrick was later forced to dismiss Martin (see below).

that four of six masters were so qualified.

The pupil teachers are an interesting group, and are frequently referred to. There are generally two at any one time. They received instruction from Merrick in a variety of subjects to further their own education. These lessons would take place mostly before school, after school or on Saturday mornings. Their attendance was sometimes erratic; this clearly irritated Merrick and he recorded the fact. The two in the spring of 1886 were T. W. Jamieson and R. H. Robinson, and were aged fifteen. Saturday mornings were spent either in study – "Jamieson here principally occupied in practical chemistry" – or in doing odd-jobs – "Robinson filled inkwells." However, they were also learning how to teach. Merrick notes: "10-11 showed Robinson R. M. how to grind (?) up his boys in the History instead of setting them to learn it." One Saturday he observes "Robinson got Monday's lesson ready"; another day "Robinson R. M. took Mr Nesbit's class first hour, self afterwards; Jamieson took Latin lesson with Robinson, R.M., and Lowes, J.H." The head master backed up his pupil teachers: "caned Hesketh T. for striking and kicking Robinson R.M., and told him I should withdraw my recommendation for his being made a Foundation Scholar." That was a severe punishment – and even more so when Mr Hesketh found out. Jamieson's time as pupil teacher ended on 23 August, 1888; he is recorded in the first entry in the log book on 1 March, 1886, and so his apprenticeship was at last two and a half years. A year later he was employed for three weeks as a supply teacher. With a small staff, both schools were dependent on them to fill gaps when members of staff were absent. In extreme cases, monitors could also be used.

Not perhaps surprisingly, boys figure large in the book. Occasionally Merrick praises them directly, but more often by implication. When boys are successful in gaining admission to further education, he announces it to the School – and gives a half-holiday to encourage others. Some boys were bright, especially the Foundation Scholars, and others much less so. Some were sensible and well-behaved, willing to give up their own time to help members of staff, and to do extra academic work, in particular in practical science. Others behaved poorly, and no doubt got their deserts. One boy deserves mention. This is Thomas Eyton. At thirteen he was told that he could not return to Mr Goodacre's class "unless he would promise to work with a good will with Mr Goodacre". A few days later he struck another master and was sent home. He apologised in writing, but his father was told he might have "to be withdrawn at the end of term if necessary." A year later he was again offensive to a master, and Merrick spoke to him "kindly if seriously about his misconduct and told him that he must express his regret for his conduct to Mr Carrie verbally or in writing tomorrow morning." Merrick clearly saw young Tom's potential, despite his misdeeds. When Thomas Eyton died on 12 December, 1954, he was much lamented by the Schools, which he supported through the Old Boys' Association, and of which he was a governor for twenty-four years. "His whole life reflected the highest credit upon his old School and his teachers: he would have been able at any time to pass an examination on *My heritage and what I have made of it* …A practising Christian… His character built on piety and true learning." (*The Allanian*, Summer 1955). Merrick would have been proud of him.

Hints of the contents of lessons appear. "Class II : Practical chemistry. Most found out the two salts given to each, but the notes were poor. Examined Class V in geometrical drawing and found them very deficient."

"5-6pm Five boys did practical electricity and magnetism." It was common for boys to stay late or come on Saturday mornings, both voluntarily and as a punishment.

Books had to be bought, initially from a bookshop, but by 1892 from the School bookshop. Foundation scholars received their books free: "gave out books to Foundation Scholars; gave out lists of books needed for next half." In English, we find *A Midsummer Night's Dream* and *Coriolanus* were read, but it is unlikely that any attempt at acting took place. "Davenport[5] and Forster still without copies of *Charles XII*", which suggests that European history was being taught. The governors became concerned at one point in 1887 at the number of subjects being taught and considered "which could be cut out": they chose shorthand and German. There was an immediate complaint about the former, and about the absence of Latin in the curriculum. Apparently Latin was returned to the timetable subsequently but numbers fell to only two boys; a new class of twenty beginners was introduced in January 1889.

---

[5] W.B. Davenport was sadly, twelve years later, to die at Mafeking during the South African War, the earliest Allanian known to have died on active service, though others must surely have done so.

Singing had been a part of the curriculum since the foundation and there was a "singing hour" at this time. When there was the annual service and prize presentation "the usual timetable was suspended to practise singing". There does not seem to have been any other form of music, certainly no instrumental tuition.

There was clearly a lot of rote learning. Merrick tells a master "to let Potts off poetry except a few lines per week," viz, to memorise it. On another occasion he "kept in boys until 5.30 to learn poetry". One hopes that they understood why this poetry was worth committing to memory. The only poet mentioned by name as being read in class was Sir Walter Scott.

Mathematics was broken down into its several parts and taught as such. But it was especially in the science field that Merrick tried to raise standards. The two laboratories were a source of great pride. "Professor Garnett brought Mr Buckmaster of the Science and Art Department, South Kensington, to see the Physical Laboratory; they also looked over the Chemical Laboratory. Mr Buckmaster urged me to try to get the school made an organised Science School." In fact it took four years (1890) to achieve it: "School recognised as an Organised Science School by Department of Science and Art". Thereafter it was necessary to keep a "science register"; the school received a grant in 1891, and "Gradon Thompson won exhibition at the College of Science in Open Competition, being bracketed first." The next year he records that he "read out to the scholars the official letters sent by the Durham College of Science to H. J. Girling and to J. P. Shepherd informing them that they had each been approved of for Free Studentships at the College for next September." Only the day before "Dr Garnett and two friends called to see the Chemical Laboratory and also visited the bookshop." Merrick was justly proud of what he had achieved in science teaching.

Meanwhile he was urging the governors to consider the introduction of technical education in accordance with the Technical Instruction Act, but it is not clear exactly what became of this. However, a manual instructor, Mr W Patterson[6], was appointed in November 1891, and a shed was quickly erected in the playground as a workshop and equipped with benches. Merrick had earlier paid a visit to Gateshead Higher Grade School to look at their arrangements for "Manual Learning". In the following June, an evening examination took place: the task was to make a lap-joint. About the same time the Northumberland County Council Technical Educational Committee's competition for scholarships was held in the schools, with about 70 boys taking part.

Other points of interest appear in the 386 pages of the Log Book. Examinations consisted of (a) the Head Master's informal tests, usually oral; (b) yearly examinations (oral and written) by an outside examiner; and (c) national examinations such as the Cambridge Locals and the South Kensington examinations. As a result of (b) promotions were made from class to class.

A bicycling club was set up, but since its activities were out of school there is no further reference. The athletic sports were however a school event. In September, 1886, Merrick records that he spent part of the morning "seeking a field for the sports". The Jesmond Athletic Ground Company lent a field, and after a day's holiday, the event took place in the early evening, and prizes were awarded. In 1890 it was the Riding School ground; these two are the only recorded sports. There was some kind of gymnastic equipment in the school yard, but there is no evidence of what, and of how it was used. In 1891, a meeting of the Old Boys' Sports Committee took place, but nothing is known of its fortunes. It is remarkable that such a body existed when it had no home ground and the School's sporting tradition was so limited.

The log book yields some information about the Girls' School in passing. Merrick's relationship with Mrs Landells and then Miss Mousley varied, but was generally rather formal. Throughout this period Merrick was responsible for sending for materials, checking the Girls' School premises, and for getting workmen to attend to problems. This was only fair: he had a school house next door. In addition, in the opening year or more he taught girls in "Elementary Natural Philosophy and Chemistry". This does not seem to have continued, and in six years there is only one reference to the girls using one of the boys' laboratories. However, in 1891 the Commissioners noted that "arrangements are now being made between them (the two heads) by which the girls will be able to attend some of the Science classes." Instead of a photographer coming once in 1887 for both schools, he had to

---

[6]After retirement, he taught at the school again, briefly, in 1912 after his successor Mr Ladds' departure.

The chemical labratory at College Street, built in 1883 and later remodelled.

come twice: sadly no copy of either photograph has survived. Another entry reports: "Girls came to learn shorthand upstairs (boys' school!). I told Mr Currie to see them downstairs, and up and down hereafter to future lessons". In some areas the heads clearly worked together – examinations at the same time and a joint annual service and prizegiving. This event took place at the end of the autumn term. In 1886, it took the following pattern. In the morning there were recitations in English and French and singing in preparation for later, and the prizes were sorted out by members of staff. At 12 noon the pupils left school and re-assembled at St Andrew's Church at 2pm. Canon Lloyd, Vicar of Newcastle and governor[7], was the preacher; he taught in school most weeks and was thus well known to everyone. At 3pm the pupils were already at the Y.M.C.A. hall for the distribution of prizes by Mr W. D. Cruddas, chairman of governors and a prominent local figure[8].

The occasion was supplemented by recitations and singing as rehearsed earlier. The following year the events took place at the same venue in the evening, but the pupils had the afternoon off. In 1888, the timing and the church were the same, but the prize distribution was in school and art work was displayed. In 1889, a different pattern was followed. Pupils did not arrive until 1.30 when they were taken to church, returning for prizegiving to the school. In 1890 it was again an evening event, with St Thomas's and the school as the venues; but the next year there was a full turnout of governors including the mayor, at the Lovaine Hall. It was clear that conditions were too cramped at College Street. The governors included Walter Plummer[9] and Edward Armorer Hedley[10] after whom two Boys' School houses were to be named in honour of their long commitment to the Schools. Others were William Donaldson Cruddas, an engineer, and Robert Gurney Hoare, a banker.

On two occasions Girls' School dances are recorded. "Girls had a dance in their schoolroom 7-9.30" – no boys. But the next year: "Girls had dancing this afternoon and night; brothers of girls present with them (who were boys in the boys' school)." In 1890, this was no doubt regarded as progressive. "Present during part of girls'

[7]Canon Arthur Thomas Lloyd was Vicar of Newcastle 1882-94 and Bishop of Newcastle 1903-07. His rich canopied effigy tomb is on the north side of the choir in the Cathedral.
[8]William Donaldson Cruddas, an engineer, and soon to become Member of Parliament.
[9]Walter Plummer, councillor and later mayor; MP for Newcastle; knighted; interested in technical education. Served for many years on the Newcastle School Board.
[10]Edward Hedley, soap manufacturer: vice-chairman and later chairman of the governors. He succeeded the Revd John Reed on the governing body in 1884.

event last night," he added the next day.

Thomas Merrick was clearly a caring man, concerned about sick or injured pupils, sending them by cab to a doctor or hospital or home, with a master or pupil teacher to accompany them. He had his own family, where the children are sometimes ill, and indeed suffered the loss of a baby. He showed understanding towards less able boys: "I offered to let him do what he could of his weakest subjects. I got some milk for the lad but he would not take any." On another occasion he told two masters not to give three boys "much memory work", and gave one of those masters "notes on those boys who have something the matter with them". He visited sick colleagues and occasionally boys, and showed a real responsibility for all.

Carl Lotinga has written about his later years (1883-91) in College Street, then newly opened. He relates how much more strenuous was a pupil's day, compared with the present, since many had to walk to school. School was from 9.00am to 12.30pm, when pupils went home for their lunches or sat in their desks to eat a packed meal. Work resumed at 2.00pm until 4.30pm, with an extension to 5.00pm or even later for the naughty or idle. The Cambridge Local Examinations provided an academic target and for a few this led to university, which meant Durham University, College of Science (later King's College) or Medicine. These examinations were held in the library of the old College of Medicine, later the Great Hall of the Sutherland Dental School in Northumberland Road. Thomas Merrick "greatly favoured mathematics and science, with the South Kensington examinations in view". He also commented on the large amount of homework – plus ça change …

"The senior boys were taken in scripture by the Vicar of Newcastle, Canon Lloyd, who was also chairman of governors of the School. He entertained all boys leaving the School at the end of each quarter to supper at the vicarage in Rye Hill. This was followed by boxing contests, and a memorable sight it was, with some rare bouts, a sport on which he was very keen. On this occasion each boy was presented with a Bible and Prayer Book by the Governors. In my day there were a number of scholarships competed for by boys attending the elementary schools. Several of those were also awarded to pupils of the School itself whom the Head Master judged worthy.

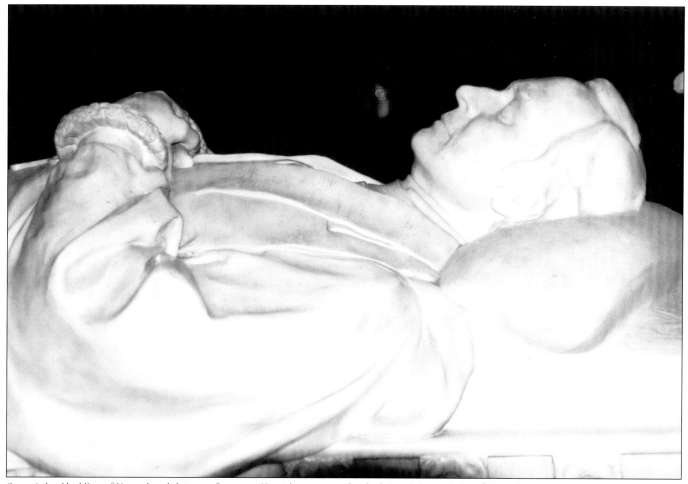

Canon Arthur Lloyd, Vicar of Newcastle and chairman of governors. He taight scripture at the school. Later he became Bishop of Newcastle.
Detail of magnificent tomb in the cathedral

These boys were known as Foundation Scholars, and received free education. A few of these were later given a higher level of scholarship which brought with it a monetary grant at the end of the year." Although similar reminiscences do not appear to exist for the girls, much of the above would also apply to the girls, though probably not the boxing contests.

Multiplication is Vexation, by Ralph Hedley (1880). Watercolour. There is also a version in oils.
Ralph Hedley was to paint Allan's girls frequently over 25 years. (Private Collection)

We have seen from the log book that Merrick also had problems with his staff, culminating with the dismissal after three years at the school of J. H. Martin in September 1887, "owing to his inability to work harmoniously with the rest of the teaching staff". But it was no doubt the lack of vision in the governing body that determined him to leave the Boys' School at Christmas 1892. The governors had erected a fine façade in College Street and had crammed 300 pupils behind it – that, he feared, was the past, present and future of the schools. Merrick recorded his last afternoon, no doubt with many regrets. "Boys and girls and teachers of both Schools presented me with a walnut writing desk in the main room. Some girls and all the girls' staff present. Mr Noble made the presentation. No word breathed to me on the subject before 12 noon today. Schools all right 10.45pm. Entd. 10.45pm 21.12.1892 T.M."

We find that he continued to live in Newcastle, where in the 1901 Census he is described as a schoolmaster "own account working at home". He was only 43 when he left College Street for a less stressful life as a private tutor. He was the last certificated head teacher of the Boys' School: in future they were to be graduates.

Thomas Merrick, Catherine Landells and Emma Mouseley had established the schools in College Street along with the staffs of the two schools. Their days had been long ones; the prospectus of October 1890 gave school hours 9am to 12.30 and 1.55pm to 4.30. Merrick's had been even longer acting as caretaker - though with the great benefit of the house. Mrs Landells had been a tangible link with the former school having taught pupils of the old foundation in St John's School. Merrick had been a dedicated and caring Head Master, championing the cause of science with his two laboratories. Miss Mouseley was proving a very successful Head Mistress, judging by inspection reports. Their achievements in the establishment of the schools were crowned with the award of grants from the Department of Science and Art from 1890 onwards. These were not inconsiderable; the school received £80 10s 1d for educating 127 pupils in science in 1892 and a further £11 10s for the instruction of 116 pupils in art. Their industry had overcome the acute limitations of the building and site and firmly established the role of the Schools in the life of the city.

Chapter Six

ALLAN'S ENDOWED SCHOOLS IN COLLEGE STREET:
THE CONFIDENCE OF THE TOWN 1893 - 1914

The years 1893 to 1915 are difficult to trace; no logbook survives from the period and much of our knowledge of the school comes from inspection reports and a very incomplete collection of Speech Day programmes, school magazines and newspaper cuttings.

In January, 1893, a new Head Master arrived in the Boys' School. The governors' choice was Edward Barrett Moffatt, M.A., Scholar of Queens' College, Cambridge, who was born in 1862 at Hexham. He had matriculated in 1882, and by 1889 he was assistant master at Sandbach Grammar School in Cheshire. We know little of him, but the 1896 report (see below) suggests that he left his successor some problems. Perhaps the governors, having experienced in Merrick a strong-minded man, deliberately chose someone academically better qualified but less determined.

Miss Dobson, Head Mistress 1894-1933

The Girls' School also found itself with a new head. Miss Mousley left in 1894 after eight years, still only 34. Her reason for leaving was marriage: she had captured the heart of Arthur Goodacre, assistant master in the Boys' School and five years her junior. She was succeeded by Miss Sarah Elizabeth Dobson, LL.A., (St Andrews) who was still in her twenties, at a salary of £250. She had been awarded the Queen's Scholarship, her Teachers' Certificate and the Archbishop's Certificate, all in the First Class, as well as South Kensington Certificates in Science. Already she had been the Head Mistress of three schools; we must assume they were small and afforded her fewer opportunities than she sought at Dame Allan's. She was to remain head for nearly forty years and was to see the transformation of girls' education. She began asserting her authority early. In 1893 the governors had decided to delegate to the heads the power of appointment and dismissal of teachers, and in 1896 she exercised it by dismissing two teachers who "have been in the school so long that they fail to recognise their proper attitude to a headmistress. They are very unpleasant colleagues." Since one, Miss Agnes Hawthorn[1], had been her deputy for two years, and the whole assistant staff was only five, the impact must have been enormous.

---

[1] Miss Hawthorn went on to set up a private school in Jesmond and sent pupils on to Dame Allan's.

Allan's Endowed Schools,

NEWCASTLE-UPON-TYNE.

THE ANNUAL

DISTRIBUTION OF PRIZES AND CERTIFICATES,

BY

THE MAYOR OF NEWCASTLE.

(ALDERMAN W. H. STEPHENSON, J.P.,)

IN THE

Church Institute, Wednesday, December 19th, 1894.

PROGRAMME.

CHAIRMAN'S ADDRESS.

| HOOP DRILL | ... | ... | ... | ... | ... | ... | ... | GIRLS. |
| VIOLIN SOLO | ... | ... | ... | ... | ... | ... | ... | F. DAVIS. |

DISTRIBUTION OF PRIZES AND CERTIFICATES.

| SONGS OF THE FOUR NATIONS AND TABLEAUX | ... | ... | ... | ... | GIRLS. |

After the conclusion of the above Programme, there will be an Exhibition of Drill and Gymnastic Exercises in the Boys' School, as follows:—

DUMB-BELL EXERCISES (Musical).

HORIZONTAL BAR EXERCISES (Low and High).

TABLEAUX.

ROPE CLIMBING.   PARALLEL BARS.

TABLEAUX.

HIGH JUMPING.   FIGURE MARCHING (Musical).

Joint Schools' Prize Day, 1894. (Oldest surviving programme to any event).

Her first Distribution of Prizes and Certificates took place jointly with the Boys' School in the Church Institute on 19 December, 1894. Before the Mayor presented the prizes, the girls did a "hoop drill" and there was a violin solo. Afterwards the girls performed "Songs for the Four Nations and Tableaux." The boys' contribution was "an Exhibition of Drill and Gymnastic Exercises" back at the school, with dumb-bells, horizontal bars, rope climbing, high jumping, tableaux and figure marching, some being accompanied by music. Exhibitions were awarded to two girls and one boy at Durham University College of Physical Science. Pupils of both Schools received certificates from the Department of Science and Art, South Kensington (London), the girls in Freehand Drawing, Model Drawing, Practical Plane and Solid Geometry and Botany, and the boys in Geometrical Drawing, Freehand Drawing, Mathematics, Theoretical Chemistry, Practical Chemistry and Shorthand. Subsequent Prize Days, as they were renamed, were held in the Church Institute in 1895 and the Grand Assembly Rooms, Barras Bridge, thereafter. The guests of honour were Mrs W. D. Cruddas, wife of the Chairman and local M.P.; the Principal of Durham College of Science; a Miss Jacob (?); and the High Sheriff of Northumberland and Mrs Burdon (jointly). Strangely the programmes do not indicate any active pupil participation such as there was in 1894 — a retrograde step.

In 1896, Moffatt left after only three and a half years, to become head master and proprietor of a school in Croydon, and in September Frederic William Brewer, M.A., became Head Master. He was born in 1867 at Preston, Lancashire, where he attended the grammar school. He was an Open Mathematical Scholar at St Catharine's College, Cambridge, from 1885 to 1889 and Senior Optime of the mathematical tripos in 1888. He joined the staff of his old school in 1891, where he rapidly became second master; concurrently he lectured at the Harris Institute in Preston in higher mathematics, mechanics and Latin. At Allan's Endowed Boys' School he taught two classes in mathematics and some Latin and scripture. For this he was paid £350 plus the adjacent house. At the time of his death in office in 1925 his salary had risen to £725.

One task that Moffatt had neglected was keeping the Admissions Register, and Brewer had to reconstruct it "from any records he could find" in October. One new entrant that year was A. F. Donald, aged nine, from "Mr Merrick's", the small school established by the former head master. In that same year, W. Tyson left the boys' school to study at the College of Physical Science, matriculating in 1894 and there may have been others before him. Moffatt may have lacked organisation, but academic standards remained high during his time at the school.

In 1897 the country and the empire celebrated the Diamond Jubilee of Queen Victoria. No British monarch had reigned as long, no nation was as powerful and no empire had covered so much of the world. The streets of every city, town and village were heavy in flags and bunting, and huge celebrations took place. Miss Dobson created an event that had been inspired by a similar one at Whitelands College in London which she had attended for two years from January, 1885, when she was eighteen. In 1881 the college, a High Anglican foundation, had instituted a Rose Fayre, with singing, dancing and drama, an idea originating with the principal's friend, John Ruskin. It was a highly successful annual event, and on 17 June, 1897, the first Dame Allan's Queen, Annie Davidson, was crowned, and so began a similarly successful Newcastle tradition. "The Lovaine Hall was nicely

Lieutenant-Colonel F.W. Brewer, O.B.E., Head Master 1896-1926

Hockey team c1895. A surprisingly early date, since regular games against other schools had to await the purchase of the fields in Fenham after 1930

decorated with flowers, festoons of ivy and national flags," wrote a local reporter. "The centre was occupied by a maypole with streamers of many hues, and on the platform was a white-draped throne." Another wrote: "All the girls from the school were there, themselves sweet buds of coming womanhood. Nearly all of them were in white, and most of them wore garlands of leaves in their hair, and each of them carried in her hand either a bouquet of flowers or a dish of fruit. The effect was exquisitely pretty. Ballot papers were distributed for the election of the queen, which was based on an absolutely democratic principle – one girl, one vote. While the voting papers were being counted, songs were sung very nicely." The result was then announced, and Annie "retired with her attendants to prepare for the coronation ceremony". After the crowning with a garland of white flowers – by whom we do not know – her subjects paid homage and presented the flowers and fruit, which were later distributed to hospitals. She in turn was to have presented Jubilee medals, but unfortunately they had not arrived in time from the Birmingham medallists. The event ended with more songs, the plaiting of the maypole and God Save the Queen. "There was a large attendance of parents, friends and boy scholars."

This festival was intended to be a one-off to mark the Jubilee and there was no similar event in 1898, but the great success it had achieved seems to have brought about the decision to have one the following year, and in all subsequent years until 1932, except during the war years 1915-18, when no doubt it was deemed inappropriate. All of these 'coronations' had an extra element since there was an opening ceremony in which the retiring queen surrendered her withered garland before the election took place. The only criteria for a flower/rose queen that we know of were that she should be "the most good-natured and show the strongest character". Good looks were not supposed to be important, but the many

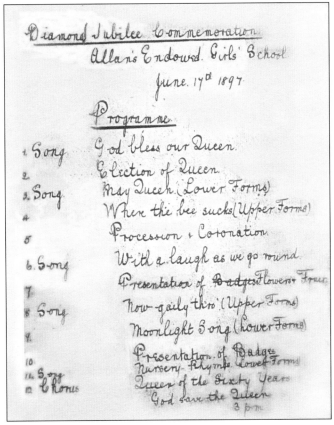

Handwritten programme for first Rose Queen event, 1897

surviving photographs suggest that plain girls stood little chance. The candidate had to be at least fifteen. We do not know if the queens were called upon to perform any duties during their year of office. Clearly there could have been problems if the School also had a head girl appointed by the Head Mistress in conflict with a popularly-elected girl of "the strongest character".

On three occasions the School's monarch was linked to the national monarch. These were in 1897, as seen, and in 1902 and 1911, when the Rose Queen distributed bronze medals specially struck for the School to mark the coronations of King Edward VII and King George V. On the former occasion, Rhoda Heppell asked, not for a day's holiday, but a week's and for both Schools: the governors agreed on the spot. As a local newspaper put it "This was not on the programme as originally drawn up, but was quite the most popular feature." More important than the election of a Rose Queen was, however, the supporting programme. All the girls took part in songs and many in solos, instrumental items and recitations. Perhaps the most significant element in the longer term was the development of drama and music theatre. As early as the opening years of the Twentieth Century these were

being performed. Initially, the subjects were fairy stories and similar, but in 1913 came *A Pageant of Women*, an original work by an Old Allanian, Miss Alice Dawson, M.Litt, which was concerned with the history of women in Northumberland. *The Evening Chronicle* wrote: "In past years the scholars have been responsible for some

Rose Queen Celebrations: One of the Muses in "The Pageant of Women", 1913. N.B. The actress in the centre is also the Rose Queen, indicated by her cross

Rose Fayre at Lovaine Hall, 1901. Bertha Dobson as Queen, with the whole school in costume, and the staff in magnificent hats

Rose Fayre
1897 - 1935

Queen Murial and Pages. July 1919

ROSE FAYRES / FLOWER FESTIVALS

Year	Queen	Crowned by	Location	Programme/Features
1897	Annie Davidson		LH	In honour of Queen Victoria's Diamond Jubilee
1898				No event
1899	G Fenwick	?	LH	?
1900	Louie Noble	?	LH	?
1901	Bertha Dobson	Miss Sybil Lister	LH	Songs, sketches, *Red Riding Hood*
1902	Rhoda Hepple	Mrs Erskine	LH	Coronation models distributed, *Cinderella* (operetta)
1903	Any Gordon	Dr Floyd, Bishop of Newcastle	LH	Songs, recitation, instrumental music
1904	Elsie Allan	Mrs Sutton	DH	Songs, *Sleeping Beauty*
1905	Mabel Dunn	Lady Owen	GAR	Songs, instrumental music
1906	?	?		
1907	Jessie McGregor	?	GAR	Songs, instrumental music
1908	Margaret Park	Lady Scott	GAR	Operetta: *In Wonderland*
1909	Bessie Pool	Lady Constance Emmet	GAR	Dramatised: *Hiawatha*
1910	Gladys Jennings	Lady Riddell	GAR	Musical Play: *Demeter and Persephone*
1911	Mildred Green	Mrs Gough	GAR	Musical Play: *Katawampus* (Judge Parry)
1912	Elsie Jennings	Deputy Lady Mayoress	GAR	Version of Tennyson's *Princess*
1913	Irene Pouter	Viscountess Ridley	GAR	*A Pageant of Women*
1914	Mary Park	?	GAR	*As You Like It* (Shakespeare)
1915-1918	No festival during war years			
1919	Muriel Williams	Mrs John Pybus	HAH	*As You Like It* (again)
1920	Winnie Kidner	?	HAH	Musical events
1921	Winnie Kidner	?	HAH	Musical events
1922	Dorothy Lowden	Lady Mayoress	KH	Songs; juniors-play with music by A F Milner
1923	Dorothy Sawden	?	GAR	Scenes from *The Talisman*; Green and sword dances
1924	Norah Richardson	Lady Montgomery	GAR	Musical selection
1925	Mabel Scott	?	GAR	Musical Selection
1926	Betty Harper	Mrs Joyner	GAR	Play: *The Dream Lady*; a cantata; songs
1927	?			
1928	?			
1929	Enid Wood	?	GAR	*A Pageant of Women* (cf 1913)
1930	Mary Galley	Mrs Bateman-Champain	GAR	Music
1931	Kathleen Clare	Dowager Countess Allandale	GAR	Musical play: *The Whispering Wood*
1932	Frances Ellison	Lady Mayoress	GAR	Music
1933 and 1934		No festival		

1935   A Rose Fayre, based on earlier festivals but organised by the Parents' Association and involving the Boys' School, took place on 30th and 31st October, and was opened on the first day by the Duchess of Northumberland and on the second by Lord Armstrong. It was in the Old Assembly Rooms at the bottom of Westgate Road.

LH	Lovaine Hall, St Mary's Place
DH	St George's Drill Hall
GAR	Grand Assemby Rooms, Barras Bridge
HAH	Heaton Assembly Hall
KH	King's Hall, Armstrong College

meritorious performances… after the crowning … and on this occasion a charming and interesting feature was introduced … It afforded considerable scope for the exercise of artistic and histrionic talent by a large number of the pupils." Clio, the muse of history, had five attendants, Piety, Courage, Charity, Tradition and Wisdom, and each of these presented women of the North East who displayed these qualities. Charity introduced not only Eleanor Allan but also Mrs Dorothy Chisholm, an early benefactress of the Schools. Wisdom presented, amongst others, the poet Elizabeth Barrett Browning, who lived for some time at Fenham Hall, and Harriet Beecher Stowe, author of *Little Women*, "who stayed in Newcastle, within the memory of some of those who witnessed the entertainment." Altogether some forty-five prominent women were presented, some who had stayed briefly but many who had lived all or most of their lives in the region. With attendants and others, the number of performers must have been half the School. In the month that Emily Davidson died in the cause of female suffrage, Dame Allan's girls were voting democratically and celebrating women's achievements, and their retiring queen was awarded a £30 Exhibition by the governors to study for a degree at the University of Durham (Armstrong College) The next year saw a standard play, *As You Like It*, which had scope for music and dance. It was, too, the first Shakespeare production. The next four years were the war years and when the coronations resumed in 1919, the play was repeated, as if to say, we go on from where we left off. Thus began the tradition of public performances of music and of drama that was to play such an important part in the Girls' School. The annual Shakespeare Festival is the current continuation of this tradition.

One newspaper reporter in 1902 was highly enthusiastic: "If the ceremony were to be repeated every day for a month running, it would require something serious to keep me, a prosy old man, back from going to see it every day… My feeling is that, if I had a hundred daughters, I should send them all to be in the happy company at Allan's Endowed Girls' School, and to be under the efficient training of Miss Dobson and her accomplished staff of lady teachers." Many years later Nora Bennitt recalled the occasions as ones of great delight. "The event occasioned much singing and dancing before … assembled parents and friends. The queen received a small cross to keep". One of these is fixed to the frame of the portrait of Winnie Kidner[3], who was queen in 1920.

The scheme for the Schools was amended in 1895, and from the next year they were the subject of annual reports. Of the Girls' School, the 1896 report comments on the unsettling effect of staff changes but states that there was promise of further increasing "the usefulness of this good school". For the boys, the examiner felt that the new head "has a difficult task before him in regulating and co-ordinating the work of the classes and in infusing the essential idea of thoroughness." The best was very good but too much was only fair. By the next year there was a general improvement in the Boys' School while it was said of the Girls' School that "there is evidence in every class of wisely devised teaching and careful oversight of the work done by the scholars". By 1898 Brewer had got his school into "a thoroughly sound and efficient condition", while the skilled teaching earlier praised in the Girls' School is

Allan's Endowed Girls' School, Newcastle-upon-Tyne.

Report for Term ending July 30th /96
Name Miss Margaret Newton Form V Division I
No. of Girls in Form 21   Position in Form 7
ATTENDANCE—No. of Times School Open 116 … No. of Times Absent 10 … No. of Times Late

SUBJECT.	MARKS.			REMARKS.
	Maximum.	Obtained.	Position.	
Scripture	373	303½	6	
Catechism	145	115	3	
Reading				Good
Spelling	120	71	19	
Writing				Good
Arithmetic	326	251	7	
English Grammar	156	121	9	
English Literature	103	90½	4	
Composition	40	38	4	
History	320	244	9	
Geography	306	245	4	
Map Drawing	90	56	16	
French	272	157	21	30 in Class
Hygiene / Domestic Economy	80	72	2	
Needlework				Good
Physiology	35	12		
Botany				
Algebra	282	180½	12	
Euclid				
Drawing—Freehand				
Do. Geometry				
Do. Model				
Do. Kindergarten				

GENERAL CONDUCT IN SCHOOL 261 · 236
NEXT TERM COMMENCES September 15
S L Dobson HEAD MISTRESS.

Report, 1896. Note "Miss Newton" and very exact marks.

[3] Winnie Kidner was to marry a Sunderland-born American naval officer who became Admiral Gordon Maclintock, Admiral in Command of the U.S. Merchant Marine Academy in New York (1948-70). At her death in 1973 she was buried in Arlington National Cemetery, Washington, and the admiral presented to the School the portrait by Tatiana Tchetchet that had been commissioned by the Women's Clubs of Long Island and New York. She played a very active role in the welfare of the young cadets, and was highly respected.
[4] Raised to 16 in line with the girls in 1899, but in fact with the agreement of the governors pupils had since 1877 been able to stay even longer.

echoed in the Boys' School. In subsequent years the word "excellent" is used of both Schools, but comments on the cramped conditions and shortage of classrooms for the girls and a leaving age of 15 for the boys[4] when "I am quite sure that boys might with great advantage stay until 17" show that they were in some measure handicapped.

Prize Giving continued to be an annual event in the 1890s, being held in the Church Institute up to 1895 and in the Grand Assembly Rooms, Barras Bridge, thereafter. Girls were already going on to study at the Durham College of Science, Armstrong College, in Newcastle. For example, nine were studying towards the B.Litt. examination in 1897; one, just embarking upon the course was Eleanor Armstrong who was to return to her old school as a teacher from January 1901 to December 1920.

The buildings, so fiercely attacked by the Charity Commissioners, continued to cost the governing body considerable sums in modifications and improvements. One project was to fit up a laboratory to the current regulations and another to increase accommodation for girls by thirty. Because of the high demand for places, the Schools were by 1895 in debt, and then sought both to raise fees to £3 18s for juniors and £4 19s for seniors and to sell some Wallsend Farm land.

The teaching staff at the time were increasingly well qualified, with the proportion of graduate and certificated teachers rising. The Boys' School staff, with the exception of the art and gym masters, were university educated. In the Girls' School, the new second mistress, Agnes Young, had studied at London University and the third mistress, Anne Hind, was among the earliest to have trained as a teacher at the Cambridge Training College, later Hughes Hall. In 1896 a specialist art teacher, Miss Ethel Cole, A.T.C., was appointed to the Girls' School. The curriculum they delivered included science subjects examined by the South Kensington Science and Art Examinations as well as preparation for Pitman's Shorthand certificates, College of Preceptors' examinations and Cambridge Local examinations. In particular, South Kensington certificates taken by pupils of one or both Schools included mathematics, practical plane and solid geometry, advanced theoretical chemistry, advanced practical chemistry, theoretical inorganic chemistry, botany, animal physiology, human physiology, freehand drawing, geometrical drawing and model drawing. We know from the record of distinctions in the Cambridge Senior examinations that pupils were examined in physiology, hygiene, English, drawing, arithmetic and religious knowledge.

As the century closed, the inspection report read, for the Boys' School, "the school has maintained all along the line the high standard attained last year and I consider English and Latin have made very considerable advances". The report on the Girls' School was even better, academic work being being of "an excellent standard" and the Schools' discipline and general conduct "leave nothing to be desired". Miss Dobson and Mr Brewer must have read these reports with great satisfaction, especially as they were all too aware of the cramped conditions under which they were working.

Students' achievements were not confined to academic excellence. When the South African (Boer) War broke out in 1899, sixteen Old Allanians volunteered to serve with the Northumberland Hussars or the Northumberland Fusiliers. One of these was, remarkably, A. B. Noble, who had been second master from the opening of College Street in 1883 until he resigned in 1898 because of ill health and moved to South Africa to convalesce. One of these men, W. B. Davenport, a former pupil teacher, was to die at Mafeking. It was not until 1913 that a roll of honour was put up in the School. It was the work of the art master and manual instructor, G. H. Cutting, and some years ago was skilfully cleaned, framed and erected in the Newsom Hall. Davenport was the first of 128 Old Allanians who died in the wars of the first half of the Twentieth Century; the sixteen were the first of 1080 who served.

In 1903 the Board of Education recognised the Schools under the Teachers' Registration Regulations. It was noted that the accommodation was poor and that "the bulk of the boys desire a more commercial training and work at chemistry, bookkeeping and shorthand". In the same year there was a proposal to address the accommodation problem by demolishing the head master's house and rebuilding as classrooms at an estimated cost of about £3000. Two years later an inspector, L A. Stephens, prepared a memorandum for the Board of Education on secondary education in Newcastle in general and Allan's Endowed Schools in particular. He found the standard of work rather low, "if judged from a decent Secondary School standard, good if judged from that

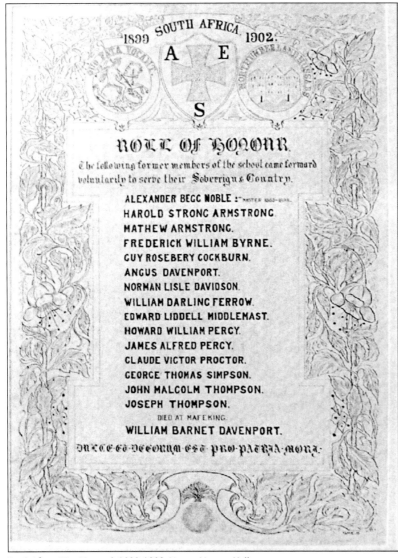

South African War Memorial, 1899-1902. Now in Newsom Hall

Within the image (Roll of Honour):

1899 SOUTH AFRICA 1902.

ROLL OF HONOUR.

The following former members of the school came forward voluntarily to serve their Sovereign & Country.

ALEXANDER BEGG NOBLE :—
HAROLD STRONG ARMSTRONG.
MATHEW ARMSTRONG.
FREDERICK WILLIAM BYRNE.
GUY ROSEBERY COCKBURN.
ANGUS DAVENPORT.
NORMAN LISLE DAVIDSON.
WILLIAM DARLING FERROW.
EDWARD LIDDELL MIDDLEMAST.
HOWARD WILLIAM PERCY.
JAMES ALFRED PERCY.
CLAUDE VICTOR PROCTOR.
GEORGE THOMAS SIMPSON.
JOHN MALCOLM THOMPSON.
JOSEPH THOMPSON.

DIED AT MAFEKING.

WILLIAM BARNET DAVENPORT.

of a Higher Elementary" but felt "no doubt that the whole school might easily be raised to a higher plane." He felt strongly that "it needs re-organisation and both the check and stimulus of inspection." Generally he felt that "a large number of boys and girls in the Newcastle Secondary Schools and Pupil Teacher Centres are receiving but a slender portion of the corporate school life that they ought to be enjoying." His recommendation was that instead of building extensions, the governors should buy the Pupil Teacher Centre buildings and move the Boys' School there, while the girls took over the whole College Street building for 300 pupils. Both schools were to take in "at the cost of their education any scholarship holders of intending pupil teachers of either the City of Newcastle or the County of Northumberland." Once they were properly housed they could apply for recognition and use the income to recoup the capital cost of the purchase of the Centre. Shortly afterwards the Board of Education turned down the application to demolish the head master's house. Stephens had talked to Canon Lister, Vicar of St Andrew's and Chairman of Governors, but seems to have found the governors unco-operative and complacent: "very suspicious of any interference." We do not have a similar record of the governors' views, but it is not difficult to see that after two centuries the Church of England clergy saw no good reason to hand over their schools to others, or to countenance secularisation. The Council's choice of nonconformists as their representatives was seen as a provocation and a sign of the way things were likely to go given half a chance. In fact nothing was done and the Schools were to struggle on for another thirty years with no significant improvement in accommodation.

We have an interesting glimpse of life in College Street in the first few years of the Twentieth Century from a boy called McNeil. He recalled as a boy of eleven following his father into the Head Master's study in his house one late summer's day in 1901. "I can still see the penetrating eyes of Frederic William Brewer sizing me up from the other side of his desk. I felt rather small under his scrutiny, which was keen but kind, but I answered his questions as well as I could, and I was accepted. Why my father chose a Church of England school for me, I never could fathom, for I don't think he ever attended an Anglican service in his life. A Scot, he was brought up in the Kirk of Scotland, but in later life he had adopted very liberal views in matters of religion. My mother was the daughter of a nonconformist clergyman and I myself had been brought up in that faith. The Anglican influence of Dame Allan's was to have its effect, however, in the years that followed. In keeping with the School's association with the Church, religious instruction was pretty thorough, and as I found out later when taking a theological degree at Trinity College, Toronto, it was as comprehensive as that required there, at least so far as the Synoptic Gospels were concerned." He praised the teaching of classics, found Cicero's *De Amicitia* "not very interesting" but "Mr Page made the *Aeneids*, particularly Books II and VI absorbing. He also acted as sports master as far as we could pride ourselves on having a sports programme. He was secretary, treasurer and wicket keeper for South Northumberland C.C. Our cricket practices took place on the Town Moor where the pitches were so bumpy as to make the bowling unplayable, or at any rate, unpredictable. We had some fun, certainly, but about

Allan's Endowed School (College Street), June 14th 1899

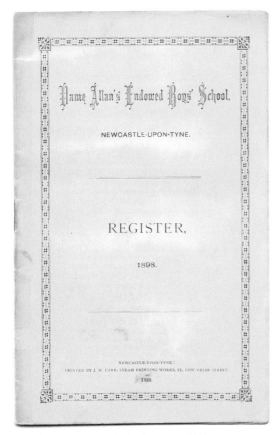

Cover of earliest extant Boys' School magazine, 1898

the only thing we really learned was to 'play a straight bat'.

"What football we played was Association. I suppose that was because Mr Brewer had excelled at it at Cambridge where I believe he won his Blue. I do know that at one time he played half-back for Preston North End when it was a top First Division club. The gym master was Mr Leblique, who, I believe, had been champion swordsman of his native Belgium." Although sport in the School had a long way to go – it was difficult to achieve much without its own playing field – at least there were masters who understood the value of sport and recreation. A fourth master "regularly spent his summer holidays tramping on the Continent".

"Early each afternoon Mr Brewer held court at the big desk in the 'Main Room'. Here he opened the big 'Book' as it was called, and sent for the luckless wights whose offences of omission and commission were deemed by form masters as to warrant the notice and judgement of the Head Master. Once in a while extreme measures would be indicated and the poor wretch would be invited to a private session in Mr Brewer's study." In the present age of league tables and manipulation of results, it is interesting to learn that in 1903 the young McNeil was persuaded to take the Cambridge Preliminary Local examination a second time, though he had already been successful in 1902, because "Mr Brewer saw an opportunity for the School to achieve some kind of record in securing the greatest number of first class honours." Candidates for the Cambridge Locals came back on Saturday mornings for special classes taken by the Head Master, most of them in mathematics and religious knowledge.

McNeil recalled Founder's Day when both the Boys' and Girls' Schools attended a special service in St Peter's Church, on the corner of Oxford Street and Ellison Place, the Schools' parish church, now demolished. "One part of the service had its amusing aspect. The Old Testament lesson was always from Ecclesiastes 12 in which occurs the passage '…. Of the making of books there is no end and much study is a weariness of the flesh." He observed that non-Anglicans were excused the service, but he did not take advantage of this nor did a Jewish boy, the holder of a scholarship from an elementary school, who insisted on going and "joining in the singing with great heartiness".

In 1905 came the bicentenary. It is not known how it was celebrated apart from the central event of the Founder's Day Service on 20 January. It was held as usual in St Peter's Church, Northumberland Road, and the preacher was the Revd Crawford Armour, Vicar of Christ Church. *The Evening Chronicle* reported that he preached on the text "When your children ask their fathers in time to come, What mean ye by these stones?" (Joshua 4:6), which he related to the founding of the Schools as Christian institutions by Eleanor Allan. Since the service was on a Friday morning, it is not unreasonable to suppose that the rest of the day was a half-holiday. It is interesting to observe that the Schools are referred to as Allan's Endowed School and Dame Allan Schools in the same article, the latter reflecting popular usage which eventually prevailed.

Girl Reading a Book, by Ralph Hedley, R.B.A (1848-1913). Hedley did a number of paintings of the Dame Allan's girls in their picturesque uniforms. Oil. (Private collection).

From 15 to 18 May, 1906, there was a first Board of Education inspection of Allan's Endowed Schools, and the report made for less than cheerful reading. First it established that there were the head and nine teachers in the Boys' School and the head and eight teachers in the Girls' School. The breakdown of geographical sources, social class and expenditure for pupils is interesting:

1906	Nos.	Homes in…..			Social Class of Parents						Per Capita Expenditure
		Newcastle	N/Land	Co Durham	Professional	Clerical	Retail	Artisans	Farmers	Other	
Boys	185	110	58	17	33	78	42	31	1	-	£8 8s
Girls	177	108	56	14	56	50	45	9	5	12	£6 14s

The fees were currently £3 13s for under eleven and £4 19s for over eleven. The Schools received £200 p.a. grant from Newcastle Corporation, and had a total income including fees and investments of £5-6000 p.a., with investments worth £40,000.

The inspectors' first comments were on the staff: in both Schools they were inadequate for the number of pupils, and their salaries were very low, especially the assistant masters, six of whom were paid under £200 p.a. The masters were described as "conscientious and industrious, but it cannot be said that they are of conspicuous ability either in scholarship or teaching power… The actual time given to class-teaching leaves insufficient intervals for the correction of exercises". Of the mistresses the report says, "the academic qualifications generally are not high, and few have had much experience in good secondary schools for girls. Their work is performed with great conscientiousness and with much patience under the trying conditions for teaching which the lack of proper accommodation imposes on them." They instance forty-five girls being taught French in a single room when two to three sets were needed.

In the Boys' School they found lack of organisation and co-ordination, in particular the lack of specialisation. The worst offender was French taught by "nearly the whole of the staff", but English, history and geography were shared too. Every subject comes in for some adverse criticism, even mathematics – Brewer's own subject – where "the teaching was generally good" but hampered by badly arranged sets with too great a range of ability. Particularly disappointing is the report on science, where "the instruction is not satisfactory, no practical work is done, and a progressive scheme of work does not appear to be followed by successive forms". Thomas Merrick, a previous head, was a science teacher, and we have seen how important he had regarded science – and in particular chemistry. The chemical laboratory was equipped with twelve benches and boys certainly performed experiments themselves, though we do not know how often. It seems that standards had declined over the previous twenty years. The high incidence of "spelling lessons" was claimed to be "an attempt to deal with a local weakness", but the inspectors felt this was not the best way of tackling the problem: it lacked "variety in methods". Music consisted only of a single singing lesson for boys under twelve: "the quality of tone is harsh and the boys are entirely ignorant of the rudiments." Considering that a number were members of the Cathedral choir, and others sang in their own parish churches, this was a severe criticism[5]. Physical education was apparently an optional extra, with classes at the Volunteer Drill Hall, and only sixty boys took it. The inspectors rightly said, "Physical education is an essential part of any complete school course." They observed that there were also no playing fields, but were unaware that cricket and football were played on the Town Moor. The inspectors commented on "the generous provision of scholarships, but for the really clever boy the school itself does not supply a sufficiently advanced course to enable him to open for himself the door to the universities".

[5]Arthur Milner (1903-09), who became a distinguished musician and taught in both Schools, recalled that he was excellently taught in English, history and languages – mathematics and science were beyond him – but music just did not occur on the timetable. "Once a year the school assembled under whichever master at the time could play the piano to learn a simple version song to sing at Speech Day … its educational value was nil, its entertainment value doubtful." Fortunately music was later taken more seriously: Sir David Lumsden was Principal of the Royal Academy of Music; Clifford Harker was composer and organist of Bristol Cathedral for thirty-six years; Michael Hall founded Britain's first fulltime chamber orchestra, the Northern Sinfonia; Dr Malcolm Boyd is a major authority on Bach; and there are currently a number of professional classical singers and instrumentalists, as well as academics.

They go on: "There is the pressing question of the very serious overcrowding of both the Schools." In the Boys' School "there is no staffroom and the Head Master's room is very small and inconvenient. There is no library or reading room and no recreation room, and the only place in which the boys may spend the midday interval (12 noon until 2pm) is the lavatory." Even the Head Master comes in for no small criticism: "there is no clear evidence that he has a comprehensive grasp either of the possibilities of the School curriculum or of discipline in its widest sense." They did, however, as we have seen, acknowledge the poor quality of his study, and also that he had clerical duties such as receiving fees. The inspectors were surprised by the lack of internal examinations, though they made no comment on external examinations. They felt that there should be an annual entrance examination rather than as vacancies arose, since the existing system "hinders a satisfactory standard of attainment in the classes".

The Girls' School fared little better. English was the central subject in the curriculum, but too much time was devoted to formal grammar and not enough to creative and independent work. The same problem existed with regard to French as in the Boys' School: it was taught by too many teachers and "it is not reasonable to expect that they should all be competent teachers of the subject". Science lacked practical work, and there was indeed no laboratory. Mathematics was, however, recognised as good. The inspectors felt that external examinations unduly influenced all parts of the School, and that younger girls should not be submitted to them at all.

There was a strong recommendation about "Housewifery". "For the girls in this school, most of whom become teachers or settle down to home life when they leave, a wide and liberal education directed to cultivating resourcefulness and discriminating taste will be the best preparation for life…. Needlework and Hygiene are included in the curriculum, but no other form of Domestic Economy or Housewifery. In view of the number of girls who settle down to home life, a course of general instruction in Housewifery for older girls … would probably be valuable." There does not seem much sympathy with the aims of Emily Davidson here.

The inspectors nevertheless concluded that "in spite of the many drawbacks, the tone of the School is wholesome, and salutary. A spirit of industry and conscientious endeavour animates the Head Mistress, her staff and the class throughout." The happiness of the institution can be attested by the fact that four of the girls educated at the school at that time would return to Dame Allan's as teachers. They recommend greater changes in the Boys' School, though they recognise "elements of vigour and vitality. The chief requirements are a wider outlook for the School as a whole, somewhat more generous principles of government, a gradually rising standard of attainment with a revised curriculum, and a more compact and effective internal organisation with the inevitable beneficial influence on discipline. If these can be secured, the School may effect much."

All of this may well have caused dismay among the governors. After all, the responsibility for inadequate buildings, overcrowding – twenty-seven girls and thirty-five boys over the design capacity of 150 + 130 – low staff pay, appointment of poorly qualified staff, and much general policy was theirs. At the same time the Schools were not wealthy and the books had to be balanced. Perhaps the inspectors had been unduly harsh – four days was not long to form an accurate impression in all areas – but clearly there had to be improvements before the next inspection due in 1909.

The new Board of Education ruled that they could not be recognised as an efficient Secondary Day Schools, but accepted that efforts were being made, and a grant was given in respect of science and art classes. This was a sad blow so soon after the bicentenary, and it had to be addressed. The first task was to reduce the numbers of pupils to the level for which the premises were built, viz., 150 and 130. This greatly increased efficiency and improved discipline. The criticism about science provision in the Boys' School might well have arisen because the laboratories had to revert to being classrooms[6]. Only twenty eight years earlier Merrick had proudly shown them off to learned visitors. The reduced numbers in the Girls' School would make it possible to set aside a room as a science laboratory. Both must have heeded the criticism of lack of practicals.

Not all problems were big ones. In the Boys' School the inspectors had noted the absence of both a globe and

[6]This was never fully resolved in College Street. The 1926 report speaks of the part-time use of the laboratory as a classroom.

large scale maps, and that slates were still used by many in mathematics. Greater specialisation in subjects was also easy to achieve in both schools, but with two small staffs, it could not be done beyond a certain point. The criticisms of teaching methods and curriculum were harder to address, tied up as they were with poorly qualified and poorly paid staff. The two heads were well qualified, and much depended on them to raise standards. Certainly within a few years boys went to Cambridge, to Brewer's old college, St Catharine's[7], and continued to go to Armstrong College in Newcastle, part of Durham University; they were pupils in the School at the time of the 1906 inspection . Other successes are recorded later in this chapter. Perhaps the inspectors were more accustomed to well housed and better endowed ancient grammar schools and in their four days missed some virtues.

Rose Fayre, 1909. "Hiawatha"

In 1909 came the second report. Over the three years the numbers had been reduced by limiting admissions from 185 boys to 150 and from 177 girls to 132. This gave classes of 25 and cost the loss of two teachers in each school, but the inspectors indicated that no more should be lost since the educational efficiency of the Schools had still to be improved, and they were again not recognised. Of the Boys' School they said that it was "doing useful work but the conditions under which it is conducted make it impossible that adequate justice should be done to the capabilities of its pupils." The Girls' staff was too small and salaries were too low. Above all, the very inadequate and inconvenient premises prevented any real progress. A letter three years later from an inspector of the Board of Education itemised the failings: no playing fields, assembly hall, art room, laboratory for the girls, insufficient classrooms and no staffroom. The most pressing need was a laboratory for the girls and an extra classroom for the boys: only then would there be the possibility of recognition. The governors replied that the considerable capital expenditure and an increase in fees "which may have the result of placing the advantages of the Charity out of the reach of some of the poorer classes" made it impossible for them to proceed further with the application. And so again nothing was done, and the possibility of a government grant was lost.

Thanks to the survival of copies of *The Register* for 1910, 1911, 1912 and 1913 it is possible to look at the situation in "Dame Allan's Endowed Boys' School". *The Register* was the forerunner of *The Allanian*, and had been in existence during the last years of the nineteenth century. Sadly, the only copy to survive before 1910 is a single example from 1898; it cannot have been the first. *The Register* came out after Christmas and marked the previous calendar rather than academic year, recording the names of governors and masters, the events of the three terms, sports results (school sports, and inter-school cricket and football), an honours list, a prize list and a school list. In 1910, the speaker on Prize Day was Professor Lebour, Vice-Principal of Armstrong College, deputising for the Principal, Dr Hadow, who was unavoidably absent. The link with Armstrong College/King's College/Newcastle University has been strong for over a century, and joint alumni must number some hundreds. In 1910, there were three Old Boys at Armstrong College and two at the College of Medicine (Durham University), as well as one at Cambridge. He spoke of the success of an Old Girl, Mary Heslop, who was "an honour not only to her old school but to her university, and to young scientific Britain. She has been engaged for some time in extremely difficult and abstruse scientific work of an original kind, and was aiding the progress of science in an very appreciable manner."[8] Girls must also have undertaken medical training in this period as mention would later be made of their war service as doctors as well as nurses.

[7]Burdus Blackburn went up to St Catharine's in 1907 and Gilderoy Davison in 1910.
[8]Unfortunately we do not know anything about her work or her future

The Boys' School staff numbered eight, including the Head Master. In 1911 the honours list included the Cambridge Local Examinations held in December, 1910. Two boys distinguished themselves in the Senior category: one was 12th out of 3820 candidates in Religious Knowledge, and 44th in Latin out of 1231, and the other 60th in Religious Knowledge, 5th out of 4228 in English Language and Literature, and 5th out of 3713 in English History. Amongst Old Boys, success at Armstrong College, with a Corporation Exhibition, was achieved by Vigo August Demant,[9] whose father had been the French master. Another section is headed "Scholarships Awarded during the Year". These were internal awards, firstly to "boys from Elementary Schools" who were given "Seconds" viz., Second Class Scholars. Several of these achieved "promotion to Firsts" as a result of their work. The second category were "to boys on Foundation", who also were "Seconds" but could be promoted to "Firsts" if they did well enough. The scholarships were given from the Third Form upwards. Almost all Fifth and Sixth Formers held the one or the other.

There were 151 boys, really the capacity for their part of the building, though it seems likely that some senior classes were held in the Head Master's house. There were 26 in Form I, 29 in Form II, 36 in Form III, 36 in Form IV, 19 in Form V and 5 in Form VI. The boys are not listed in alphabetical order, however, but "arranged in order of Merit, in English, Art and Science subjects for the (autumn) term". Why Latin, French, Geography, History and Religious Knowledge played no part in the order, though studied, assessed and reported on, is difficult to understand. The eminence of Art at this date is also surprising. To the world of education today the publicity given to an exact order of merit might seem a little harsh – for boys at the bottom at least.

The annual sports were held at the Gosforth Cycling Track in 1910 and 1911 and at the Medical College grounds in Heaton in 1912 and 1913. The events were throwing the cricket ball, long jump, high jump, cavalry race (piggyback?) and 80/100 yards, all with under-13 and over-13 events, plus 220 yards and quarter mile for over-13 only, and half-mile open. The 1912 sports were expanded, with a quarter-mile under-13 handicap, with thirty-one runners, and a half-mile open handicap, as well as an Old Boys' 220 yards final. Good numbers of parents, friends and Old Boys attended these sports, "a large and fashionable attendance," said the *Newcastle Daily Journal* in 1910 and it is recorded that in 1913 no fewer than 142 out of the 150 boys at the School entered events.

News of Old Allanians also appears in *The Register* in those years before the Great War. The Revd B. R. Blackburn (also St Catharine's College, Cambridge) and the Rev. A. L . Duncan (staff) were ordained priests, Dr W. A. Slater became the Assistant Medical Officer to the Newcastle Education Committee, J. M. Klitgaard became principal bass of Moody-Manneres Opera Company, G. Johnson became Town Clerk of Jarrow, S. Hardy played for Newcastle United, G Davison, St Catharine's College, Cambridge, coxed his college boat and Arthur

Cyril Foggin's Blackburn aircraft. This is a large model; the original cannot be photographed satisfactorily in the museum

Milner gave an organ recital in St Peter's Church. C.L. Foggin escaped virtually unhurt when he crashed his aeroplane at Eastbourne, but on 19 October, 1912 received his full pilot certificate No. 349, from the Royal Aero Company, flying a Bleriot monoplane.[10]

Then, as later, Old Allanians were representing their county in cricket, rugby and golf. On 27 January, 1912, two old boys and the School's classics master were members of the Northumberland Rugby team that defeated Lancashire to become

[9]The degree he received in 1913 was B.Sc in Applied Science. Surprisingly he was to become a priest and Canon Treasurer of St Paul's Cathedral, and finally Regius Professor of Moral and Pastoral Theology at Oxford. He preached at the 250th Anniversary Service in the cathedral in 1955.

[10]Cyril Foggin took delivery of an aircraft, a single-seater monoplane, the seventh of its type, from Harold Blackburn at Leeds at Easter 1913, but sold it on the outbreak of war. He served in the R.F.C. and R.A.F., (Major) but was killed in 1918. This aircraft, fitted with its original 50h.p. Gnome rotary engine, is now in the Shuttleworth Collection, at Old Warden Aerodrome near Biggleswade, and is the oldest British aircraft still able to fly.

champion of the Northern Section. Finally, on 29 January, 1912, following the Annual Service (later called Founder's Day) in St Peter's Church in Oxford Street, the Old Boys met and formed an Old Allanians' Association, with W.R. Lowe as secretary. This was to falter during the war years, but be revived subsequently.

Such was the Boys' School on the eve of war. Sadly there are no similar sources for the Girls' School. It was not expected to produce women for the professions, apart from teaching. Nevertheless it is clear that Miss Dobson and her staff were not content to educate young ladies simply to be wives and mothers and nothing beyond that, though many parents would have been satisfied with that, and Society would largely have supported them. The North East had produced its own prominent martyr in the cause of Votes for Women in Emily Davidson of Morpeth, who was fatally injured by the King's horse when she ventured on to the course during the 1913 Derby. One can imagine that the School simply got on with its lessons, games started to play a larger part in school life, and there were the special events such as the Rose Fayre, Prize Day and the Annual Service. We know that academic results were good, since they were commented on by – for example – the Archdeacon of Durham on Prize Day, 1912. Girls were, as we have seen, going on to university. The Rose Fayre brought more music, both vocal and instrumental, dance and drama to public performance. Speech Days for the Schools continued to be held jointly in the Barras Bridge Grand Assembly Rooms. The speakers (all men, of course) seemed to direct their comment mostly to the boys, but in December, 1913, the Lord Mayor, Councillor Johnstone Wallace, "observed that whilst they had heard a good deal that night about the boys (the cadet corps had just been formed), he believed that the chief need of today was for good women. He often thought that those who were most heroic were the women who stayed at home, for whilst the men might go abroad fighting the battles of their country, the severest ordeal was for the women at home wondering what had befallen their loved ones. He wanted the young girls of today to grow up to be womanly women, sweet, good and gentle. Such girls would make the men a great deal better." Nearly a century later these words might seem a trifle patronising but frighteningly prophetic, for within months both girls and boys, both women and men, were to be put most severely to the test.

The next inspection was in January, 1915, and of course nothing had changed. The problem of provision after the leaving age of sixteen for those intended for the local university had been partially addressed: pupils could stay on but no further Scholarships were available to help them financially; most have a period of private work. There was a lack of school kitchens, gymnasium, specialist rooms, staff provision and even sufficient classrooms: "at times as many as three divisions have to be taught in the same room. This is only an extreme instance of the way in which the teaching is hampered at every turn." The confidential notes not included in the issued report are most revealing. The inspectors observed that "the Head master and head mistress are kept at a distance (by the governors) which is quite unusual when there is no evidence of lack of confidence. "So long as the autocratic chairman[11] is in possession, it is futile to effect any alteration." The governors said that the city had confidence in the School and there was always competition to fill vacancies. The problems arose from lack of funds, and the governors complained that the Board of Education had failed to guide them to possible grants. The Board had clearly questioned the absence of women governors, but the existing governors claimed that such were not permitted under the existing scheme. However, the Board disagreed, and it was clear that any future scheme would have to ensure that there were women on the governing body. The Schools then looked into the possibility of renting additional accommodation nearby and sought to raise fees to pay for this and for increased staff salaries. Until the restrictions on building works and loans were relaxed after the war, nothing else could be done.

Academic standards were rising and the teaching staff was strong, but the Schools continued to face the problems of lack of space and overcrowding due to the great demand for places. The inspectors noted that, despite their difficulties, the schools maintained "the confidence of the town." In the face of adversity, this was a very valuable asset and a strong tribute to the work of Elizabeth Dobson and Frederic Brewer.

[11] Canon Lister, Vicar of St Andrew's, had been a governor for thirty years and retired in November 1916.

Chapter Seven

THE GRAMMAR SCHOOLS IN
COLLEGE STREET:
THE GREAT WAR AND THE FINAL YEARS IN COLLEGE STREET, 1914-1935

The growing tension in Europe was reflected in Dame Allan's by the creation of a cadet corps for the boys. The driving force for this was the Head Master, and he was strongly supported by the Governors. The matter had been discussed and plans made during 1912, and the proposed corps had been commended to parents by Mr Brewer at Prize Day on 18 December, 1912. On 15 March, 1913, the first drill was held in St George's Hall, and on 2 May the corps was officially recognised by the County Territorial Association and became one of the first cadet corps in the North East. In June, recognition of the corps was published in Army Standing Orders, and on 17 June the uniforms arrived, no doubt to great excitement. On 9 July, Charles Nichol photographed the cadets beside the school, looking very smart and very solemn, the officers with swords and the smallest boys with rifles. This made possible the first annual church parade at St Peter's Church on 20 July. Five officers and thirty-two cadets were inspected by Alderman Sir Walter Plummer, Vice-Chairman of Governors. By Speech Day later in the year the number of cadets had grown to fifty, which was a third of the School. On that occasion, Canon J. Moore Lister, vicar of St Andrew's and Chairman of Governors, said in praising this response by the boys that "if he were dictator for two years, he should decree that no one between the ages of 18 and 35 should be allowed to attend a football match unless he had first qualified himself to defend his country. People were too ready to say we were quite safe and that there was plenty of time to prepare, but the time to get ready was now (applause) Young men of today were so keen for their games that their work was a boredom and their country very much a cipher. The establishment of a cadet corps in connection with the School was a highly commendable step." (*Newcastle Daily Journal*). Dame Allan's lacked the playing fields such as those on which Etonians prepared for Waterloo, but the drill hall, the playground and the Town Moor served them well enough when the time came.

On 25 January, 1914, the cadets paraded for the first time with the 6th Battalion of the Northumberland Fusiliers, to whom they were attached, to St Silas' Church, and on 1 March with the Gosforth Detachment of the 5th Battalion to Gosforth Parish Church. On 10 March they again paraded at the Cathedral for the Laying up of Old Colours. "Two cadets, who were also choirboys, carried the colours to their permanent resting place after they had been handed over to the care of the Church." Clearly the presence of a cadet corps on parade occasions was important to territorial units, and the Dame Allan's cadets were called upon quite frequently, and later, when they had a fife and drum band, they were even more popular.

But it was not all drill and parades. A soldier's job was to kill or capture the enemy, and rifle shooting was a vital skill. From the first the cadets were highly trained and became very competitive. On 6 May, 1914, Dame Allan's cadets took part in the competition for the Imperial Challenge Shield, Junior Division. Although they came 438 out of 900, they won a prize of 10/-. On 24 May, in the Empire Day Parade of Territorial Units they marched with the 6th Battalion, to which they seem now to have been attached. From 20 to 28 June they attended their first camp with the Northumberland Territorial Infantry Brigade at Greystoke near Penrith. It was reported that "the food was good although some cadets wanted puddings every day". Obviously the youth of Britain was already in sad decline and going soft. When the cadets attended their second annual church parade at St Peter's Church on 12 July, they no doubt felt themselves as seasoned veterans, and to encourage them, Herbert Shaw, Sheriff of Newcastle and a governor, presented a challenge cup for shooting, first competed for a week later[1].

---

[1] The cup was competed for until 1927, and again from 1950 to the disbanding of the cadet corps in 1959.

1912		Headmaster and Governors propose creation of corps. 18 December: Commended on Speech Day
1913	15 March	First drill in St George's Hall
	2 May	Official recognition by County Territorial Association
	c.8 May	Recognition published in Army Standing Orders
	17 June	Uniforms arrived; corps included in Army Orders
	9 July	Photograph of corps
	20 July	Five officers and 32 cadets on first church parade at St Peter's Church, inspected by Sir Walter Plummer, vice-chairman of governors
1914	25 Jan	First parade with 6th Batt. Northumberland Fusiliers. Further parades.
	20-28 June	First camp with Territorial Brigade near Penrith
1915		Cadet shooting team first place amongst cadet corps of secondary schools affiliated to territorial battalions in England
1916		Shooting team again came first. Winner of Lucas-Tooth Competition for most efficient C.C. in Northumberland
1917		Two officers and 57 cadets. Again winners of Lucas-Tooth Competition
1918		Three officers and 82 cadets. Harvest Camp at Netherton, visited by Major General Montgomery. Sheriff of Newcastle presented cup to be competed for at rifle shooting: shooting teams competed in national event.
1919		Guard of honour for Admiral Beatty and Field Marshal Haig; the latter inspected them.
1920	17 April	Guard of honour inspected by Prince Albert (later King George VI) outside Commercial Exchange
7 May		Guard of honour inspected by Prince Henry, Duke of Gloucester, when Lt-Col. Brewer received OBE. 64 cadets.
1921		Junior shooting team: highest performance of all English School Cadet or Officer Training Corp in Imperial Challenge Shield of National Rifle Association
	23 April	War Memorial unveiled by General Montgomery
1922		Two officers and 69 cadets. In Imperial Challenge Shield, of 1800 teams throughout the Empire, school team was placed 15th in UK teams.
1923		Two officers and 61 cadets. In ICS, school was 4th in UK. In King's Shield competition for cadet units (UK), the team was 7th out of 95 teams.
1924/25		Two officers and 60 cadets. No national competitions
1926		First annual camp at the Rifle Range, Ponteland
1927-39		The cadet camps gradually became school camps
1930		Government recognition and support of all cadets corps withdrawn
1939		Two flights of Air Cadets formed
1940		Army cadets established at Windermere; affiliated to the Border Regiment (Carlisle)
1941-43		Very active period, with good quality training, including camps at military bases. Experience of wide range of weapons.
1944		Re-formed in Fenham: affiliated to Northumberland Fusiliers
1945		Cadet camp: peace parades
1946		F Coy Army Cadets: two officers and 55 cadets: harvest camp and cadet camp
1947		Cadet camp
1948		Major P C Stronach (OA) and 41 cadets
1949		Combined Cadet Force: 48 cadets. L/Cpl Alan Yeoman* gained highest mark in War Certificate "A" examination, Part 1
1950		63 cadets
1951		102 cadets: plans to create RN and RAF sections with Royal Grammar School
1952		RAF section created at Dame Allan's
1953		Basic course plus army and airforce at Dame Allan's. Naval cadets at RGS. Slingsby glider provided for school field.
1954-59		All three sections of CCF operating successfully
1960		No further references to cadets in *The Allanian*; reason for closure unknown.

*Later major-general

9 July, 1913. Photo by C. Nichol, O.A.

The cadets were not only active physically, but intellectually too. Cadet E. C. McGuinness came first in a competition for an essay on the Battle of Waterloo given by the Imperial Cadet Magazine. The prize was a trip to Canada with British Cadet Five Unit as a guest of the Canadian Government. He stayed in Quebec for three weeks, and returned to a different Britain and a different world.

The decline into war was hastened by the assassination of Archduke Franz Ferdinand on 28 June, and the first declaration of war was on 28 July when Austria-Hungary declared war on Serbia. On 1 August Germany declared war on Russia and on 3 August on France. The next day, Britain declared war on Germany, and Germany invaded Belgium. The Great War had begun.

Commemorative medals for the coronations of King Edward VII (1902) and King George V (1911). Presented to pupils by the governors.

Dame Allan's was quickly affected. Many Old Allanians were already in territorial units. George Jameson, for example, had joined the Elswick Battery in 1909 and later, because he liked horses, had transferred to the Northumberland Hussars Yeomanry, and was within weeks sent to France. On 16 September two masters were promoted to Captain and went off to war. On 12 October, J. W. Pape was congratulated and immediately promoted by General Smith-Davison "for gallantry in rescuing a wounded comrade under fire". Later the same month (21) W. R. Boiston was awarded the Distinguished Service Medal after a naval action off Heligoland. The citation said "he showed great ability and coolness in taking charge of the after boiler room (of *H.M.S. Laurel*, a destroyer) during the action when an explosion blew in the after funnel and a shell carried away pipes and seriously damaged the main steam pipe." The first casualty seems to have been Edward Laidlow, who was killed on 1 November in the London Scottish charge as Messines, near Ypres. A visitor to the School on 11 December was an Old Boy, William Walton, whose tinted photograph as a boy in 1865 still hangs in the School; his five sons were serving in the armed forces and all survived the war.

1915 was to see the casualty list mount. On one day alone (26 April) one Old Allanian was killed and five wounded in a single fierce action involving the Northumberland Territorial Infantry, and on 24 May two O.A. captains were gassed and had to be invalided home. Cadets took part in the Junior Imperial Challenge Shield of the National Rifle Association and came thirteenth out of 154 teams from Britain and the colonies; they were first amongst cadet corps of secondary schools affiliated to Territorial Battalions in Britain. At Christmas boys sent parcels containing handkerchiefs, footballs, chocolate, tobacco and other useful items to the Sixth Battalion of the Northumberland Fusiliers. It is certain that the girls did something similar, no doubt with some of their own knitting to give a personal note. For them as for the boys, fathers, older brothers and other relatives would be serving on land or sea. No doubt all pupils helped in many sorts of fundraising ventures.

In May the Head Master appointed a woman to the staff. This was Miss E.M. Turner, B.Sc (London) M.Sc. (Sheffield), who was not only highly qualified but who was so successful in her part-time post that in September she became full-time. She was to be joined by others as the war progressed. Other vacancies were filled by men too old to fight, among them Arthur Inglis, known as "Daddy". Bill Johnson later recalled, "He possessed a double-sided blackboard duster which he would hurl with amazing accuracy at any miscreant."[2]

In February Capt. P. D. Forrett, a science master at the School, was killed by a shell: "an excellent officer," wrote his colonel. Another master, Capt. J.E.B. Heads (classics), already a victim of gas attack, was again invalided home with trench fever[3]. In the autumn Sergeant R.S. Robinson, Royal Fusiliers, was awarded the Distinguished Conduct Medal. "During a very heavy bombardment he succeeded in digging out two men who were completely buried, although he himself was nearly buried two or three times by bursting bombs, and it was at the unanimous request of the men, who did not even know his name, that he was recommended for the

[2]He was to stay at the school until 1926, retiring aged 65. He was a Cambridge-educated lawyer, admitted to Lincoln's Inn in 1881, but he took up teaching in 1887. He taught languages, having been educated himself for some time in Switzerland.
[3]For the rest of his life, boys recall his body would be wracked by prolonged bouts of coughing. John Heads was to die on 12 December, 1930, whilst still a member of staff. The staff book simply records: "Died from effects of gas received during the War."

decoration." Two months later Second Lieutenant John Kent of the Durham Light Infantry was awarded the Military Cross. *The London Gazette* said, "He led a raid with great courage and skill, himself going to the flank under intense fire, and withdrawing the covering party. He has on many previous occasions done very fine work." On 31 May, William Atkinson was killed, together with 1265 other men, when, at the opening of the Battle of Jutland, H.M.S. *Queen Mary*, a battlecruiser of 26,350 tons, was hit by a salvo of shells and blew up. Since 52 Old Allanians received orders and decorations, and 28 were mentioned in despatches, let these few stand for the rest; they all were brave men and a credit to their parents and their school. By the end of 1916, 35 were killed or missing, 56 gassed or injured, and a further 400 serving.

The cadets were very active throughout 1916 with training inspections and parades, and again two rifle teams entered for the Junior Imperial Challenge Shield came 22nd and 52nd out of 194 teams. This made the first team top of all cadet corps of secondary schools affiliated to territorial Battalions in England, and both teams did better than any of the Junior Officer Training Corps teams. Later they were to win the Lucas-Tooth Competition for the most efficient cadet corps in Northumberland, receiving a cash prize and a medal for every cadet. This distinction was repeated in 1917 and 1918. In the shooting competitions of the same years similar performances were achieved but also with entries in the senior competition; against similar cadet corps, Dame Allan's senior team came second and the junior team first. It was a remarkable record.

In the autumn, the Revd Canon Lister, D.D., Chairman of the Governors, completed thirty years as governor, and the Schools marked the occasion with a holiday. This must have been one of the longest periods of service as a governor in their history, but as we have seen, he had latterly been heavily criticised by inspectors. He retired as vicar of St Andrew's soon afterwards, and he was succeeded as Chairman by Sir Walter Plummer, for long a good friend of the Schools. He died in office only a year later, to be succeeded by the Rev. Canon G. E. Newsom, Vicar of Newcastle, who was in turn to prove an outstanding chairman. It is easy to overlook the immense amount of work put in, without remuneration, by chairmen and by other trustees/governors over the past three centuries. Many of them were very busy people with heavy responsibilities elsewhere, and without them the Schools could not have survived.

With so many men away at the war and costs rising quite steeply, teachers were in heavy demand. There was competition for labour of all kinds, and teachers' pay rose proportionately. When the Girls' School staff found in 1917 they were not included in this, they threatened to resign *en masse*. They got what they wanted. The girls' school staff was relatively stable during the war years and four of the seven assistant mistresses were old Allanians[4] and included the last of the pupil teachers, Effie McNeil, who was appointed in 1912 and stayed until her marriage in April 1919. Her training must have been felt to have been good as she returned briefly to cover staff absence in 1921. From these years comes a mystery. In January, 1964, Elinor Brent-Dyer[5] gave an interview on television to Brian Redhead in which she gave the impression that she had been a pupil of the Girls' School between c1905 and c1910. However, later research for a biography of her, *Behind the Chalet School*, by Margaret Moncrieff, drew blanks with her contemporaries of those years, and the School's admissions register and staff register

[4]Eleanor Armstrong B.Litt., Florence Weddell B.Litt., Hilda Watson B.A. and Effie Stenton McNeil.
[5]Elinor Brent-Dyer was the author of a very famous series of girls' stories about the Chalet School. She was born, the daughter of a naval officer, at South Shields in 1894, and her early education was in Westoe Village. Her books were published from the thirties to the sixties.

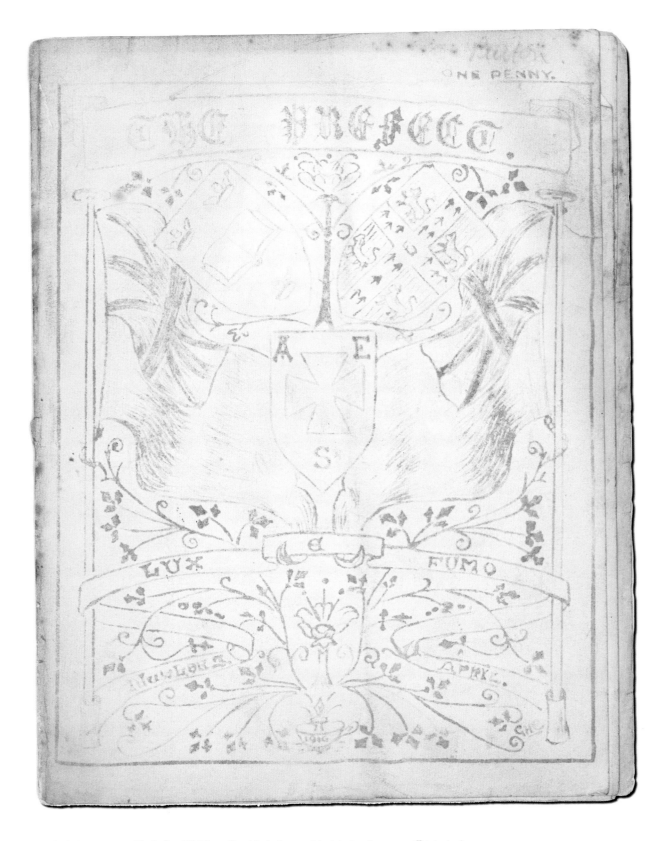

Sixth Form magazine: The Prefect. 1916 'Lux e fumo' (Light from smoke) might have been an unofficial school moto

Fifth Form magazine: The Fighting Fifth. 1916. The half-price rival.

no longer exist. The only supporting evidence was the "surprising number" of books by her in the School library, but of course that might simply be the result of enthusiasm for a local author on the part of the teacher/librarian, and indeed might have been matched in many girls' schools. She seems to have visited the School on several occasions and been accepted as an Old Girl. It is more likely that she was briefly a junior teacher between 1916

As You Like It. *1919. The earliest Shakespeare production of which we have record*

and 1918, having just qualified from Leeds Training College. It seems that Miss Dyer did not confine her imagination to her novels, and was known by her friends to mix fact and fiction. We shall probably never know. Certainly the Chalet School does not seem to bear much resemblance to Dame Allan's, except, of course, as a happy community.

Maj. Edward Liddell Middlemast, Fort Garry Horse.

On the morning of October 9th, 1918, he was in charge of advanced guard squadron of the regiment, and located the enemy with many machine guns in the Bois-du-Mont Aux-Villes and Bois-de-Gattigny. After successfully sizing up the situation and timing himself with the advancing infantry, he charged the wood with the sword around the enemy's right flank, killing large numbers and capturing approximately 200 prisoners and 20 machine guns. Although wounded in this charge, he, after having his wound dressed, resumed command of his squadron and did valuable work during the remainder of the day.

London Gazette supplement, 30 July, 1919

At Easter 1917 another member of staff, J.W. Earnshaw, joined the army; every form gave him a present. He was succeeded by a second woman, Miss Mabel Thompson, B.A. (Dunelm), to teach English, Latin and Mathematics. Again at Christmas a collection was taken for the Sixth Battalion, and, "as chocolates could not be bought, the money was expended on footballs, in response to a request from the men". In September 1918 a third woman, Miss Mildred Green, B.A. (Dunelm), an Old Allanian, arrived to teach Latin.

As 1918 began, *The Register* was dominated by the names of the men of the armed forces. The vast majority were in the army, and many of those in the Northumberland Fusiliers, though 120 different units in the army, navy or airforce were being served by the 560 Old Allanians. The number of killed or missing had risen to 57, with 93 wounded and three prisoners of war. 183 had gained commissions, and already nineteen former cadets were serving. Yet another member of staff, C. L Wilson, left to join the Forces, and for one term there were three female members of staff to four men. There is no entry for 11 November – Armistice Day – but the cadet corps was providing a guard of honour to the flag two days later. The Head Master, meantime, thanks no doubt to the great success of the cadets, had been promoted from captain to lieutenant-

The Great War memorial, formerly on the stairs in the College Street building, and now in the Newsom Hall. Dedicated, 23 April, 1921

colonel. He led a harvest camp for a month during the summer holidays at Netherton near Rothbury. There were thirty-one cadets and they worked at seven farms, mostly on turnips and hay. The bugle band led them to church on Sundays, and there was a shooting match with the local Volunteers, which the cadets lost, lacking, no doubt, the others' frequent practice on rabbits and pigeons. They also had bathing, fishing, football, rabbit-catching, sports, competitions and a concert. Major-General Montgomery visited and expressed his approval. This camp was important as the first of a series of camps that gradually through the twenties and thirties evolved from a cadet camp into a school camp, when boys who were not cadets were welcome to join, increasingly on an equal footing. In 1918, beside Lt-Col. Brewer, Lieutenant Cutting and Second Lieutenant Earnshaw (all staff) and C.S.M. Webb, there were two companies, O and U, totalling eighty-one cadets out of a school of 150 boys. J. Maxwell Hough recalls joining the first form in October, 1914, when the war was two months old. "Apart from the fact that at least two masters were in the Forces, the war had had very little effect on school life. Later, changes came very rapidly. The younger masters gradually went and older men came out of retirement to fill the gaps. Eventually the time arrived when a lady (Miss Turner) was first appointed to the staff. It is not appreciated what an epoch-making event that was, but how quickly and quietly the change was accepted.

"There were no organised games and no playing fields available. Unofficially, soccer and cricket matches were organised by the boys and very occasionally a match was fixed up with Newcastle Modern School, which was

Field Marshall Haig inspects Dame Allan's cadets. 1919

situated in Park Terrace. These matches took place on the Town Moor. On a very few occasions a paper chase was organised on a Saturday morning. In 1920 the School sports were held for the first time since the outbreak of war on the College of Medicine ground on Heaton Road.

"There was one activity that became a most important part of the school life, the Cadet Corps, and this was very successful. In the summer of 1918 there was a camp to assist the farmers with the harvest. This was open to all the older boys whether cadets or not. A very pleasant time was had by all in that delightful place, Netherton, near Rothbury. Some of us stayed on with the farmers after camp broke up."

It was some time after the war ended that a complete list of those who had served, with lists of the fallen and of the decorated, could be prepared. The Old Boys' Association decided that a brass memorial tablet should be erected on the staircase and that a leaving scholarship be established. Donations came from all quarters, and the tablet was prepared, bearing the names of the fallen and the following words:

STA PUER ET REVOCANS HOS ALMAE MATRIS ALUMNOS VIVERE PRO PATRIA DISCE MORIQUE TUA

(Stand, boy, and recalling these Old Boys of the School, learn to live and to die for your country).

On the side panels are the 51 decorations earned by members of the armed forces, and across the bottom the statistics:

Served : 652   Fallen : 84

It was unveiled by Major-General Sir R.A. Kerr Montgomery, K.C.M.G., K.C.B., D.S.O., and dedicated by the Vicar of Newcastle on St George's Day, 23 April, 1921. On that occasion the general commented on the extraordinarily high level of casualties for a school of 150; he felt it must be one of the highest in Britain. The memorial was moved to the Newsom Hall on the Fenham site in 1935.

H.R.H Prince Albert, Duke of York, later H.M King George VI, inspects the school Cadets, 17 April, 1920

Percy Stronach, c1923, head choirboy of Newcastle Cathedral and later head of School. After degree and war service, returned to teach at his old school until retirement.

Although *The Register* in the immediate post-war years seemed dominated by the war and by the cadets, much else was obviously happening. Games, which had been somewhat curtailed by the war, and swimming, which had frequently been impossible in school hours because the baths were restricted to servicemen, resumed their former importance, but the lack of facilities at the Schools remained a serious problem. Old pupils who had been unable to complete or indeed start their university courses were once more receiving degrees. Medicine had already started to be a popular subject with Allanians: through the rest of the century very many in both Schools chose this career. One who obtained his B.Sc in 1922 at Armstrong College (the Newcastle branch of Durham University) in Applied Science (Naval Architecture) was Capt. G. B. Jameson, M.C, who had fought throughout the entire war. In the intermediate examination of the Institute of Chartered Accountants, Old Allanians took first and second places in England. An Old Allanian, Frank Platt, was the first person in the North to be awarded the Cromwell Badge by the Boy Scout Association. On the half-term holiday the Head Master and three other masters "took 86 boys in three charabancs to see the Roman Wall" plus Chesters and Housesteads forts. It was not yet possible to regard such an excursion as sufficiently educational as to hold it on a school day, but it was a step forward nevertheless. It was clearly a success, since the next year another tour took place to Alnwick, Bamburgh and Wooler. In 1925 the two senior boys' forms went to the Theatre Royal to see Sir Frank Benson's Company in *Twelfth Night*. This too seems to have been a first, and the first of hundreds of theatre visits by both Schools as the century progressed.

Each year the Annual Commemoration Service took place in St Peter's Church near the Schools in late January, and each year too there was a prize distribution in the Schools by the Chairman of Governors. This was clearly a retreat from the pre-war position when the Schools combined in a single event in a spacious setting and had a guest speaker. There must have been two separate occasions, and desperate overcrowding, since the largest place available was the double classroom. Did only prize-winners attend with their parents, or were parents excluded? The likeliest answer to why the prize distribution was downgraded was the cost of hiring a suitable hall, plus a reminder to everyone that the existing buildings were totally inadequate and that a move to a much bigger site was a matter of urgency.

At some point, perhaps at the end of the war, the headmaster moved out of his house beside the Schools, and caretakers moved in. In the 1920s, Mr and Mrs Scott lived there and did many duties outside the normal role of caretaking, such as lunchtime supervision, tuck shop and first aid. Part of the first floor became a boys' classroom; a similar plan for the girls seems not to have happened despite their equally urgent need of more space.

The cadets meantime had provided guards of honour for Field Marshal Earl Haig and Admiral Lord Jellicoe, and for Prince Albert, Duke of York, later King George VI. In May 1920, a very proud guard of honour was provided for Prince Henry, Duke of Gloucester, when he came to hold an investiture at which the Head Master received the O.B.E. Their final inspection of that year was by Lt.-Gen. Sir Charles Woolcombe, Inspector General of Cadets. The following year a new boy joined the cadets: his name was Percy Stronach, and he could not have imagined what was to follow his decision. He must have been very busy, since he was also chorister at the cathedral and later head chorister.

In 1921, the first men were appointed to the Girls' School staff, James Mitchell and Arthur Milner. The latter was an Old Allanian, and was for the next thirteen years a most able music teacher. The only men who had previously taught the girls were clergy governors and Thomas Merrick.

Within a few weeks of the war ending, a note was added to a letter from the governors recognising that the Board was committed to placing the Schools on the grant list "as soon as possible after receipt of an adequate application for an amending scheme." The Board of Education required the following from the Schools in return for recognition and a secondary school grant:

(i)   A new scheme
(ii)   Eight free places should be awarded to boys and six to girls from 1 January 1919.
(iii)   Pupils should be limited to 150 boys and 120 girls while the Schools remain in the existing premises.
(iv)   The governors must submit proposals for providing satisfactory accommodation of a permanent character without undue delay.
(v)   Physical exercise must be included in the syllabus without, as hitherto, an extra charge.
(vi)   Pupil age limit to be raised to eighteen.
(vii)   Heads would not have to be practising Anglicans.
(viii) The School could be permitted to take boarders.
(ix)   Tuition fees to be raised from the present £3-£5 to a maximum of £12
(x)   A reconstituted governing body, with a lower proportion of clergy, more representatives of the City Corporation, at least one woman, and a representative of Durham University.
(xi)   The name of *Allan's Endowed Schools* might be changed to *Dame Allan's Schools* by which name they were popularly known.

The financial problems could not however be solved simply by receiving a grant from the Board. The income for the Schools came from the Wallsend Farm and the property in The Side, investments, fees and — since 1904 — an annual grant of £200 - £250 from the local education authority. Rises in costs meant that the Schools would become financially dependent on the LEA, but that body could not be expected to fund pupils from outside the city, currently 30%, and the governors were unhappy about charging higher fees for them.

On 7 February, 1921, a new scheme for the Schools was approved by King George V in Council. This replaced the scheme of 11 July 1877 made under the Endowed Schools Acts, and altered by three minor schemes. Allan's Endowed Schools were in future to be known as Dame Allan's Schools, and were to have twelve governors: the five ex-officio members of the Lord Mayor and four vicars, four representatives of the Newcastle Education Authority and three co-optative governors, members of the Church of England and appointed by the other governors. Very importantly, in the second and third categories there should be at least one woman in each. This no doubt was a by-product of the recent granting of votes for women over thirty. The quorum was four governors. The Schools were to be maintained as two public secondary schools and their Anglican ethos was fully preserved. The scheme allowed for boarders, but this section was not taken up, nor, for twenty years, was the introduction of a preparatory department, either one for each school or a joint one administered by the Girls' School.

Dame Allan's Girls School 1920
Queen Winnie with her Pages and Bodyguards

The minimum age of admission was ten, and it was possible to stay until eighteen, and no one was to be admitted without passing an entrance examination. Forty boys and twenty girls were to be exempt from tuition fees. Of these, half were to be awarded to children from Anglican public elementary schools (or from any school if there were insufficient suitable Anglicans), and, all things being equal, preference was to be given to children from the parishes of St Nicholas and St John. Any of these children exempt from tuition fees who did well and deserved the distinction were to be called Foundation Scholars. In addition, maintenance allowances could be paid by the governors at their discretion to any of these pupils; a minimum expenditure of £60 for the boys and £30 for the girls was expected, and there was no upper limit. The governing body, in consultation with the appropriate head, was to appoint or dismiss assistant teachers; latterly the heads had done both without necessarily consulting the governors. The governors were also given considerable powers over curriculum, school terms and similar arrangements; this was much as before. Either head could make proposals for changes directly to the governors, and had control over "the whole internal organisation, management and discipline" of his or her school. Parents could claim exemption for their children from any religious worship or lessons; this had long been the case. Leaving exhibitions could be awarded to pupils proceeding to higher education, also as before.

The annual tuition fee was fixed in 1921 at not more than £12 without Board of Education agreement. In 1930 in a modification of the 1921 scheme, the number of governors was raised to eighteen, two more from the city council, a representative of Armstrong College and three more co-opted members. There was now a university representative on the governing body as of right for the first time.

Academically, the schools were also in a phase of transition. The old system of Form Teachers, in which several subjects were delivered to one year group by one teacher, was gradually being replaced with increased subject specialism among the staff. In December 1920, the Girls' School lost the services of Eleanor Armstrong, an Allanian who had taught at the school for twenty years. She had been Form Mistress in Form V, also teaching history and geography throughout the school. In the early 1920s the school was to make some very good appointments in Audrey Cuthbertson, another Allanian, Jessie Dodd, Janet Ramage and Stella Lippett. All were to make an enormous contribution to the School both in the

F.M Osbourne. Head Master April-December, 1926

final years of College Street and in the new building. The Boys' School also saw the retirement of the long-serving Arthur Goodacre in 1923. He had taught at the school since 1885 and been second master since 1898. He and his wife, formerly Miss Mousley, Head Mistress of the Girls' School, were to stay in touch with the school and visit from time to time. The part time gym master, Leopold Leblique, left for a full time post at the Royal Grammar School in 1919 after 26 years at the school. A Belgian by birth, he was reputed to be a champion swordsman and was a member of the Academie d'Armes de Londres.

The Register of 1925 came out as F. W. Brewer had drafted it, but he was already dead when it appeared with a postscript in memory of him. He was in his thirtieth year as Head Master, coming to Newcastle from Preston Grammar School where he had been both pupil and master. During those years he had built up the Boys' School as an important element in the life of the city. His enthusiasm and far-sightedness had brought about the foundation and growth of the cadet corps, and its success had been recognised by his promotion to lieutenant-colonel and later by the O.B.E. The dreadful losses of so many that he had taught were borne with courage. "His simple Christian faith, his lofty purpose, his unselfish devotion to his life's work, his scornful attitude towards anything that savoured of dishonesty and intrigue, his dislike of what he termed 'window dressing', all these were apparent to those who had the privilege of his friendship." The present author owes him a debt of gratitude too, since in 1897 he wrote some notes on the early history of the School, really for his own interest and information. Nearly thirty years later he added some more material that he had since come across, and had just typed the fair copy when he went to take evening prayers for the last time. Those notes have survived, and have been used in compiling the present work. He does not cite sources for any of the material, and it is certain that many of them are lost, but I have felt that such was the nature of the man that the notes are quite reliable.

In November, 1925, the clerk to the governors, Robert Muckle, wrote to the Board of Education about the increasing urgency of a move from College Street. He said that there was little land within the current city boundaries, and the governors were looking at two estates in Fenham. Here there was no secondary school (apart from the convent school) and there was extensive building of houses. Although there were financial problems, they felt they could acquire sufficient land for playing fields and then plan buildings for 250 pupils in each school. Official notes agree with the governors' plans in all particulars. "Dame Allan's Schools have been quite full for many years past and each year many applicants are refused... they would have little difficulty in filling the additional places from the Church element." A further note observed that the LEA might increase its maintenance grant "with tactful handling", and commented; "The School really wants a second founder." He further observed that they stood socially "midway between the Grammar and High Schools on the one side and the Provided Schools on the other". Neither the governors nor the Board wished fees to be raised to anything like the levels of those two schools[6] since that would mean competition with them, and would also exclude some of their present clientele. Canon Newsom, though quite determined that his Schools should be rehoused – and soon – was pessimistic about increased L.E.A. grant, and also about the scale of voluntary contributions: "There are," he said, "not many rich people in Newcastle at present."

A.K Wilson, Head Master 1927-1953. Under him the Sixth Form rose from 6 to 60

The inspectors' report in 1926 simply confirmed what was already known about the inadequacy of the premises, but it gave a sense of urgency to the situation. "Modern improvements in other schools and the raising of the standard of

---

[6] £30 and £20 10s respectively; the LEA fees were £8. The suggestion for Dame Allan's was £12 or 12 guineas (today's £12.60), later revised to 15 guineas (£15.15s), in 1927.

Miss F.A. Elliott, Head Mistress. 1933-53

accommodation in secondary schools generally, serve to accentuate the heavy handicap imposed upon these schools in almost every detail of their work. The utterly cramped condition of the building sorely restricts the life of the schools... The early provision of new and up-to-date premises is a matter of vital importance to the success of the schools." The opening of Heaton Secondary School two years later showed the standard to be expected of such schools; ironically, when a month later, King George V and Queen Mary came to Newcastle to open the Tyne Bridge, and visited the new school, the guard of honour was provided by the Dame Allan's cadets.

The two Heads and staffs could not be expected to overcome all or even most of the problems presented by the buildings, and the danger was that they would move to more congenial surroundings and that good new staff would not come. Fortunately Miss Dobson, who had been Head Mistress since 1894, was a woman of determination, but she was not very far from retirement. However, in the Boys' School an alarming warning had occurred. The death in office of Brewer meant a new Head Master, F. M. Osborne[7], had taken over in April, 1926. We can only speculate that the inspection of that year influenced Osborne's decision to resign and leave in December to join the inspectorate himself.

One did not need to be committed to the easy life to see which job seemed more attractive. An Old Allanian, Bill Johnson, recalled that, in his two terms of headship, Osborne "blew in, blew around and blew out". In fact, cometh the moment, cometh the man. The governors chose A. K. Wilson to take over in January, 1927: in three centuries they could have made few better decisions on any matter. Alfred Kenneth Wilson; born in 1889 and Hastings Exhibitioner in mathematics at The Queen's College, Oxford, had been Head Master of Ludlow Grammar School since 1921; one must suppose he wanted a challenge. Other fortunate appointments around this time were Robert Muckle as Clerk to the Governors, and Henry Mallinson to teach mathematics; both were also to prove great assets.

It was recognised that the Schools could only expand and develop by moving to a new site, and in April, 1927, a conditional agreement to purchase 12.88 acres at £650 per acre in the suburb of Fenham was made with the trustees of the Hospital of St Mary the Virgin. A report was required on the abandoned mine workings under the site; these did not seem to constitute any problems at the time but minor problems were to arise during the construction of the biology block in 1994. In June 1929 the governors sold trust stock to buy the land, and on 1 November paid £8348 for it. A year later the ground was ready to use, and a handsome pavilion was soon added. At this time the farsightedness of the governors also extended to the treatment of the staff. Miss Enid Doull, the French and English mistress of the Girls' School was given sabbatical leave in 1929 to pursue a course at the University of Madrid; on her return she would teach Spanish at the school[8]. The Boys' School had gained a Spanish master, Charles Davies, the previous year. This was the first extension of modern language teaching in the Girls' School since German had been dropped after the Great War, perhaps owing to post-war hostility.

One of A.K. Wilson's first acts, in the spring of 1927, was the introduction of a new scheme for the formation of four houses. These were named after "benefactors or great men who have rendered signal service to the School".

[7]Francis Marden Osborne, M.A. (Exeter College, Oxford), MA (Ed.) (King's College, London) was house master of Whitgift Grammar School, Croydon, before his move to Newcastle. Osborne gave an account of the educational aims of the School at the Prize Distribution in December, and it is clear that he had some good ideas about the School's future development. One of these was the building up of the Sixth Form, currently nine boys. He said that boys were allowed to choose their subjects: "there is no attempt to force them into a particular group such as science and mathematics in order to claim an additional grant from the Board of Education for an advanced course." Currently four were doing Modern Studies, while after Christmas at least six would be doing science and mathematics. He urged the more academic to stay on in the sixth form.

[8]During her absence Mary Clark, Old Allanian, filled her place. She had trained at the Royal College of Music and the Universities of Nancy and Madrid. She is the earliest girl studying beyond Newcastle or Durham of whom we have record.

Brewer's: Frederic W. Brewer, head master, 1896-1925
Hedley's: Edward Hedley, soap manufacturer, governor and chairman of governors.
Plummer's: Sir Walter Plummer, M.P., Lord Mayor, governor and chairman of governors.
Ridley's: The Ridley family had supported the Schools over many years. The Home Secretary, Sir Matthew White Ridley, 1st Viscount Ridley, is probably the one honoured.

A boy's house was determined by the initial letter of his surname. At a day school, the house system struggles to be more than a convenient arrangement for games and athletics, and it would be unrealistic to imagine that it was ever significantly more than that in the Boys' School. The Girls' School, perhaps valuing games a little less, seems to have made greater efforts in enlarging the scope of houses – but that lay in the future. In 1934, the girls established their four houses, named after the four ancient parishes of Newcastle, namely St Nicholas', St John's, St Andrew's and All Saints', the vicars of which still served as governors.

One group of boys at this time were a special group within the School. They were the cathedral choirboys. They numbered about fifteen, of whom no more than twelve might be called upon for choral services at any one time. They could leave early for evensong and also for special services. The agreement was that the cathedral paid the fees, while parents paid £1 5s per term for books and other materials. The cathedral did this in return for the boys' singing duties. The cathedral agreed to pay these fees for up to fifteen terms, and a boy was expected to stay until he was sixteen. The choirmaster would make the choice of boys "as far as is compatible with the rules of the School and with a reasonable standard of learning", though not necessarily as high as the paying pupils. It was understood that when they were withdrawn in school hours, "all school hours so lost shall be made up by boys in private study." Thus a chorister, possibly academically weak though vocally superb, was to be trusted to make up for lost lesson time.

When the Governors decided to raise the annual fees from twelve to fifteen guineas (£12.60 to £15.75), the Provost[9] and Chapter objected quite strongly, but were faced with an even stronger reply from the Head Master in a letter of 19 October, 1931. It was pointed out that the services caused "a considerable interruption to their ordinary school work, which is reflected in the low percentage of cathedral scholars who pass the (School) Certificate examinations." Further, when a boy's voice broke, the cathedral ceased to pay his fees, and parents were expected to pay the full fees – indeed had signed an undertaking so to do. Many, however, could not afford it. The School found that financially and academically the cathedral boys were a liability. Since 1916, of the 41 cathedral scholars who had stayed on to take the School Certificate, only 14% passed. The School felt that in the long run the system was not to the advantage of the boys either. The School governors proposed that the cathedral authorities paid seven guineas a year and parents eight guineas a year until the boy was sixteen. Thus both the cathedral and the parents made a five-year commitment from the first, and the breaking of a boy's voice made no difference to his education. Indeed, if it were early enough, he stood some chance of catching up. The Provost and Chapter agreed to this.

Stanley Davidson (1942-48), who held a choral scholarship, tells of the tough regime. He and the other choristers left school at 4pm, had tea, practice and evensong, frequently not leaving the cathedral until after 7pm, when it was home to face homework. On Sundays there were three services. In addition, there were special services for civic and similar events, weddings and funerals. Percy Stronach was able to be head chorister *and* a cadet *and* do well in his school work in the thirties, but it must have been hard.

Later, the cathedral was to found its own (day) choir school, teaching up to the Fifth Form, and some boys then transferred to Dame Allan's for the Sixth Form. When the choir school ran into financial problems in the 1970's, one proposal was that it might be absorbed or partially absorbed into Dame Allan's Boys' School, but the problems were too great; in particular, the high academic standards of Dame Allan's at that time, with ten boys competing for each place, could not be reconciled with voice tests. When the cathedral choir became a voluntary choir, Dame Allan's boys participated in it, and have continued to do so to the present day.

---

[9] The Vicar of Newcastle became more usually known as the Provost of Newcastle around this date; in 2000 the head of the cathedral became the Dean of Newcastle.

The inspectors' report seems to have encouraged more extra-curricular activities despite the accommodation problems. One boy, J. W. Blakey, recalls joining the School in 1930; he left in 1935 after enjoying only one term in Fenham. A vivid memory is of "Mrs Scott's tuckshop at the far end of the bicycle shed. For games the YMCA ground at Henry Street in Gosforth was used, and when the ground was too wet for rugby, runs took place up the North Road, across the Town Moor and down Claremont Road. Very shortly after I started school, we moved to the present playing fields. Here I distinctly remember changing for rugby in the new pavilion amongst the joists before the floorboards were in."

He remembered the developments in those last years in College Street "We started a chess club and a stamp club; in 1930, Volume 1 Number 1 of *The Allanian* was published replacing *The Register*. In 1931 we held our first swimming sports; in late 1931 the Musical and Dramatic Society was formed, the first production being *The Morrison Tableaux* in 1932 and the first large scale production being *HMS Pinafore* in the Spring Term, 1933. In the season 1931-32, J. Weatherston was awarded an international rugby cap for the England under-14 side v Wales."

As J. W. Blakey recalled, *The Allanian* replaced *The Register* which had begun c.1895 *The Register* had appeared annually and *The Allanian* was to do the same. There had been an enterprising pupil-produced publication, *The Prefect*, of which two early copies survive dated 1916. It contained stories to appeal to school boys and we do not know how long it lasted. It was produced by the Sixth Form, and priced 1d. The Fifth Form launched a rival, priced $^1/_2$d, called *The Fighting Fifth*. The girls' school produced a magazine twice a year from 1934 containing "a comprehensive record of school events, news of old girls and original compositions of past and present pupils". The first five seem to have been typed and duplicated, but later ones were printed. No copies have survived of the duplicated issues, but the 1936 printed number exists.

The cadets, as we have seen, flourished under Colonel Brewer in the immediate post-war period, but then suffered two blows which effectively brought them to an end. The first was the death of Brewer, who had founded and led Allan's Cadet Corps. The second was quite different and is part of our national history. The government in 1930 withdrew recognition and funding from cadet corps, made it unlawful to wear military uniform (though cadets could wear out existing uniforms provided they removed all military badges) or to take part in any military

Rehearsal for H.M.S Pinafore. 1933

instruction. Moreover, although the Commanding Officer, Capt Mallinson, was a reservist, he could not wear uniform while drilling "a body of men or boys whose organisation is not recognised by the War Office." The cadets continued with swimming and physical drill, - the former in the City Baths and the latter in St George's Drill Hall across Vine Lane - and the annual camp in the rifle range huts at Ponteland, now clearly called the School Camp, continued to be held. These government decisions might seem, with hindsight, to lack foresight; whether they were guided by economy or pacifist sentiments or both, they cost a lot. The camps continued to prosper and fostered a sense of community as well as being just plain enjoyable. In a letter, a German schoolboy called Herbert Seidenstucker, son of a judge, wrote about his stay at the July 1931 camp thus: "At first I was astonished at the friendly relations, at the comradeship which existed between masters and boys and there was yet discipline. It is a pity that in Germany only very few schools have institutions which can be compared with such a camp... Besides all kind of sport fit to strengthen the body, I could also admire mental performance, as *The Review*, which was shown by the boys, was an absolutely good one, especially the songs...(The boys) did not treat me as a stranger but as one of their school comrades. I was pleased that I could speak about the World War with teachers and boys in quite a fair and reasonable way." There is a terrible irony here.

The Schools had used the Northumberland Road Baths for many years: they were extremely convenient for the College Street building. Strangely, it was not until 1931 that boys' swimming sports were held, though swimming lessons in school time and swimming by the cadet corps had flourished. The same year also saw the first organised venture abroad, when a party of fifty-one spent a week sightseeing in Paris. The cultural programme was a full and thoughtful one, but "what little space of time each day we had left after our visits was our own, and we were allowed to go out alone. At night we used to go and see the lights of the city."

Another first that year was that Sports Day was held on the Fenham ground, and the first building on the site, the pavilion, was formally opened, when the Schools were congratulated on "the admirable facilities for games." The staff and pupils of the Girls' School had generously donated a cup for the boys' Mile, and Miss Dobson proposed a vote of thanks; was it a joint sports day? The Old Boys' rugby and cricket teams took advantage of the new ground for their home fixtures immediately.

"Twelve Days for £12": School cruise on S.S. Montcalm 1932

Even a glance at the School Roll is fascinating. At the end of the summer term, two first-formers, rivals but great friends, are fighting it out for top place: Alasdair Christison[10] and Eric Rees[11]. In the second form, well up the order, is Philip Charlton[12].

Also new in 1931 was a joint Parents' Association. Formed initially to raise funds for the new building, it quickly found other ways to help the Schools, including a garden fete on the new ground and teas on Sports Day.

Drama was flourishing in the girls' school. The performances given at the annual Rose Fayre were of a very high standard and with most impressive costumes. One of these on 20 June, 1929, was a repeat of Miss Dawson's *A Pageant of Women*, first given in 1913. It was confined to the history of women in Northumberland, and was an enterprising in-house production. Mary Wylie, recalling it seventy-six years later, spoke of its colourful costumes and liveliness. She played Margaret Widdrington of Unthank Hall; others were Grace Darling, Josephine Butler, Margaret of Anjou, Phillipa of Hainault, Ellen Richardson, Margaret Tudor, the Cullercoats women – and Eleanor Allan, of course!

Music was more difficult to pursue in the cramped conditions in College Street. Arthur Milner, part time

[10]Alasdair Christison won an Open Scholarship to Worcester College, Oxford, where his particular friend was Richard Adams, later the author of *Watership Down* and numerous other novels. Christison was killed in the Western Desert in 1943, and a plaque to commemorate him, the gift of Richard Adams in 2002, is in the Newsom Hall.
[11]Eric Rees became a priest, a fine baritone and minor composer, whose songs have been performed in Stockholm, Paris and Brittany as well as in Britain, and recorded. He was an early interpreter of Mahler songs. He remains in touch with the School.
[12]Philip Noel Charlton (1917-89). Joined navy in 1938, and served in Fleet Air Arm, flying from aircraft carriers *Courageous*, *Glorious*, *Ark Royal* and *Victorious*. He shot down 6 enemy aircraft plus 2 probables. Lt.-Cdr., D.F.C., D.S.C., King's Commendation.

The Most Reverend Dr William Temple, Archbishop of York, launches the appeal for the Fenham building on the announcement of the aquisition of the Fenham site. Speech Day, City Hall. 2nd Dec, 1929. All the guests have copies of the appeal brochure. The choir members wore Eton collars, and some wore boots

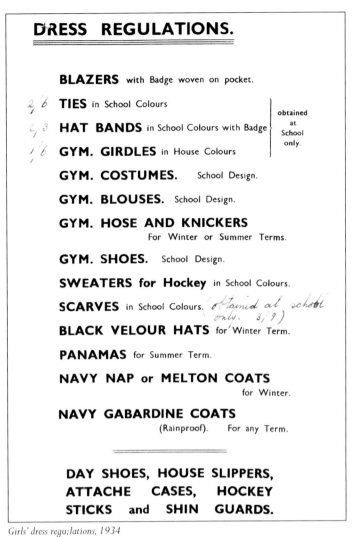

DRESS REGULATIONS.

BLAZERS with Badge woven on pocket.

2/6 **TIES** in School Colours

2/3 **HAT BANDS** in School Colours with Badge — obtained at School only.

1/6 **GYM. GIRDLES** in House Colours

GYM. COSTUMES. School Design.

GYM. BLOUSES. School Design.

GYM. HOSE AND KNICKERS
For Winter or Summer Terms.

GYM. SHOES. School Design.

SWEATERS for Hockey in School Colours.

SCARVES in School Colours. *(obtained at school only. 3/9)*

BLACK VELOUR HATS for Winter Term.

PANAMAS for Summer Term.

NAVY NAP or MELTON COATS
for Winter.

NAVY GABARDINE COATS
(Rainproof). For any Term.

DAY SHOES, HOUSE SLIPPERS, ATTACHE CASES, HOCKEY STICKS and SHIN GUARDS.

Girls' dress regu;lations, 1934

music master in both Schools and himself an Allanian, recalled the problem of teaching singing when only a wooden partition separated his class from another. Nevertheless, as one of his girls recently said of him, "He was an inspirational teacher … he was responsible for instilling a love of music into many of us, if not all of us." Later M.F. Larcomb would recall, " We had no school hall in the accepted sense, and plays and concerts took place with the added danger of falling over desks and furniture which had been piled in the corridor. The important thing is, however, that they *were* performed."

The Boys' School seems to have been slower off the mark (but records are incomplete), but a musical and dramatic society was formed in 1931 and it met on Friday evenings in the pavilion. They formed a four-part choir, held play readings and had gramophone recitals. A violin class of fifteen boys was started, and the whole society joined in performances of the thirty scenes of *The Morrison Tableaux*, which were about a remarkable Morpeth man, Robert Morrison, F.R.S. (1782 – 1834), who in 1807 was the first Protestant missionary to China. He translated The Bible into Chinese, prepared a grammar and then a dictionary, all by 1821. Tableaux are very demanding, and an unusual choice for a boys' school, but it was at the request of the committee of *Other Lands Exhibition*. This appears to be the first major dramatic activity on record, and proved the way for the enterprising choice of *HMS Pinafore* the next year. It was performed in the hall of Jesmond Parish Church in January, 1932, under the skilled baton of Bill Little, with a cast of fifty-two, all in superb costumes, as a surviving photograph shows. Twenty-three were female roles played and sung by the younger boys. Thus began the tradition of Gilbert and Sullivan operettas that was to last for over twenty years.

In 1932 there was another overseas trip by the boys, again under Messrs Little and Davies. This was a "students' cruise – 12 days for £12" on *S.S. Montcalm* from Liverpool to Madeira, Casablanca and Gibraltar. One boy,

Original design for Fenham building, 1929. A statue of Eleanor Allan and a flagpole were intended to stand opposite the main entrance; the former was not carried out.

Raymond Chapman, met a girl from Bolton on the ship and, after a decent interval of years, married her.

While the governors and the two heads were much concerned with the future, teachers and pupils were getting on with the present. The boys' Sixth Form, only formally introduced in 1929, numbered nineteen within two years[13] and the Board's inspectors felt that "the head master has worked wonders in spite of the difficulties"; all start Latin at eleven and then as alternative to Spanish the next year; Greek was an optional extra; chemistry was still the main science subject, but biology and physics were now available in first two years. They said that the standard of work "has improved out of all knowledge in the last two or three years". The inspectors observed that Miss Dobson was close to retirement, and ventured the observation that "it seems very probable that the governing body will appoint the Boys' head master to take charge of the two schools and make them into one mixed school when they move to the new buildings... He is a very capable man, who in a quiet and unobtrusive way has accomplished a great deal for the school." He was of course to achieve much more – but not as head of a mixed school.

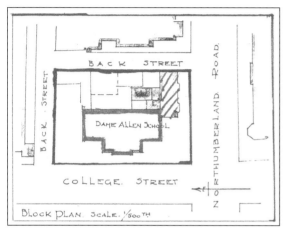

Plan of 1932 showing very restricted site. The shaded building is the former headmaster's house, by now occupied by the caretaker minus one upstairs room occupied by the boys.

A girl, M. F. Larcomb, writes of the problems of the last years in College Street. "The school, in spite of its material shortcomings, had a very corporate life. There was a very strict segregation of sheep and goats; although the boys' school existed and made itself manifest with a great deal of noise, we were supposed to ignore it. "We had no facilities for domestic science and no laboratories, and gym was carried out at some risk of splinters in the Y.M.C.A. Hall in Saville Row. Netball took place on a cinder patch. School meals were cooked on a filthy gas stove in a corner of the cloakroom and eaten on desks. Term ended in a horrible orgy known as 'a beano', in which large quantities of totally unsuitable food was consumed."

She observed that the world of women was changing. "There were in fact still quite a number of mothers who were hurt if it were suggested that their daughters should work after leaving school. Indeed two or three years at college could seriously jeopardise your chances of marriage." But times *were* changing for women, and the arrival of a new headmistress and the move to Fenham seemed to mark a new era. Mary Wylie (1925-32) was one of four girls in the Sixth Form, doing Spanish, French and English for highers. They had a tiny room just off the entrance hall. She loved the School – "the good old school". Another girl, J. M. Hunt, who joined in 1933, concurred with the above, but, "it had the most ghastly cloakroom." Yet she rapidly felt at home in the school and on games afternoons on the playing fields in Fenham, she and the other girls could see rising the new buildings, and think of the splendid accommodation to come. One annual event she recalls is the buying and selling of textbooks. In those days books were not supplied as part of the package, but had to be bought. If you could buy ones second or third-hand – or even more – from girls moving to a higher form, you could save money compared with a new copy. It had the advantage of making pupils look after books with more care. Exercise books also had to be bought.

The problems facing the governors were immense. It was one thing to buy the Fenham site: it was quite another to raise the funds to build the schools. The assets in 1920 consisted of the site and buildings in College Street, the farm at Wallsend with 69 acres left of the original 141, (including the sites of the two small hospitals), the property in The Side and assorted stock vested in the Official Trustees of Charitable funds; this stock amounted to a nominal value of £43,000. This was around half of what was needed, and indeed £5000 had already been spent on the land, drainage and other works, and the pavilion. The annual income from its properties was £1740; this would fall to a mere £25 if both the remaining Wallsend properties and the property in The Side as well as the stock were sold. The Schools would have no income from them and no reserves for a rainy day. Clearly an appeal was vital, and it had to go to a wide range of people.

[13] Alan Simpson (1913-98) won a Major Scholarship at Merton College, Oxford and was later a Commonwealth Fellow at Harvard. Professor of History and Dean at University of Chicago 1959-64. President of Vassar College NY. "A very warm, very humane person and a very intelligent man" (Chicago Tribune). The School has recently (2005) recovered from America via E-bay his 1925 prize for drawing.

Unfortunately, it was a very bad time to appeal for money. The world was sliding into depression, and local industry was badly affected. Unemployment was a serious problem which had lasted from soon after the end of the Great War, particularly with the decline of shipbuilding. The economic situation affected all levels of society, and there was no real chance of large donations in significant numbers. It would have to be done by strenuous efforts at small-scale fundraising and by many small donations.

On the other hand, the North-East Coast Exhibition on the Town Moor was intended to boost local industry and perhaps raise the spirits of Tynesiders. Opened by the Prince of Wales on 14 May, 1929, it stayed open until 26 October, and had nearly $4^1/_2$ million visitors. Marjorie Coates, now 16, "visited regularly" and found "every pavilion fascinating". To children the fun fair, especially the switchback railway, was the greatest attraction. It was spectacular and greatly enjoyed, but largely failed in its main purpose. Both Schools made educational visits.

The governors invited the architects Messrs Cackett, Burns Dick and MacKellar to design a building for the new site to accommodate 250 boys and 250 girls. It was to lie parallel to Bolbec Road facing east across the playing fields to the pavilion. The design for the centre block was a handsome two-storey building, twelve bays on each side of a classical portico of six columns and pediment surmounted by a clock tower or steeple. Behind were a boys' quadrangle and a girls' quadrangle separated by the assembly hall. To the north of the girls' wing was to be a dining room (shared) and to the south of the boys' school a gymnasium (shared). The site allowed for future growth north and south without impinging on the playing field.

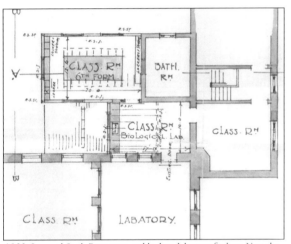
1932. Proposed Sixth Form room and biology labratory for boys. Note the classroom in the caretaker's house.

An appeal brochure was prepared and launched by the new Archbishop of York, the Most Revd Dr William Temple, on Speech Day, 2 December, 1929, in the City Hall. The preface was by the former chairman of governors and Vicar of Newcastle, the Revd G. E. Newsom, now Master of Selwyn College, Cambridge. "When I was chairman (1918-1928) I formed the opinion that there was no escape from the dilemma of either new buildings and a future of high promise – or annihilation." Fortunately he himself had led the way with the decision to acquire a site and launch an appeal. His successor as vicar and chairman was the Revd Canon J. R. Bateman-Champain, who was also resolute that the matter should be pushed forward with energy. The brochure makes clear that the governors wished to keep the Endowment Fund intact, since it gave "a certain measure of independence and scope for progressive development". Moreover they did not wish to raise fees and gain income that way since they wanted to maintain "a high standard of education at fees within the reach of the class it is intended to benefit". After the sale of the College Street premises, they would require a sum of £20,000.

No doubt the appeal began with high hopes of a quick and satisfactory response, with many lively events to raise the money required before building could start. Despite the eminence of the launcher of the appeal, the very presentable appeal booklet and the clear need, the result was a disaster. The Board of Education noted in 1932: "the governing body launched a campaign for voluntary subscriptions two or three years ago, with great hope of raising money enough to start building the new school, but the results were almost negligible and brought in a few pounds only. Since this was before the present financial crisis[14], there appears to be not the faintest hope of the money for the new building being forthcoming for many years to come." This was clearly a tremendous setback, and the governors put forward a plan to extend the College Street premises by adding an upper floor to a single-storey wing at a cost of £450. The principal need was for Sixth Form space. "In recent years the standard of work has increased very greatly and the number of pupils who pass the School Certificate every year has led to a steady growth of the Sixth Form, which now promises to be a regular feature of the

[14]The great economic depression started in America a few weeks before the appeal was launched, and quickly spread around the industrial world. By Christmas 1930 unemployment in Britain had risen from a million to $2^1/_2$ million. Tyneside was very badly affected.

organisation. It is the work of the Sixth Form that is most badly hampered by the lack of space, because they are divided up into small groups, which have no place to work in. There is a real need for a small biological laboratory as an extension of the passage which serves the purpose now." The extension would have provided both – but only for the boys, unless, on Miss Dobson's retirement the next year, a step towards coeducation was contemplated.

Despite the cramped conditions for biology students, it is evident from one source that standards were high. The sketchbook for dissections and microscopy of William Snowdon (1927-34) is in the School archives and shows astonishing artistic skill. He was evidently studying biology at the Higher Level; a pencil copy of Wright's painting *The Alchemist* shows that he should also have been studying art. In fact he became an architect's assistant in the Ministry of Works.

Although the Board approved this proposal, the governors reconsidered their position and made a momentous decision: they would sell the Schools' investments to pay for the building work. It was not a good time to sell but it was a good time to build. Canon Newsom had been right about the appeal, and perhaps they remembered his warning: without new buildings the Schools faced "annihilation". The design was extensively modified to a simple thirties design of no architectural pretentions – no portico and no clock tower. It was indeed to be much less handsome than Johnson's building of 1882, but it turned out to be far more practical – what we call today "user-friendly". Moreover, there was space to build further so that there are now almost a thousand pupils on the site.

As 1933 drew to a close, an offer of £17,000 was received – they had hoped for £20,000 – for the College Street buildings, the proposal to raise fees to eighteen guineas had been accepted, and plans were drawn up and submitted for the new school. During the first part of 1934 the governors, the architects and the Board of Education discussed details. The Board argued that there should be two halls: the interesting but unsatisfactory compromise can be seen today, with a huge wooden sliding screen that can separate the girls' western hall from the boys' eastern hall. They also urged larger laboratories and libraries, and argued against joint use of other areas. By September the Board had approved the estimated cost of £36,319 and the acceptance of a tender by Alexander Anderson of £33,285. Work could now begin.

The last flower festival took place in 1932. There is nothing in the newspaper account of that year to suggest it was to be the end of a tradition. Kathleen Clare abdicated and Frances Ellison was crowned by the Lady Mayoress. The fruit and flowers were distributed as usual to hospitals, while a collection raised funds for the Eye Infirmary Appeal Fund. Perhaps there was a feeling that it had become rather old-fashioned, and minds were concentrating on what would become possible once the Fenham buildings came into being. Its inspiration had been Miss Dobson's and she was on the point of retiring. Whatever the reason, the years had produced spectacle, music, drama, dance, recitation and vast enjoyment to performers and audiences alike.

When in the summer of 1933 Miss Dobson retired after thirty-nine years as Head Mistress, an age seemed to have come to an end. The College Street premises, which had seemed fine enough on her arrival, were now quite inadequate and the move to the Promised Land of Fenham was close. After her death in June, 1952, one of her former pupils wrote: "When as a child of ten I began my school career at Dame Allan's, the personality of Miss Dobson created the strongest of all the new and bewildering impressions I received. She was so handsome and awe-inspiring as she swept through school with her gown billowing around her, producing an absolute hush merely by her approach, and fixing wrong-doers with an eye that could quell the boldest. She seemed so far removed from ordinary mortals that I remember feeling quite surprised to hear that she had a mother. In later years, with a juster appreciation, I lost none of my admiration, and recall with real gratitude her genius for actual teaching. Later still, as a member of staff, I learned her capacity for organisation, and grew to know and love the warm and affectionate nature behind the façade of head-mistress. She had the gift of inspiring loyalty and any difficulties and personal problems met with ready understanding, sympathy and support." Another wrote: "Quite lately I was told of her affection for her staff and how each day she praised them at close of school." A third wrote: "Although the standard she met herself and required from others was high, painfully high to us, we never considered it impossible or undesirable." In those days it was not possible to be a woman teacher – never mind a headmistress – and married, but four years after her retirement, whilst on a world tour, she met and subsequently married a Mr Clark. They found great happiness together. Old Girls of the School raised sufficient funds to endow an Exhibition in her name, and this was awarded for many years. She was succeeded by Miss F. A. Elliott M.A. (Cantab.). Florence Annie Elliott was born in 1895 and was brought up in Kent. She had read English at Girton College, Cambridge, before completing a teaching certificate at Halsey Training College in London. She had taught in four girls' schools before coming to Dame Allan's, most recently at Rutherford College Girls' School in Newcastle. At some point the idea of a mixed school under A.K. Wilson had been lost but for the Schools the exciting move to the new buildings awaited.

The failure of the original appeal meant that a further invitation was required. This took the form of an appeal to people to "buy" a window or bricks along the façade of the buildings. It was launched by the Chairman, the Vicar and Provost of Newcastle, John Bateman-Champain, in November 1935. The bricks and the windows were already in place and pupils sat behind them, but everyone needed reminding that much was still needed to complete the work. There were eleven upper windows and thirteen lower windows on each side. The Clerk to the Governors and Bursar, Robert Muckle, who knew the financial situation better than anyone, gave the clock tower window. Eleven former Rose Queens clubbed together and gave the Girls' Library window; Form III (boys) also caught the spirit of the thing and paid for a window. Others donated one or more bricks at one shilling each. A donor wrote or signed his name on a slip of paper and stuck it on a corresponding blank on a page in the large record book. Thus you could identify "your" brick on the building. Some whose names appear elsewhere in this history, such as Nora Bennitt, E. Rose, E.V. Rees, Alan Simpson, Dorothy Hornsby and Arthur Milner, have their own bricks to this day facing the rising sun. Some had left long before and wanted to say thank you: Joseph Asquith Hodgson Curry Roberts 1888-92 was one. Adjacent bricks read P.M. Laws 1893-1902 and P.M. Laws 1930-193_; the latter was still a pupil there. Antonio de Camos Viana (Lisboa), his wife and daughter were no doubt reminding the Schools of England's oldest ally.

Sadly the record book shows that this appeal was far from a huge success. Windows went metaphorically unglazed and the intervening walls failed to rise from their foundations. If Form III could do it, so could others, but they didn't. Of course, many had already contributed in one way or another, and some would have economic problems of their own. The donations undoubtedly helped, but there was no quick solution to the financial difficulties.

Up to March, 1937, the expenditure had been £59,050:

Site	£8,531
Roads	£2,746
Laying out playing fields and pavilion	£6,763
School buildings	£36,68
Caretaker and groundsman's houses	£1,238
Furniture and equipment	£3,091

This was paid for by the sale of stock, sale of College Street buildings, sale of Threap Moor and wagonway at Wallsend, and other sources. The cost of the girls' gymnasium, further boys' classrooms, dining hall and kitchens were estimated to be a further £16,000. The Schools were empowered to raise £11,000 on mortgage, but undertook to replace stock over sixty years to build up reserves.

The pavilion, the first building on the Fenham site, 1930

Chapter Eight

THE SCHOOLS IN FENHAM:
EARLY DAYS IN THE NEW BUILDINGS 1935-1939

At three o'clock in the afternoon of Tuesday, 15 October, 1935, the Bishop of Newcastle, the Rt Revd Harold Bilbrough[1], unlocked the main door of the new school, and declared the new buildings open. When everyone was seated, a short service took place, and then there were speeches by the Provost and Vicar of Newcastle and Chairman of Governors, the Very Revd J. N. Bateman-Champain, by the Lord Mayor, Councillor R. S. Dalgliesh, and by Sir George Lunn, Chairman of Newcastle Education Committee, which had made a "small grant" to the Schools. The hall was named after the late Canon Newsom, of whom the chairman said: "One of his greatest ambitions had been the building of a new home for its scholars; it was largely through his efforts that such an accomplishment was made possible."

DAME ALLAN'S SCHOOL, NEWCASTLE-ON-TYNE. (7A)

Front of schools from south. From 1935 to 1940 there was a gap between the main block and the boys' gym, with an entrance set well back. In 1940 an air raid shelter was inserted, later used for storage, and a labratory built above. These and the boys' gym were demolished to make way for biology block

"Probably the first thing that appeals to most of us about the new school is the sense of space, of light and of air. The old buildings had a strong claim to our affections, but the general atmosphere was too suggestive for comfort of a crowded cupboard or a popular store during a sale. Here we sit in many windowed rooms or stroll along open passages in full enjoyment of sunshine and fresh air." (*The Allanian* 1936).

It is important to understand exactly what existed. The Newsom Hall, divisible into two parts, the girls' on the west and the boys' on the east, lay between two quadrangles, both open on the far side. The front and the rear wing looked much as now. A gymnasium lay at the south end, and was initially to be shared. This was much less than the governors had intended, but funds were insufficient to carry out the intended development in full. It was hoped that the governors, staff and pupils would demonstrate by their determination that they deserved support.

J. M. Hunt recalled her delight: "the spaciousness was almost too much for us at first" after the six classrooms, cloakroom and "a playground the size of a postage stamp." There was the choice of domestic science or science

[1]Bishop Bilbrough presented the Schools with many learned books from his library when he retired in 1941.

in proper accommodation, a geography room, an art room, "a marvellous gymnasium, which we shared with the boys, and best of all a beautiful library." The increased space meant that immediately another 11+ form could be introduced, and the School had become two-form entry. By 1939, the first three years (called Second, Third and Fourth Forms) had so developed, but the other two (called Lower Fifth and Upper Fifth) were still single stream. The Sixth had only two girls.

As part of the fundraising, a final and very spectacular Rose Fayre took place in the Old Assembly Rooms on 30 and 31 October, 1935, organised for the first and only time by the Parents' Association. The first day was opened by the Duchess of Northumberland and the second by Lord Armstrong. J. M. Hunt recalled: "We were all dressed in shades of pink organdie trimmed with rosebuds, and all the stalls were covered with paper roses which we all helped to make. It was very colourful indeed. This was the first time the boys' and girls' school really joined forces and the result of the combined effort was very successful." She does not say if the boys also wore pink organdie, but we may safely assume not. They did, however, run the Fun Fayre and the Boys' Concert Party, while the girls helped on the fruit and handicrafts stalls, and gave displays of country, maypole and sword dancing. An Old Allanian, Sal Sturgeon, a well-known actress and star in the early days of radio, delighted everyone with her Tyneside sketches. A local reporter described the rooms as "transformed into a scene resembling Tennyson's *Rosebud Garden of Girls*." Certainly the Old Assembly Rooms, one of the very finest public rooms of the Eighteenth Century in England, supplied a splendid setting, and over £1000 was raised.

DAME ALLAN'S SCHOOL SCHOLARSHIP EXAMINATION

GENERAL PAPER   March 1936.

1.   From what source are the following materials obtained:-
        rubber, linen, steel, sugar, petroleum?

2.   Write five lines (no more, no less) about ONE of the following
        rivers:-   the Nile, the Amazon, the Rhine.

3.   Who wrote the following works:-
        (a) Hamlet,   (b) The Last Days of Pompeii,   (c) Pickwick Paper
        (d) Tom Brown's School-Days,   (e) Robinson Crusoe?

4.   Name a work by each of the following authors:-
        (a) Milton,   (b) Wordsworth,   (c) Coleridge,   (d) Tennyson,
        (e) Rudyard Kipling.

5.   For what are the following important:-
        (a) The Duke of Marlborough,   (b) Captain Cook,
        (c) David Livingstone,   (d) General Gordon,   (e) Colonel
        Lawrence?

6.   Name in order the four English Sovereigns who came before
        H.M. King Edward VIII.

7.   Name the part of speech which describes the words underlined in
        following sentence:
        The mice made up their minds to put a bell on the cat's
        neck thinking that they would hear her as she ran swiftly
        towards them.

ARITHMETIC   March 1936.

        Show all working
        You may answer the questions in any order.

1.   A train 440 yds. long travelling at 33 ft. per sec. meets another
     train 220 yds long travelling at 77 ft. per sec. on a parallel
     set of lines. How long will they take to pass each other?

2.   A cubical box has a volume of 343 cubic metres. What is the total
     surface area?

3.   If eggs at 2 a 1d are mixed in equal quantities with eggs at 3 a 1d
     what is the average price?

4.   If our coinage were revised so that £1 = 10 florins, 1 florin =
     10 cents, 1 cent = 10 mils, express £3:7:8½. in the new units to the
     nearest mil.

5.   Find the value of $3 - \frac{2}{5} + \frac{6}{11} - \frac{71}{110}$

6.   A motor-car was timed to do ¼ mile in 34 seconds, and the time may
     have been 1 second out. Between what limits did the speed in m.p.h
     lie?

7.   A man sells 3 dox. cycles for £4:2:6d each. How many must he sell
     at £3:7:6d each to realize the same total sum?

There were two other papers, in English and in numerical accuracy, the latter making generous use of imperial measures of distance, weight and money. Today such a test for 10- and 11-year-olds might be regarded as excessive.

Meanwhile school activities continued to flourish. The girls had a geography/biology field trip based in Grasmere Youth Hostel, which included an ascent of Helvellyn, and also a school visit to Lucerne – both enterprising undertakings for the late thirties. The boys also made a tour of Belgium. The two Speech Days were at last on home territory and the Founders' Day Service was transferred to the Cathedral after many years at St Peter's, Oxford Street. The old buildings had been close to St Peter's, but it was more appropriate that the service should be at the Cathedral, with which the Schools had been linked since their foundation. Moreover, St

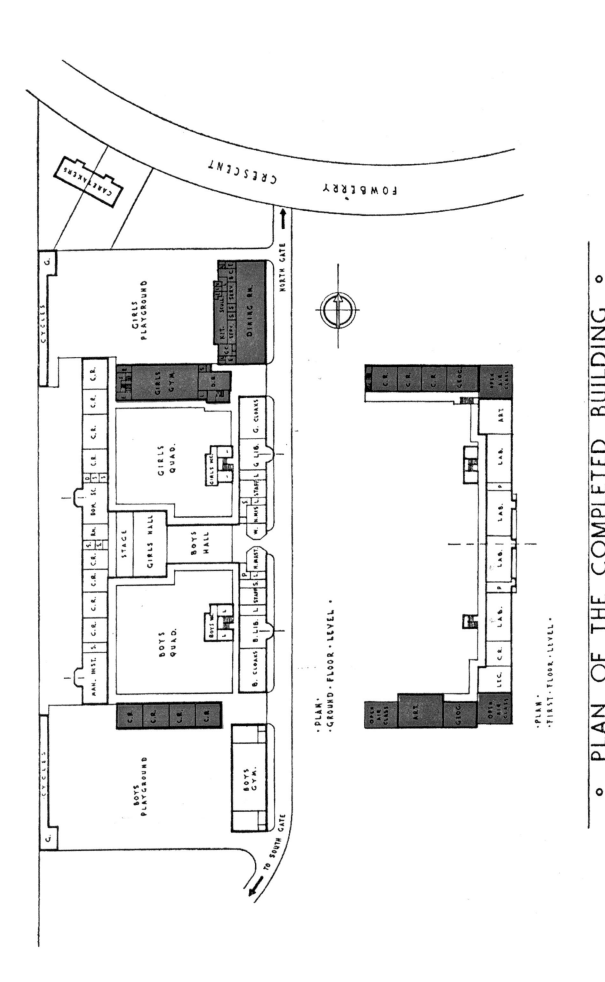

○ PLAN OF THE COMPLETED BUILDING ○

In outline, the buildings opened in 1935; in red the second phase completed in 1938

Peter's was shortly to be made redundant and demolished, but it should be remembered that for over half a century it had been Dame Allan's parish church and a part of the Schools' history, together with its vicars who took great interest in the Schools, notably the Revd J.J. Pigg, who taught part-time in both Schools.

Both Schools were delighted in their new libraries, and appealed for funds or books to stock the shelves, since the number from College Street was relatively small. The Old Boys were especially helpful to the boys' library, providing shelves, tables and chairs as well as books. Old Allanians were making an impression in the world with appointments as an Assistant Keeper in the British Museum, as a house surgeon, a manager with Imperial Airways in Singapore ("His recommendations for landing have been officially adopted"; what did they do before that?), and a holder (as Oxford graduate) of a Commonwealth Scholarship at Harvard.

The statistics for 1936 are interesting. Of 139 girls, 95 were from Newcastle, 33 from Northumberland and eleven from Co Durham. Of 170 boys, 100 were from Newcastle, 45 from Northumberland and 25 from Durham. The average age of leavers in the Girls' School was 16.4 and of boys 16.7. Nine girls had gone to training colleges over the previous three years, and twenty-one boys to universities. It must be remembered that although Dame Allan's girls had been going to university for some twenty-five years, it was still not a common route to careers; those who went to training colleges for teachers were no doubt as bright as those boys who went to university. It was the different expectations of boys and girls rather than abilities that created the difference; Tyneside was, in this sort of thing, deeply conservative.

By October, when the first inspection in Fenham took place, the numbers had grown to 198 girls and 227 boys, with nine teachers in each school. 80% of pupils had come from public elementary schools, and 25% had City free places, for which the LEA paid £6 a head plus a small block grant. The Board of Education gave a direct grant. The Foundation Scholarships, covering part fees, had been discontinued a year or so before the move from College Street for financial reasons, but maintenance allowances of from £1 to £3 per term were given by the governors "in necessitous cases to Free Place holders". The inspectors observed that in the new buildings the curriculum and organisation were close to the normal. "Given adequate staffing there is every reason for anticipating a higher level of attainment in the future...and the outlook is promising." The inspectors also commented on the flourishing out-of-school life.

Meanwhile, between 1935 and 1937, Japan attacked China, Italy occupied Abyssinia, and Germany marched its troops into the Rhineland and sent its air force to bomb the civilian population of Guernica in Spain. King George V had died, King Edward VIII had abdicated and King George VI had come to the throne. The economy and world trade were still in difficulties though improving, but in the old industrial areas such as Tyneside there was still mass unemployment.

The boys' quad, with Newsom Hall as built in 1934-35; this part remains unchanged, as does the corresponding view from the girls' quad

The first production in the Newsom Hall by the boys was their second Gilbert and Sullivan operetta, *The Pirates of Penzance*. Ian Maciver, later to be a distinguished doctor, played Major-General Stanley, and his daughters were astonishingly lady-like. Michael Scott[2], N.B. Hall and D. C. Elder displayed a demureness to which we are unaccustomed. The sight of Peter Easton and Angus Bird as young ladies was in itself worth the price of admission." Young Angus is elsewhere described as "diminutive but his tackling was a strong feature" in junior rugby and in cricket as "a most promising young bowler and opening batsman." The girls, too, quickly employed the hall for short plays by junior forms and for house plays,

[2]The diplomat Sir Michael Scott, KCVO, CMG, ambassador to Nepal 1974-77 and high commissioner to Malawi 1977-79 and Bangladesh 1980-81; Secretary-General of the Royal Commonwealth Society 1983-88.

ASSEMBLY · HALLS · DAME · ALLANS · SCHOOLS · NEW · BUILDINGS · FENHAM·

Newsom Hall: architect's drawing, 1934

but did not embark upon anything of the scale of the 1929 pageant.

Domestic science room c1935

Staff and pupils had from the first looked after the development of flowerbeds and lawns, and the site was quickly made very attractive by their efforts. Building work resumed in 1937 with the construction of a block of classrooms to complete the boys' quad, presumably because this was the most urgent. "Lessons are carried on," wrote the editor of *The Allanian*, "to the accompaniment of a series of bangs and thumps." Pupils in 2003-4 will readily recall their own experience of this kind of thing. The next phase was the girls' gymnasium, thus closing the north side of their quad. The final phase was the dining hall and kitchens, and these were opened on 2 November, 1938, by the Rt Revd J. N. Bateman-Champain, the new Bishop of Knaresborough, and, until some months earlier, chairman of governors when he was Provost of Newcastle. He had presided over the decision to move to Fenham and over the realisation of it; it was wholly appropriate that he should be the opener.

The new buildings allowed for the growth of the school and this necessitated a growth in staff numbers. In their last year at College Street, A K. Wilson and Miss Elliott had presided over staffs numbering seven full time for each school with two part time teachers in the Boys' School and three in the Girls'. At the move to Fenham Miss Elliott gained a further two full time members of staff and two part time mistresses took on additional hours. In the Boys' School, Bill Little, until then a part time teacher, became full time. By September 1938, with the further buildings also in place, Miss Elliott was assisted by a staff of twelve teachers; eleven were full time.

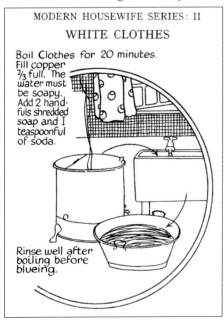

MODERN HOUSEWIFE SERIES: II
WHITE CLOTHES

Boil Clothes for 20 minutes.
Fill copper ⅔ full. The water must be soapy. Add 2 handfuls shredded soap and 1 teaspoonful of soda.

Rinse well after boiling before blueing.

From domestic science book, used in Girls' School in 1935

A.K. Wilson had a staff of twelve full time masters and one part time master. These pre-war staff were very well qualified[3] and committed to their profession - three would later lecture in higher education and a fourth became a local authority adviser.[4]

The new facilities made possible the extension of the girls' curriculum as they at last had a properly equipped domestic science room. The 1877 reconstitution had made provision for "Domestic Economy and the Laws of Health" as well as needlework but now cookery and laundry could be taught for the first time. Miss Doris Weightman was appointed to teach "Needlework, Cookery and Laundry work". The domestic sciences, long urged by inspectors, were especially welcome. A delightful little textbook, *Laundry Work*, price 1/-, owned by Olive Nixon (IIa) and dated Autumn Term, 1935, was used in that first exciting term, and survives in the school archives. Miss Weightman also had responsibility for another new feature of the schools with oversight of school dinners, supervising the kitchens and preparing the menus. The charge of school meals, including accounts, was to remain the responsibility of successive domestic science mistresses until 1948.

[3]In an age when physical training teachers were rarely graduates, it is interesting to note that, of the four Boys' PT teachers at Fenham, three were graduates, one holding an MA in Latin, and the fourth had completed three years at Balliol College, Oxford, before leaving without taking his degree.
[4]Vernon Jones lectured in Physical Education at Swansea University, Granville Allen lectured in Art and Woodwork at Bangor College and Arthur Pennington lectured in Science Education at Durham. Vera Burkett became the Music Co-ordinator for Aberdeen.

The Mikado (Boys' School)

The appointment of a master with graduate qualifications in both art and woodwork meant that the latter reappeared in the Boys' School curriculum in 1936, after a gap of a decade. Another addition to the staff as an "occasional visiting master" was a young curate from the cathedral, already a good friend of the School, the Revd Charles Hay. That summer he took his first group to Bruar Camp, an association that was to last for over thirty years. In May, the coronation of King George VI and Queen Elizabeth took place, and the occasion was marked at Dame Allan's by a service with "an enthusiastic address on England and the Empire", and a whole week's holiday. Drama was important in that year, with, for the first time, a professional company performing in the Newsom Hall, theatre visits and three performances by the boys of *The Mikado*. It is interesting to note that the boys' swimming sports were held in the Northumberland Baths on a Saturday evening, and that at the athletic sports the Parents' Association provided refreshments; both seem to have been social occasions as well as sporting events. This seems to have been equally true for the Girls' School. The girls gave a gymnastic display in the Newsom Hall in which everyone took some part; sword dancing was the most unusual event.

The new buildings allowed the growth of other activities. "Attempts had been made to form an orchestra while in our old premises, but the handicaps had proven too strong," wrote Bill Little. "With the removal to the new buildings, the idea was resuscitated, and in January, 1936, ten boys began lessons in violin and viola." Eighteen months later, the number had grown to thirty-six, with the addition of the cello to the other two instruments, and the orchestra had performed on Speech Day with considerable success. The girls made a slower start, with three violinists by May, 1936, but their enthusiasm and their teachers' skill led quickly to better things. At Easter, 1937, the temptation of the new stage proved too much for the staffs, and they joined forces to produce three one-act plays.

The Old Girls' Association took advantage of the new facilities. In hockey they had regular Saturday afternoon fixtures with other clubs, while the tennis courts were used on Saturdays and evenings in the summer. A gym club gathered on Tuesday evenings, there was a summer outing and attempts were being made to put on a play. Miss Elliott had asked former pupils to write to the magazine about their careers and interests, and one, Marjorie Coates, replied, regretting that she had been unable to study science at College Street, "for I think I have a scientific brain". Instead she had read history at Armstrong College, becoming interested in Egyptology and then Romano-British archaeology, in which she was required to use scientific methods. The provision of a laboratory for the girls in the new building would mean that a scientific career would now be much easier to follow.

The Old Boys' Association used the facilities in Fenham for cricket and rugby. Golf was played elsewhere, the Annual Dinner was held at the Royal Station Hotel, and the monthly lunches at the County Hotel. They had in 1938 a membership of 481, but many lived away from Newcastle and took little interest in the Association. Over ninety attended the 1937 dinner.

The Parents' Association, having made a tremendous effort for the Rose Fayre in 1935, had an intentionally quiet year in 1936, but when the Governors informed them that £3000 were needed to cover the cost of the dining hall, now nearing completion, they responded by promising to raise this sum as quickly as possible. Planning was begun for another major event over two days in October 1939, and it was hoped that this and other events would raise half of it by Christmas 1939. It was not to be: others had less charitable intentions.

G.L. Anderton, English Schools' Rugby Union captain, 1938-39. He played against Wales at Coventry.

Despite the increasingly worrying situation abroad, school continued as usual. The expansion to two-form entry, already observed in the Girls' School, had also taken place in the Boys' School and by the summer of 1938 the first three years had X and Y forms of thirty each, whereas the fourth and fifth years had single forms of thirty each. There were seven boys in the Sixth Form, and the total was thus just under 250 compared with the 150 of College Street days only three years earlier. The Sixth Form, though small, had at the highest level, considerable success, with three open scholarships or exhibitions at Oxford, Cambridge and Durham, while the Cambridge School Certificate had a fine array of very good, good and credit in a wide range of subjects.

By the autumn of 1938 both Schools had seen the two-form year group move through to the fourth year, and by the autumn of 1939, the process was complete. Despite the availability of school dinners, the tuck shop did well. At a higher level, plans were made to landscape the substantial area between the boys' playground and the Nun's Moor gate. Both Schools lined Fenham Hall Drive to cheer the King and Queen on their visit in February 1939, with the rest of the day a holiday. Speech Days, Sports Days and Swimming Sports were held in their due season. Staff came and went, and the new Provost of Newcastle, the Very Revd. G. E. Brigstocke, became chairman of governors. Dances were held for the first time for the Girls' and Boys' Schools Staff Dramatic Society and for the Boys' and Girls' Schools, with parents, old pupils and friends at both events. A Chamber Music Club was formed and met on Saturdays from 5pm to 7pm: that takes a special kind of pupil and teacher. Ian Richmond, the leading authority on Hadrian's Wall, gave two lectures on the subject, and, very interestingly, a priest serving with the Society for the Propagation of the Gospel (S.P.G.) gave a talk on the Japanese occupation of China, with the deliberate "bombing of universities and schools an essential part of their programme of making the Chinese a subject nation". He felt that "Japan's real difficulties would arise after the war was over, when she would have to revert from a war basis to a peacetime one." We now know how Japan solved the problem. Another dark note in *The Allanian* for July, 1939, was the creation of two flights of Air Cadets. "In view of the importance of 'air-mindedness' in these days and of the National Service fulfilled by membership, those who have not yet joined are strongly urged to do so." The most ominous statement was this: "Under the Government's Evacuation Schemes, Wigton in Cumberland has been assigned as the place to which, in the event of war, the school will be sent."

Provost Brigstocke, speaking at the Boys' School Speech Day in December, 1938, had commented on the gathering gloom. "We ought to be thankful that we live in Britain where young people are taught to think for themselves. There are not many places in this strange new world where this is a fact." Many in his audience were to be killed and injured in the next few years to keep Britain from the fate of China.

19th April 1939,

EVACUATION OF SCHOOL CHILDREN

1. <u>TO PARENTS OF ALL PUPILS</u>:

Arrangements are being made by the Governors of the School To participate in the evacuation scheme being prepared by the Newcastle upon Tyne City Council.

In the event of a national emergency this School would be evacuated to a place of comparative safety where it would be attached to another secondary school for educational purposes. The pupils will thus have the opportunity of continuing their secondary school education under secondary school conditions whereas on the other hand it is extremely doubtful if there will be any educational facilities for those who remain behind in the areas from which evacuation is effected. If orders for evacuation are issued by the Government the school party will be transported by rail to the reception area and there dispersed to billets in private houses where the householders have indicated their willingness to receive them. We are unable at the moment to state the probable destination of the Dame Allan's Schools but it is hoped to billet both Boys' and Girls' Schools in the same town or village.

Parents will no doubt appreciate that in a time of national crisis it is in the interests not only of the children but of the nation as a whole that children should have the best possible education in spite of the difficulties of war. With this in view the Governors sincerely trust that if the necessity for evacuation should arise it will be possible to continue to conduct the Dame Allan's Schools as a unit transferred to another district. It is hoped that all parents will consider this matter carefully in the light of the information given herein and that they will agree to their children participating in this scheme.

P.T.O.

Notice to Parents, 19 April, 1939

Langdale Pikes by Richard Laws, who came to love the Lake District so much in 1940-44 that he has returned many times. This was painted in 1980 and was a scene familiar to boys and girls of the evacuation years.

Chapter Nine

THE LAKE DISTRICT YEARS:
WAR AND EVACUATION, 1939 - 1944

The years of work in maintaining the cadets by Captain Mallinson and others during the twenties seemed by 1939 to have been wise. The creation of two flights of air cadets at Dame Allan's in that year recognised the huge development in the nature of warfare, particularly following the bombing of Guernica by German aircraft in 1936 during the Spanish Civil War. The threat to the civilian population of Newcastle in the event of war with Germany was also recognised by the city authorities, and, as we have seen, plans were drawn up for the evacuation of schools to the west side of the country. A letter with an application form went out to all Dame Allan's parents explaining the need for this as early as 19 April, 1939.

The Schools went on holiday for the summer. The Scouts went off to camp at Edmundbyers where they had a particularly good time in excellent weather. Late in August, Charles Hay, a young curate based on the cathedral and with many connections with Dame Allan's, was phoned in Hawick where he was on holiday. His caller was the Very Revd George Brigstock, Provost of Newcastle and chairman of governors. He said that evacuation was "almost certain" to begin next day, and that the Schools were to go to Wigton in Cumberland. He asked Charles to drive over to Wigton to assess the situation. At the council offices "we found utter confusion and apprehension, and no one could tell us anything". He returned to Hawick where he found a summons back to Newcastle where he arrived mid-evening. Going immediately to the Provost's house, he was asked if he were willing to go with Dame Allan's to Wigton the next morning, as five of the staff would be called up, immediately or shortly, to the armed forces. He agreed at once, and went to see A.K. Wilson who was engaged in "packing up the family silver to be taken to a safe place".

A.K. and his staff and Miss Elliott and her staff had been hard at work for days in preparation for something that might not – and they profoundly hoped would not – happen. The pupils and their parents were likewise deeply apprehensive. Some pupils no doubt felt it would be a great adventure, but others would see that it was not the same as going off to Guide or Scout camp for a week or two. Their parents perhaps recalled the almost universal opinion of twenty five years earlier – that it would all be over by Christmas – without mentioning in which year; some may have repeated it to comfort their children.

The Boys' School roll on 1 September, 1939, was 260; the Girls' 211. Some did not join the evacuation, but 470 children, staff and helpers gathered in Northumberland Road that Friday morning "with knapsacks on backs (change of clothes), gas mask in its cardboard box and strange labels on coats", and walked to Manors Station to board their train at the station. They were given a paper carrier bag of rations, including a tin of corned beef and a Kit Kat. They left at 11.40 with pupils from St Andrew C.E. School. An earlier train for Wigton at 10.15 had already taken a nominal 570 children from Cruddas Park, St Aloysius R.C. and Canning Street Schools. Charles Hay, having seen off the pupils, drove with a companion up the West Road, "looking over our shoulders for the crash of the first bombs and almost expecting to see Newcastle going up in smoke and flames. This was the general expectation." When the train arrived in Wigton, many children feared a gas attack had started and reached for their cardboard boxes, but soon learnt that Wigton always smelt like that: it was carbon disulphide released from the cellophane factory, a strong and unpleasant smell to which they were to grow accustomed – or nearly so. The army of children walked along Station Road, the girls to the Thomlinson School, the boys to the Nelson School. Here the local hosts were waiting in the sunshine.

The arrival of the evacuees at Wigton station, 1 September, 1939

"The intended drill", one Old Allanian recalled, "was for children to go in groups into the school building, there to be registered and then allocated to suitable hosts, at the best a very rough and ready exercise. But outside, impatient of waiting and with shrewd anticipation, the good people of Wigton went around making their own choices of children who looked suitable". Another boy later described it as resembling "the local cattle market auction". They were then whisked away "without further ceremony, unregistered and disappearing into the unknown". There was a marked preference for girls, and some local families were to be disappointed. "Evacuee billets was often compulsory if people had spare accommodation, and contrary to popular belief, not everyone who was given an evacuee appreciated it. My first billet was definitely in this category." At 10/6 for one evacuee and 17/6 for two, no Wigton resident was expecting to get rich from their guests.

Some were very fortunate in both the kind-heartedness of their hosts and the material comforts of their accommodation, others in the one, and yet others in neither. "My best friend and I were taken on foot by our hostess to a street of small houses, gas lit, one cold tap in the wash-house for two houses and an external shared toilet. Our adoptive parents were extremely kind and had gone so far as to give their bedroom to us.

Charles Hay and five boys were the only ones left by late afternoon and were taken together to "The Grange, where we were greeted with excitement and open arms by the most kindly and generous Mr and Mrs Johnson". The headmaster and his wife, on the other hand, were lodged "in a large house where their hosts were exceedingly mean and grudging. As in every community there were those like the Johnsons who were kind beyond the call of duty and there were those who were heartless and selfish beyond the understanding of ordinary folk. In the middle were the bulk of those who just did their best in trying circumstances, trying both to host and guest."

The experiences of Bob Colston show the variety of fortune that befell the evacuees.

"My first billet as an evacuee of eleven years was at Wigton with a middle-aged couple, the Holidays, who had no experience of children. We were marched into the Market Square at Wigton like slaves in ancient Rome and the locals came to inspect us and say how many, and of which sex, they wanted. Females were popular, as they could double up as domestic servants better than boys. The Holidays' surname proved to be a misnomer. Mrs Holiday said she would take two boys and Gwyn Bevan, a friend of mine from the primary school, grabbed me and said, 'Come on, Bob!' and we were off into her house. No other evacuee was allowed in – ever.

"The Holidays were very religious people. Wigton was a strong Quaker Centre but they were Wesleyan

Methodists. Godliness was the main concern in that house. The Holidays would have loved us to convert to their particular brand of religion but they knew we attended a Church of England school. To complicate matters, their niece Madelaine, a lady of some thirty years, lived with them and was a member of the Plymouth Brethren. It became her aim in life to convert Gwyn and me to her sect as members. God tore at us from all sides. All things enjoyable were frowned upon at Market Square. The radio and card-playing were despised; I'd enjoyed both of these at home in Newcastle. Anything vaguely interesting or exciting to us was dismissed as the work of the devil. To the general horror someone sent me a mouth-organ as a present. Shock! Non-hymn music was sinful.

"Gwyn and I had our day's work judged at night by Madelaine's Box. This contained about a hundred rolled up biblical texts, some good, some bad. We had to pick one each before we went to bed. A good text, "The blessing of the Lord be upon you!" earned you a sweet and a pat on the head for being a good boy. But a bad text, "The wrath of God be upon you!" got you a clip on the ear, and sent to bed in disgrace, for being an evil little monster. Some nights Gwyn got a sweet and I got a boxed ear. Sometimes it was the converse. On a good night we both won. It was our first lesson in Applied Religion and Bigotry. The Holidays did not like having evacuees. They complained to the billeting officer. Gwyn and I shared the blame for all things that went wrong in their home. Our running down the stairs had stopped their grandmother clock… our loud behaviour had scared their goldfish so that it died. We had to go.

"I was on my own in the second Wigton billet. This was with a young couple, Sid and Irene Harrington, at South End. Sid was 24; Irene was 19. They had a lovely little baby daughter, Nora. We got on like a house on fire. Although they had a tiny house and were poor, they made me very welcome and I had a great time there. When we went back to Newcastle in April 1940, I was very sad to leave them. My parents sent presents for Nora because they had been so kind to me."

Denis Wardle (1939-44), too, while finding the evacuation very traumatic, met kindness from a "dear, plump lady in a small terraced house" and, when later moved, from a railway worker, his wife and daughter, with whom he was to stay in contact for many years afterwards.

Sheila Mitchell was one who had a tough time at Wigton, and not simply because she was both starting a new school and being evacuated. She had a pretty and bubbly friend who insisted they stayed together, and at the "market" they were picked by a very pleasant and caring couple with a girl of similar age. All seemed well enough, and then "auntie" found she was pregnant and the couple had neither time nor space for the evacuees. The two girls were taken, without any prior checking of the suitability of the accommodation, to a council house on the outskirts of the town and lodged with a woman and her daughter. They quickly discovered why there were no other members of the family around: the husband was in prison and the son in borstal. Mother and daughter departed to the cinema after the first meal, leaving the girls to wash up. Instead, the girls repacked and called at the post office to get money from their accounts for the train fare. The postmistress, realising the situation, contacted Miss Ramage and Miss Cuthbertson who came and took them back to their own hotel for the night. The two mothers arrived from Newcastle the next morning and had to go from door to door in the town begging for someone to take them in. Eventually a local bank manager and his wife agreed. They found it difficult to cope and the girls often felt hungry and no one seemed to have real concern for them. "We had to look after ourselves."

Melvyn Bragg, in his splendid history of Wigton 1900-75, *Speak for England*, quotes a local resident who was a boy in 1939. "We had two types of evacuees. We had the Dame Allan School which came, which were the grammar-school people, and they of course were the upper crust. We had the other evacuees that came with the short hair-cut… They were townies as against us country lads. I can't remember any evacuees ever playing in our immediate circle… They were alone to themselves." But see later for evidence of integration at another level.

For the next fortnight there was no school. Two days after the evacuation, Britain and France declared war on Germany after its attack on Poland, and the evacuation seemed a wise precaution: Newcastle, with its heavy industry, looked a likely target for air raids. The girls shared the premises of the Thomlinson School, the local girls' grammar school. The Thomlinson pupils worked in the mornings and Dame Allan's in the afternoons. "The idea of half-day school, though bemoaned by the mistresses, was greeted with jubilation by the girls." The senior

Girls at lunch at Thomlinson School,Wigton. Autumn, 1939

school, however, also had morning school, and one of them recalls "lessons in the Friends' Meeting House, where during the winter, we read Shakespeare around a slow combustion stove." The school's facilities were poor compared with Fenham's, with inadequate science facilities, no gymnasium and only the yard for netball. The Friends' School, a mile away on the outskirts of the town, lent the use of their laboratory, and the Victoria Hall was available in the mornings, "while the presence of frisking bullocks on the hockey pitch was an added interest".

The staff consisted of Miss Elliott and most of the existing mistresses. All were unmarried, and the move to Wigton was thus easier, but nevertheless must have produced considerable problems. Pastoral care, lessons in less than ideal conditions, billeting, the break from family and friends must have made life difficult. One response to the increased needs of pastoral care – homesickness must have been common – was the increase in the number of out-of-school activities. On Saturdays was the very popular mixed dance, held in the two Schools. On Sundays church attendance was encouraged, poetry reading and similar activities were held and in the evening the mistresses organised games for the juniors and afterwards held a short service followed by a discussion led by Miss Elliott and the Revd Charles Hay. On other days girls were instructed for the St John Ambulance certificates, and a Guide Company was formed. The usual games were played, and the 1st Hockey XI accepted a challenge from the Boys' School. "The girls lost the match 11-0 but certainly learnt many new hockey tactics."

Boys 11, Girls 0.Wigton, Spring 1940

The boys meanwhile were having similar fortunes. They too had afternoon lessons from 1 to 5, and mornings were taken up by games, supervised homework and jobs. The latter arose from the desire for pocket money on the one side and the shortage of land workers on the other. Many boys were billeted with farming families, where help was expected whether for pocket money or not. One-sixteen-year-old found himself on a Clydesdale stud farm, "so most glorious mornings were spent working on the farm, for a man I much admired and who was only too willing for me to try everything. I was there for a year and then back again for the harvest of 1941, before I joined the army. I learned how to milk cows and loved the smell of the byre on a cold November morning, and their warm flanks against my forehead during the milking. Looking back, it seems like a lively dream and an isolated interlude in my life. Those experiences have never left me".

The availability of mornings for sporting activities brought a gleam to the eye of Charles Hay: here was an opportunity to build "a superb rugby team. It was important to start young. By the time our Second Form was the Sixth Form we had an unbeatable team." In particular Fenwick Allison, Gwyn Bevan and Gordon Anderton were to play at international level. Bob Colston (quoted above) admits "I was useless at rugby and wished the school played football. But it was banned." The School was too small to do both well. Bob, however, became a football reporter, reading the football results for ITV for a quarter-century. "I only hope Charles Hay never knew."

Nelson School, Wigton

A.K. Wilson had serious staff problems because of the loss of the masters to the armed forces. It seemed that no sooner had he replaced one, then another – or even the same one - was called up or volunteered. Fortunately he had three experienced schoolmasters of the best kind. The second master was Ted Finch, "a most gifted and scholarly person, fierce and even terrifying to naughty or thoughtless boys, but also possessing great understanding and kindness." The second was Captain Henry Mallinson (Mally to all), a remarkable man, "loved by all, one who had a good word to say for even the worst of sinners, and with an extraordinary gift of encouraging boys to make the best of what they were, though no administrator."The third was the music master, Bill Little, whose interests and energies covered all aspects of school life, "whatever was for the benefit of the pupils." To these was added the young Charles Hay, a fifth who was to give so many of his active years to the school. Besides the fluctuating body of younger masters, there were a number of women teachers, of whom Sylvia Boykett made perhaps the deepest impression.

Within a short time of arrival, the next Gilbert and Sullivan operetta resumed rehearsal; it was *Ruddigore*. Herr Hitler might have caused the minor inconvenience of removal from Fenham, but no jumped-up little corporal was going to interfere with the larger things of life such as G & S. On the morning of the first performance, Rose Maybud was ill, Sir Despard walked out and Sir Ruthven lost his voice completely. Bill Little trained replacements for the first two and played the third himself, as well as conducting and producing. No sooner had this been performed than plans were made for a revival of *The Mikado* for performance before Easter. Both were considerable successes, and were supported by local people both as members of the orchestra and as audience.

27th Carlisle (1st Wigton) Scouts, ie. Dame Allan's

Charles Hay and Richard Stringfellow[1], already Scouters, realising that they had many scouts with them and aware of the need for such an activity, formed a School Troop based on the 22nd Newcastle (St Nicholas' Cathedral) Group, but containing members of the 1st Tyne Sea Scouts, the 4th, 8th, 11th, 27th, 33rd, 49th, 63rd and 100th Newcastle and 7th Whitley Bay. This troop was "to last for the duration of the emergency," and, since there was no scout

[1]Richard Stringfellow joined the RAF and was killed in action in the Middle East on 18th June, 1942. He left a valuable legacy to the school.

group in Wigton, it became 27th Carlisle (1st Wigton) Group. Two more Scouters joined, one of them the former Gosforth Park Camp Chief and a Scout Commissioner, and the latter maintained the troop with a number of local boys who had already joined when Dame Allan's returned to Newcastle. The troop was very successful and had to operate in two groups, meeting in the school gymnasium.

Maureen Symington recalls picking and packing apples in the orchard next to the Thomlinson School in the autumn, social evenings and dances with the Boys' School (suitably chaperoned), a sewing class (mainly darning their own stockings) and visits to "a very small, very uncomfortable cinema." Despite the weather – it was a hard winter – rugby practice and games took place; as with the girls, the mornings were much used. Both girls and boys also took advantage of the countryside for cycle rides and walks.

On 16 November, 1939, the Board of Education produced a report on the evacuation conditions in Wigton. Already 27 boys and 47 girls had returned to Newcastle; 20 more girls intended to leave at Christmas. "The billeting situation is the worst reported by any Secondary School in Cumberland, Westmorland or Durham. From what the Head Master says it seems questionable whether the school can remain here and survive. The standards of the houses in which a large proportion of the boys are billeted are said to be low in respect of washing, sanitation and comfort: many have no bath or indoor water closet, the kitchen sink is commonly used for personal ablutions and in perhaps nine cases out of ten the boys share a double bed, sometimes with a boy of the household. There has been an outbreak of skin diseases, affecting some twenty of the boys to date and there are no means of isolation – the only resort is to send cases home. But the unwillingness of the householders to receive or keep boys is apparently an even worse factor in the situation. Ten boys a week are said to be turned out and some have to be sent home until new billets can be found – a matter of increasing difficulty and constant anxiety, devolving largely on the Head Master … In regard to Christmas holidays the Head Master sees little hope of retaining the boys – the boys themselves are in a state of tension, the parents will demand them and the householders will throw them out."

The situation with regard to the girls was just the same as for the boys, though girls had often been chosen in preference to boys in the original "cattle market" on 1 September. "The resources and goodwill of the district seem to have been overstrained and the impression is given, whether just or not, that the local billeting organisation has not been effective."

The Cumberland Evening News of 22 November commented: "Children have come from 'higher class' homes in Newcastle. We can only give them what we have. We cannot give them Jesmond suburban villas in Wigton … The burden upon Wigton of both a boys' and a girls' secondary school was far too great, and they should be relieved of it." One must have some sympathy with this view, since the town also had Newcastle primary schools.

The clerk to the governors wrote to the Board three days later pointing out that the haemorrhage of pupils was also a haemorrhage of finance and that the Schools could sustain neither. In mid-January the Board met the Director of Education and LEA representatives to discuss a possible return to Fenham. The director said that the Royal Grammar School had kept 631 of its 790 pupils in Penrith but no doubt someone pointed out that Penrith was a very different place from Wigton. He feared that if Dame Allan's returned it "would attract a lot of new entrants who would normally have entered other schools, and would insist on the parents signing an agreement to keep them at Dame Allan's to the end of their school life," thus weakening those other schools. He asked that pupils should be free to leave to enter other schools, and the Board agreed on a clause to that effect. The situation at that point was that the Girls' School had lost 131 out of 256 pupils and the Boys' School 98 out of 304. On 2 April, the LEA gave final approval for a return to Fenham provided that the governors agreed not to tie pupils to the Schools, which they accepted. They also agreed to build air raid shelters at the schools.

Meanwhile back in Newcastle, the period of the phoney war saw none of the expected air raids. Neither on land nor in the air was there significant conflict; only at sea was there fierce activity. After the fall of Poland, the Russian attack on Finland on 30 November and the ensuing war, ending on 12 March, 1940, was the focus of interest. Many had returned home for a Christmas break, and this had been unsettling. Some mothers had come as helpers in September, but were attracted home and sometimes took their children back too. Miss Elliott later reported that "billeting conditions and the unexpected quiet in Newcastle resulted in a gradual, and then a rapid, trek home. By Easter it was obviously impossible to stay at Wigton". On 2 April, the two Schools learned that they were returning to Newcastle four days later, and that the summer term would be in Fenham. Two days after the return, the phoney war ended as Germany invaded Denmark and Norway, and on 10 May, Holland and Belgium, followed by France on 13th. On the 26th, the evacuation from Dunkirk began and on 22 June France capitulated. The whole of the coast facing Britain, from beyond the Arctic Circle to the southern end of the Channel, had passed into enemy hands.

About that summer term one girl wrote that its "vividness depended upon the eloquence of familiar things. Yet even the familiar had undergone some change. It was not without a jolt that we realised that we must pass a sentry in order to indulge an enthusiasm for Pythagoras and irregular French verbs". The reason for the sentry was that in the months since the evacuation the school buildings had been used for civil defence purposes, and the girls' gymnasium had become a First Aid and Decontamination Centre. This it remained when the Schools reoccupied the rest of the buildings. The familiar sound of building work, remembered from 1938-39, was still present: air-raid shelters were going up. The first seems to have been at the boys' end, between the main block and the gymnasium, and then along the back of the Schools. It was only when these were finished that a full complement of pupils could be admitted, the seniors taking priority.

"School regained much of its former tone: the usual mob besieged the tuckshop daily, and the habitually careless had more than their usual scope with identity discs, gasmasks and bicycle padlocks to lose."

The boys too settled in to something of the old routine of lessons and games, and most of those who had returned to Newcastle early or had not gone at all rejoined their classmates. Yet the war could not be forgotten: the news on the wireless, the men and increasingly the women in uniform about the streets, air-raid practices, the blackout, the rationing and shortages. More masters were called up; every man under 41 was conscripted. Senior boys – but not senior girls – did some firewatching. It was becoming increasingly evident that a second evacuation was imminent.

The last straw was on 2 July. Evensong was in progress in the cathedral as a German raider dropped a bomb aimed at the High Level Bridge. It missed but struck Spiller's Mill nearby "with a most tremendous bang and the whole cathedral was violently shaken." The choirboys had much to tell their classmates the next day. There had been considerable damage in Newcastle and down river at Jarrow, with thirteen killed and over a hundred injured.

Not all parents wished their children to be evacuated, but some three-quarters did. At least one parent, a Methodist minister, opted for the third possibility; evacuation to Canada, and in August, J.M. Udy, aged twelve, crossed the Atlantic. It is very likely that a girl, name unknown, did the same, since a letter from her in Ontario simply about her school was printed in the 1943-45 magazine. This option was effectively closed when the *City of Benares* was torpedoed by a submarine the next month and many children died. On 7 July the boys assembled as before and the train took them to Windermere. "It was a brilliantly sunny day and the landscape was beautiful." This time the billeting seems to have been better organised, and the accommodation generally to have been superior. Billeting resources were no doubt less stretched, with 150 rather than 400 to be accommodated. Boys, too, most of them with the earlier experience, were better able to cope. The arrangements with the host school, Windermere Grammar School, were also far better. The headmaster of the school, Mr Knowles, was called up for the army (sadly he was to die in captivity in the Far East), and A.K. Wilson became acting head of that school also. Dame Allan's assemblies were held each morning in St John's Church, and W.G.S.'s in the hall/gymnasium, and registers and similar were separate, but lessons were taught together and essentially the two operated as one. Temporary wooden classrooms soon provided extra space.

On 8 July the girls' school also travelled to Windermere, where they transferred to buses and continued to Ambleside. One girl recorded how very different this experience was. "For one thing, it was a considerably smaller school on this occasion; for another we had been expecting and were prepared for the issuing of this evacuation order, whereas before events moved so rapidly that few were ready when the summer came. Also the spirit of excitement and thrill of adventure were lacking this time. Nearly all of us gathered there were hardy veterans of the evacuation scheme and we knew its difficulties; in consequence, our behaviour was more orderly

Windermere Grammar School in 1940. Now Demolished

Windermere Grammar School in 1940

and passive. Grey-stoned, irregular little Ambleside, seemed pleasant and kindly as we drove through to the billeting centre, where cars were waiting to take us to our new homes immediately." Most were in Ambleside itself, with a few at Lakeside and Rydal. Ambleside already had evacuees, with elementary school children from Newcastle and several private schools in large houses. The wisdom of the move was confirmed by further bombing on Tyneside on 18/19 July, and then at intervals through August and September.

The billets in Ambleside were generally more satisfactory than in Wigton. Barbara Purvis recalls the eighteen months she spent with the kindly landlady of a small hotel, the Bowfell, on the shores of the lake at Waterhead, a mile from Ambleside. Initially she shared with another DAGS girl, but she soon returned to Fenham.

"I was never asked to take part in any of the work involved in running the hotel. I just had to look after myself and my belongings and not get in the way. A corner was found for me in the busy all-purpose kitchen-cum-livingroom where all the action was based, and it was here I did my homework and wrote my weekly essays. If I was only reading, I was allowed to sit in the Residents' Lounge, which had a spectacular view over the lake. But I also found it fascinating to watch how everything was done in the kitchen and with a minimum of labour-saving equipment but a maximum of satisfaction for the guests, many of whom had been visiting Bowfell for years. There was a small wooden jetty, and during the summer months I used to sit there and fish. I caught only an occasional perch, but my kind-hearted hostess would always fry it for my next meal." Her parents and her sister were able to stay during holidays, especially half-terms. The position of the hotel meant she had an appreciable journey to and from school, which was situated on the lower slopes of Wansfell and a steep quarter-mile above the main road, itself a mile from the lake. This was sometimes helped by a bus for part of the journey, but the journey had to be made four times a day. In the winter, even when there was an evening activity, "I sometimes preferred to stay at home. I could always read, keep Mrs Bell company and knit gloves and seamen's oiled-wool socks for the war effort."

Maureen Symington and Joan Craig were taken to a large house, where the lady viewed them with some displeasure: "Haven't you got some boys?" It seemed that she had four older sons, and was thus used to boys and not to "town girls". In fact the girls immediately took to the open air life and rejoiced in it. Maureen recalled "I swam regularly in Windermere from Whitsuntide until late September." She was to walk repeatedly on the hills, Loughrigg, to the west of the town, being her particular favourite. "I have wonderful memories of climbing up there after school to skate on Lily Tarn, with skates fixed to old hockey boots."

Sheila Mitchell, who had had a bad time at Wigton, fared little better at Ambleside. She and another girl were first lodged with a very kind couple. Unfortunately the couple moved away but arranged for them to live with friends of theirs. These people were good in various ways, but had strange notions of hygiene. Fortnightly all the clothes were washed in a boiler in a wash house. The same water was then used successively in a tin bath by

Kelsick Grammar School, Ambleside in its beautiful position

the husband and wife, with the girls at third and fourth. Sheila found the water so disgusting by this time that she refused to use it. Further, the wash house had no curtains at the window, and passers-by could look in. There were compensations, however. She and her companion had freedom to roam in the beautiful surroundings without giving any account of themselves. One memorable day they climbed Loughrigg. Sheila was impressed by the standard of education; she felt it to be better directed and organised than it had been in her first three terms. She recalled one brush with Miss Elliott. The girls to reach school had to descend to the main road and then go up again to the school, both being on Wansfell. They discovered that it was possible to go much more directly by going along a low dam wall across a stream. Miss Elliott found out, and gave them a strong lecture on taking unnecessary risks. Returning home for Easter, 1944, she looked so scruffy and neglected that her mother did not immediately recognise her. It was quickly determined that she should go to the Fenham Dame Allan's and not return to Ambleside. Looking back, she knows it was an unpleasant experience, but recognises that it was character-building and gave her independence and determination.

The older pupils were thrown into Cambridge School Certificate only two days after the evacuation but the rest of the girls were on supervised holiday. Each morning they met at the YMCA hall for prayers at ten o'clock, and events were arranged for the rest of the day. Sadly the fine weather that had greeted them to Ambleside was promptly replaced by a fortnight's rain, and most activities took place in the hall – plays, games and dancing. At the end of this period, Kelsick Grammar School broke up for their summer holiday, having skilfully arranged a massive improvement in the weather. Thereupon, Dame Allan's took over their premises for lessons, two hours in the mornings and ninety minutes in the afternoons. In reality Miss Elliott and the staff recognised that there was more to education than classroom lessons, especially if you are newcomers to the Lake District, and many outdoor activities were enjoyed to the benefit of soul and body.

After three weeks, the official summer holiday began fully for all except senior forms who had some science lessons. No one was allowed to return to Newcastle but girls could meet parents for holidays in safe areas. For the rest, the holidays were supervised, with many outdoor excursions, including ascents of Helvellyn, Scafell Pike and lesser fells, and much use was made of Lake Windermere for swimming.

For the boys too, similar arrangements were made. Most were quite satisfied with their accommodation and treatment, though one recalled that he quickly got chickenpox and his guardians would not have him back. He was sent to another house where "there was obviously a severe domestic problem", but then was moved "to a new guardian, Mrs Haworth, who was very kind, and I stayed there until the school returned to Newcastle in 1944. She took me to tea with her friends, including the Lord Lieutenant of Westmorland. In later years I stayed in contact with her and took my family to visit. This continued until her death fifty years later." Others report similar experiences of becoming part of their guardians' families, and likewise staying in touch for many years.

Gordon Anderton[2] recalls looking after a hundred chickens at Wigton, but at Windermere he lived with a retired banker and his wife: "charming people. He liked to play chess with me and was so kind I couldn't stand beating him. Fortunately, that didn't happen often! He taught me a great deal about climbing in the Lakeland hills." Denis Wardle, fortunate in his accommodation in Wigton, was again lucky when he stayed with the manager of Martin's Bank, Bowness and his wife. He well remembers Mr Nicholson's fine baritone. The Nicholsons had no children, and Denis and another boy, Robert Waters, became sons of the family, remaining there until 1944. They were to remain in touch for sixty years.

[2] Gordon Anderton played rugby for England Schoolboys against Wales. He became an aeronautical engineer, working on the Comet for De Havilland in Britain and then for Boeing in America, where he was responsible for stress analysis for wing-body intersection and landing gear for the Boeing 747.

TEAL LANDING

RML

Richard Laws drew wildlife during his Windermere years, 1940-44

Richard Laws and his friend Bill Harrison, after temporary lodgings, were moved to a fine modern house in a glorious garden with splendid views across Lake Windermere. Even better was the remarkable couple, who looked after them. They were in their fifties and had had no children; the two boys could not have fared better. "It was an idyllic place for a teenager with interests like mine, a life unlike anything I had experienced before .... A new and different world and culture ... a very formative period of my life." Other formative influences besides the Woods were the devoted members of staff mostly mentioned elsewhere, but one important to Dick Laws was Mrs Friend, the art mistress, who encouraged him in his growing interest in drawing and painting, especially of flowers, birds, butterflies and other insects. The Royal College of Art had been evacuated to Ambleside and the students held an annual exhibition. The Woods knew several Lake District artists and he had the chance to talk to them and see their work. Once, visiting friends of the Woods in Ambleside, he met a German artist and refugee, Kurt Schwitters, and saw his last great work, Merzbau, on a barn wall – one of the first people to see it.[3]

The other great influence was the magnificent scenery: "I developed a deep love of hills and mountains, which will remain with me until I die." Within the days of arriving at Windermere he joined a party led by Charles Hay on the Langdale Pikes and "I never looked back". The Woods had been keen climbers, and Dick was introduced to rock climbing by Bentley Beethan, who had climbed on Everest, and other well known climbers. His second climb that first day was the Mitre, done in nailed shoes. One person with whom he climbed was Miss Joslin, his physics teacher, whom he had already found impressive in the classroom. Like other boys he also used his cycle extensively, and would cycle back to Whitley Bay (110 miles) for holidays.

It was not of course always an easy relationship. Growing boys – and, for that matter, growing girls – are not easily accommodated by their own parents, never mind proxy parents. Trevor Storey recalls how he and his friend Bill Casson restored a canoe with a tarry substance that somehow transferred itself to their clothes. On seeing them, their guardian, a good

SCHOOL HOUSE - WINDERMERE GRAMMAR SCHOOL
BILL CASSON VANCOUVER 1997

The hostel, Windermere Grammar School, formerly the head's house. Watercolour by Bill Casson, Old Allanian. Done in 1997. Both the house and the school have been demolished

3 Dismantled and taken to the Hatton Gallery, Newcastle University, where it is now displayed.

Christian woman, employed language of a sort that shocked both parties, and caused her to feel that she was unable to go to church for some weeks. This further upset her, and she realised that coping with two fourteen-year-olds was now beyond her. The hostel was the only answer. In fact, one of the boys became deputy director of education for Newcastle and the other an architect and housing officer of British Columbia, but clearly she did not spot the potential in them, well, not that sort of potential anyway.

High Borrans, near Windermere. Second hostel, but also a private home. Now an outdoor recreation centre

Thirty of the younger boys had a different experience, since they were accommodated in a large house at the school. The hostel had four dormitories, with rooms for Major Mallinson and Bill Little, and dining and recreational rooms. Mrs Knowles, wife of the WGS head then on active service, was matron. "There were the unforgettable cricket matches, most of the time being occupied by arguments as to whether Horace was out, or if Jack should be allowed to play without brushing his hair". A newspaper called *The Boarderer* and later another "known by its editor as *The Hostel Opinion* and by others as "that rag" made brief appearances, and there were attempts at concerts by "the few bright boys". A second small hostel was set up at High Borrans with a small group of boys, with Charles Hay in charge. For cyclists it was a "wonderful downhill ride to school", but was less good on the return.

Bob Colston again had the experience of two billets, very different but both good. "The first was with two old ladies, Miss Brady and Miss Peacock. Emily Brady was an extremely rich old lady who lived in a luxurious house in Windermere. She had had it specially built to look straight up the lake from her dining table so that she had the Langdale Pikes, Harrison Stickle and Pike o' Stickle, framed in the very centre of her window. She had several servants who came and went during the day, like the gardener and the maids, but the cook/house-keeper, Jenny Peacock, was resident. She was a second mother to me. She even wrote to my parents offering to adopt me in the event of their being killed in the war-time bombing. I remained in contact with Jenny for many years after the war right up to the time of her death in the sixties. She was a great lady.

"In 1941, after I had only been in Windermere a few months, Miss Brady died and her house was to be sold so I had to leave. While a new billet was being sought for me I was sent to the hostel, the school boarding house, in the school grounds where there were some thirty boys and two teachers resident. The boys were in four dormitories and they were under the charge of Henry Mallinson and Bill Little.

"What a difference from my quiet life with the two old ladies! After only one night in the boarding house I knew that this was the place for me. Plenty of life and action. Plenty of young boys to talk to, to laugh with, to tell my jokes to. I had plenty of jokes. My father was a Music Hall comedian so I knew all his patter and passed it off as my own. Night after night I held forth in the dorm. I loved having an audience.

"I asked Mally (Captain Mallinson) if I could stay in the boarding house instead of moving out into a private billet. He referred me to the Headmaster, who, to my great delight, readily agreed. I returned to the staff room and informed Mally of the Head's decision. Mally seemed happy. He was a wonderful man. He was what people called a character when he was alive. Now he is dead he is a legend. Mally was on permanent duty all his life at Windermere while he was in charge of us boys. He held all the keys for everything. He kept lists and rotas. He organised the hostel on military lines. The thirty boys were split up into five orderly rotas to serve the meals, wash up and peel potatoes on a daily basis.

"Mally referred to the boys as "Gents!" He was a maths teacher by trade but he taught us many many other things: manners, organisation, cleanliness, trust, kindness, efficiency, tolerance and a great insight into his war, The First World War. The man was a gem. He invented 24/7. He was always there for you. His loud army voice bellowed out throughout the hostel in the mornings "Stand by your beds. Prayers!" And while yelling out from memory the matinal ritual, "Almighty and most merciful Father who hast safely brought us to the beginning of this day......" he rushed through all four dormitories to ensure that all boys were correctly praying and dutifully standing by their beds, before rounding off the proceedings with The Lord's Prayer in which we all joined, chanting from the various rooms of the establishment. After the last Amen, Mally blew his whistle and yelled "Gents. Orderlies!" And the six duty boys would rush off to the kitchens to serve the breakfast in the dining room.

"At bed-time Mally's cry was : "Gents! Sick, Lame and Lazy!". All lads who had cut fingers, bruised knees or any kind of ailment went and queued up at Mally's room which smelt like a chemist's shop, for a dose of this, a pill for that or a bandage on the other. This nightly medical surgery was held all the time Mally was in charge.

"Some nights Mally or Bill Little, the English and Music teacher who shared the duties at the boarding house, would tell us boys bed-time stories. Mally's stories were all of a military flavour. They were tales of his war with himself as the leading character and his two side-kicks, Blackbeard and Gorilla, who abetted him in all his doings. They must have been based on real life privates who had much brawn and no brain. This trio always managed to put one over on the enemy. And the enemy wasn't always the Boche. Sometimes it was their senior officers who seemed a wholly incompetent set. Sometimes it was another platoon. Whether it was fighting in the trenches for extra rations or whatever ... our gallant trio always came out on top.

"We learnt about the terrible conditions in the trenches, the damp, the cold, the general lack of everything. We heard about the hopeless conduct of the war. We heard about the armistice at Christmas time between the troops when Germans and English met together in No-man's Land and swapped cigarettes, chocolate and names and addresses and a promise to look each other up after the war, if they survived. We heard about the gallantry of the young troops who were ordered to their deaths by the thousand to save the reputation of some idiot in Whitehall. Mally made light of the whole affair. He dismissed medals as things that were won by fools too stupid or too drunk to realise what they were doing. The death and glory boys, he called them. It was only much later when I had left school that I learnt that he himself had been awarded the Military Cross. He never mentioned it to us.

"Bill Little's story-telling technique was quite different. He didn't walk up and down in a great coat like Mally. He turned the lights off and lay on a bed and smoked. We only saw the glow of his cigarette in the darkness. He built up atmosphere. His tales were of the James Bond type. His heroes visited foreign locations and met characters with strange names. There were always shady criminals, spies, crooks, thefts, chases and thrilling incidents. Later I realised that Bill was probably giving us the plot of a book he had just read. But at the time, as schoolboys we lapped it up. And story nights meant that it was late when you went to bed. When in July, 1943, Bill and Mally decided to call it a day and hand over the boarding house to others the boys were shattered. The new teachers to take over were Charlie Hay, (History, Scripture and Rugger-Rugger-Rugger) and Sylvia Boykett (French) - Bessie to the boys behind her back. Both of these teachers were strong disciplinarians. When I met Miss Boykett years later and told her how terrified we were of her, she told us that it was because she was terrified of us. There were several female teachers in the school now. There had been none at the outbreak of war. But with the drift of the men off to the forces the female teaching ranks swelled. And excellent ladies they all were too.

"The school rule was that all boys should be in two organisations extra to the school curriculum. I was already a scout and when Bill Little began the Air Training Cadet flight, I joined that to make up my two. We met in the ATC hut in the village on Tuesdays and Fridays and learnt marching, drill, astronomy, aircraft identification, Morse Code and other allied requirements for future air personnel. Out of school at Windermere our entertainment comprised: boating and swimming in the lake, climbing the hills and mountains, cycling everywhere, and indoors we had the usual games, monopoly, totopoly, chess, cards and all the games that thirty boys had brought with them from their homes. I recall that we had so much rail-track that it stretched right across the playing field of the school. Extra cash was earned by helping lake boatmen tidy up. Mally invested in a billiard table and a radio and he bought us an engine (The Brahman Moor) for our trains. The radio came in handy on Thursday evenings to listen to Tommy Handley in ITMA, the big hit radio show of the war. Bill Little had taught us ballroom dancing in the gym on Saturday nights so that we should not disappoint the young ladies of Windermere whom we invited to our socials and hops. Charlie Hay introduced us to bridge and we formed a bridge club. The head organised a tennis tournament at Nab Wood tennis courts where we were allowed to indulge in mixed doubles with more young ladies. I decided to organise entertainment to liven up the long dull winters. I drafted several luckless lads to learn my scripts and play the parts in my sketches. We had a ready audience of the boys and the staff and they were pleased to laugh at anything.

"As a church school we held services every weekday before lessons at St John's Windermere and we also had Sunday services at St Martin's at Bowness. Stage craft, drama and public reading were vital training grounds for me, as I was to use voice and body in teaching and broadcasting for well over fifty years". Bob taught for several years and then successfully worked for BBC Newcastle, Associated Television, London Weekend and ITN London, largely in announcing of sports results.

Miss Pat Deans, who was appointed in August 1942, recalled in 2003 some of her memories of duties and responsibilities some sixty years earlier. "Part of our job as staff was to visit boys in their billets and ensure all was well. Some boys were not allowed to use ink in case they spilt it, but the majority were all right. In order to take the boys out of their billets as much as possible, we had school on six days, with half-days on Thursdays and Saturdays, with some organised games on those afternoons – and detention for malefactors. Mr and Mrs Wilson lived at the Nabwood Hotel near the ferry at Bowness. Mrs Purves (Latin teacher on W.G.S. staff) and I used to take some of the less happily billeted boys for tea and table tennis on Sunday afternoons". Since Pat Deans was in charge of junior P.E. and games (for which she was qualified, despite "no personal experience of rugby and cricket), as well as teaching history and French, it is obvious she had little time for herself. She helped with cadet dances "teaching them to waltz and quick-step", collected salvage for the war effort, organised "a huge 'posh' jumble sale, when the gym was packed with goods to raise money for Mrs Churchill's Fund for Russia. Being from a farming family, I was pressurized by one of the Windermere boys to start a Young Farmers' Club. We had a couple of allotments in early 1944, but only cos lettuce had been grown before the return to Newcastle. However, one of the members, Graham Rose, did go on to make a name for himself as gardening correspondent of *The Sunday Times* and to write *Landscape with Weeds*". It is clear that all the teachers from Dame Allan's who were at Windermere worked extremely hard, physically, mentally and emotionally. To Messrs Wilson, Mallinson, Finch, Little and Hay, to the Misses Boykett, Ramage, Joshin, Deans, Patterson and Humble, to Mrs Wilson and Mrs Knowles, and to the six Windermere teachers, Dame Allan's Boys' School owes a deep debt of gratitude.

The scouts were quickly re-established during the term in Fenham as 22nd Newcastle, and it was during this brief spell that the link with Col Warde-Aldam of Healey was made with the first of numerous forestry weekends. At Windermere the 27th Carlisle/22nd Newcastle became the 6th Windermere – though it was the only one in the district. Again it was immediately successful, with large numbers, ideal scouting facilities and strong staff support. "Tree-felling at Nab Wood, weekend camp at High Borrans, the forestry camps at Healey, exciting adventure hikes and first class journeys across the fells, an Air Scout section, some remarkable wide games, and gang shows, first produced in Windermere and brought on tour to Fenham: these are some of the highlights of four interesting years."

Windermere Grammar School: classrooms and gymnasium. Gwyn Bevan (13) on his Raleigh bike. December, 1940

A "book of excursions" details some of the more energetic activities for 11 to 16 year olds. The first was on Tuesday, 13 August, 1940. It had been intended to climb Scafell Pike, but weather conditions, with cloud base at a thousand feet and rain, limited them to an ascent of the Langdale Pikes; nineteen boys and two masters took part. Three days later seventeen boys and three masters took a lower level walk on the hills between Esthwaite Water and Coniston. The following week twenty-two tackled Helvellyn via Striding Edge, and eleven took High Street in their stride. Clearly the Lake District was there to be enjoyed. The cadets resumed their activities with an added sense of purpose: what they learned might one day save their lives and the lives of others.

The Girls' School was not integrated with Kelsick Grammar School in the way that the boys were with Windermere Grammar School, since the situation was quite different. Kelsick was co-educational, and the two Schools occupied the same premises at the same time, with all available space fully employed. One Old Allanian recalled: "It seems strange now but I cannot recall having any contact, formal or informal, with our opposite numbers, though it was really quite a small establishment." Latin, mathematics and geography in the School Certificate year only, and some Sixth Form work were, however, taught together, and the two staffs sometimes assisted each other. "It says much for the organisational skills and the patience of the staff of both Schools that normal life – assemblies, classes, exams, homework – all seemed to proceed in an orderly fashion." The head master of Kelsick, Mr Mander, and his colleagues certainly did their best to make it all work.

Maureen Symington recalled that Kelsick Grammar School was in a very beautiful position with a spectacular view, but its facilities were, like the Thomlinson's, well below the standards the girls had enjoyed in Fenham. Again there was no gymnasium and gym lessons were held in the school hall with a minimum of equipment. There was a science laboratory, but it was poorly equipped. "There was no domestic science as such but we had some cookery lessons in the kitchen, which was also used for some lessons, particularly in the Sixth Form." Netball and rounders were played on the school yard, while hockey was in Millan's Park, half-an-hour's walk away. "The ground was very uneven, and sometimes we had to chase sheep away: they kept the grass cropped. We had a wooden pavilion for changing rooms, but no showers.

"Everyone in my form could swim and so Miss Ball, our games mistress, put us through our life-saving drill. One rather chilly afternoon we were examined by a man from the Royal Lifesaving Society for our bronze medals. He said it was the first time he had conducted the exam in a lake rather than a swimming pool." Miss Elliott ruled that no girl could swim in the lake without an adult, but she had not reckoned on the ingenuity of her charges. "The housekeeper and gardener from our billet would often be willing to accompany us and stand on the shore; neither could swim." Sometimes the girls would swim in the river, which likewise broke no rule. No wonder Hitler lost the war.

Four Dame Allan's girls on winter walk on Kirkstone Pass, c 1941

The gardener also taught her to row, and they would go char fishing and also look after a number of traps which caught perch. These were sent away to be processed and canned to replace sardines and pilchards which were no longer imported.

Netball and hockey were resumed and games were even played with old rivals, since Newcastle Central High School was in Keswick, and both Sacred Heart Convent and Heaton Secondary Schools were in Kendal. The guides were re-established by Miss Burton and Miss Bell and numbers quickly grew. Saturday evenings were frequently given to dances and games, and on Sunday evenings there were "short services with lantern slides". There were drama productions, for example the Sixth Form wrote and produced an entertainment called "If Bacon wrote Shakespeare, why can't we?" The local cinema had one programme on Mondays and Tuesdays and a second on Thursdays and Saturdays. At 4d and 6d on hard seats at the front, it was popular with the girls.

Meanwhile, back in Fenham term had begun for the hundred pupils left behind. With the provision of air raid shelters, this alternative was possible as it had not been in September of the previous year. Those pupils who had not gone to Wigton had had a serious interruption to their education. Some had gone to other schools, temporarily or permanently, some had had work sent by post – one girl expressed her gratitude to teachers who had done this – and some seem to have had little or no education. No doubt some were taught privately or at home.

The first air raid shelters were built at the boys' and girls' entrances from the drive; the heavy construction can be detected at the latter entrance but was destroyed at the boys' entrance when the biology block was erected. Others were put up behind the School.

There could be no alternative to combining the two Schools. One girl wrote: "Both parties were at first aloof and cold. The boys, like the girls, had been divided on the subject of amalgamation. Some maintained that it was a violation of their rights, as peaceful citizens; others, of a more sociable disposition, were pleased with the event. The girls spent much time on the first day in discussion of their strange form-mates, voicing the disadvantages and advantages of their presence, and the former won the day. But gradually they forgot their disagreements and friendly peace reigned." Another recalled that when numbers allowed it, there would be a boys' form and a girls' form, rather than two mixed forms, but of necessity some classes were mixed. By the summer of 1943, the girls' magazine records: "With the exception of Form 2c, the girls are now working apart from the boys." Miss Lippett and two other mistresses joined Mr Finch as the combined staff. Increased unpleasantness from across the North Sea in no way deterred the pupils from preparing an end-of-term concert in year groups. "We (the girls) were surprised to find that a turmoil of muscular legs and slightly wilting net skirts was a ballet by the Remove boys (14/15 years). The long-suffering and harassed Fifth (15/16 years) produced a drama which even the Remove had to admit was well done under the circumstances: its subject was the Red Terror in Russia." This last should have sent everyone home happy for the Christmas holidays. Russia, it should be remembered, had shared Poland with Nazi Germany in September, 1939: it was not to be an ally of Britain until it was itself attacked in June, 1941.

One girl recalled the air-raid shelters as seeming "flimsy". "Occasionally we had to file into these dismal dank buildings, most usually for practice sessions and only rarely on account of an alert. The daylight raid of 15 August, 1940, in which the R.A.F. inflicted very heavy losses on the German bombers, was most likely responsible for one of these rare occasions. The alerts were probably all false alarms. The shelters never lost the smell of damp concrete and even in mid-summer felt cold and forbidding." Nevertheless, the war was a serious matter that impinged on ordinary life. Masters had to do fire-watching duty, viz., to stay overnight in the school to tackle incendiary bombs should any be dropped. Mr Ross claimed that he was too old for that duty, but in a letter to Wilson, Finch claimed that Ross was younger than he was.[4]

Despite the relatively low numbers of boys, the 22nd Newcastle Troop was revived, and besides operating its own programme, joined the Windermere Troop in summer camp at Healey. Although a guide company was set up in Ambleside, none was formed in Fenham.

TAKEN OVER BY THE MAYOR OF NEWCASTLE-ON TYNE
FOR A GIRLS HOSTEL FROM DAME ALLEN'S SCHOOL
NEWCASTLE, Oct. 10th 1940 TO Oct 1st 1943.

Entry in the guest book of Smallwood Hotel. Last holiday guest, 22.09.40; next 05.04.44.
The school actually left on 19 July

The absence of so many pupils in the Lake District meant that there was spare accommodation in Fenham. At the same time the parents of existing pupils urged the creation of a junior department for their younger children. To this the Governors agreed "as a war-time proposal, but they visualised the possibility of a properly organised junior school of much larger dimensions being developed". (Letter of October, 1949, from Clerk to the Governors to Miss Elliott). The junior school opened on 28 April, 1942, with twenty-two pupils, thirteen boys

---

[4] He was right. Robert Ross was five years younger than Finch. Ross had taken a temporary war post teaching science, geography and maths at Fenham and stayed until he retired in 1950. He had studied chemistry at Oxford and had been a headmaster in Shanghai until 1932, when he retired to England.

Smallwood Hostel, Ambleside. The low building, now a restaurant, was in 1940 part of the hostel

and nine girls, aged eight and nine. There was a waiting list of ten, and by 15 July a second form was created and there were over forty pupils. Within a year there were fifty. Miss Patterson and Miss Fletcher of the staff started a cub pack from these juniors, and they too took advantage of Healey camps.

The Smallwood Private Hotel in Ambleside was taken over by Newcastle Education Committee and converted into a girls' hostel, similar to the one occupied by the boys at Windermere. On 28 October, 1940, thirty-one girls and two mistresses moved in, the girls being mostly newcomers both to Dame Allan's and to Ambleside. A matron and "lady helpers" completed the family. Two young residents recorded at the time that the hostel was "not a grand place, but a happy and busy one, and we all agree that we are splendidly fed" – no mean achievement under rationing. The first two mistresses at the Smallwood were Miss Nobbs (French) and Miss Goodman (mathematics), succeeded by Miss Tinson (Science) and Miss Cuthbertson (Scripture),

Dame Allan's cadets on parade in Windermere, c1941. Bill Little is the second officer. Local boys were later allowed to join. At the side of the road are other Dame Allan's boys wearing caps.

and later by Miss Clarke (history) and Miss Burton (English). The dining room was in a wooden annexe which still exists, now as a separate restaurant. The lounge of the hostel was sometimes used for sixth form lessons, particularly history and English, and the informality was greatly appreciated. The hotel entertained nostalgic Old Allanians for years afterwards. Miss Cuthbertson left the school in December 1941. She was an Old Girl herself and served the school for twenty years, many as Senior Mathematics Mistress.[5]

The cadets had lapsed during the Wigton period and it was in fact the Air Defence Corps, formed shortly before the outbreak of war, that re-established itself first as the Air Training Corps. It was led by Flying Officer Bill Little, assisted by a member of the Windermere Grammar School staff. It was highly successful and additional flights had to be formed for local boys and for the evacuated Ashville College from Harrogate. Thus Dame Allan's was able "to give to Windermere the makings of a very fine tradition in youth organisation". Annual camps were held twice at Millom and once at Blackpool.

M.V. Tern, 1891, (H.M.S. Undine). H.Q. of Sea Cadets on Windermere

With the help and encouragement of the Windermere Home Guard, the Dame Allan's Army Cadet Company was re-established on 18 February, 1942, under the command of Major Mallinson. They were affiliated to the Border Regiment, based in Carlisle, and wore the regiment's cap badge, initially in nickel and later in a plastic material. "Our first taste of real action was in searching a wood for escaped German prisoners, with one rifle between five but supported by police with truncheons. Although the Germans failed to materialise, their suspected presence made that exercise an unforgettable experience." The first camp was in July at Wray on the shores of the lake, and it was rather scout-like, but at the 1943 camp, at Hazelslack in Lancashire, the cadets "under expert tuition, learned how to handle various weapons such as the Sten, Bren, Browning, Vickers and 6-pounder anti-tank gun and various types of grenades, bombs and mines." Astonishingly the full company returned to Windermere unharmed.

Those with a nautical bent were also satisfied in 1942, when a Sea Cadet Corps was formed. Starting with an old café converted to "a shiplike H.Q." and a ship's mast, the corps acquired a whaler, a cutter, three ship's lifeboats and a gig, and in late 1943 "a lake steamer from the L.M.S., a railway company that in peacetime operated such vessels on Windermere. It was lent on condition that it was returned in the same condition as it was when borrowed." It was indeed kept in very good order, painted and repainted in battleship grey in the best traditions of the Royal Navy.[6] Sadly, with teachers very fully occupied with education, games, scouts, cadets, boarding duties and pastoral concerns, the formerly lively world of drama and music was largely restricted to concerts and gangshows.

Dame Allan's Guides with Stan and Billy, driver and horse respectively, collecting waste paper.

John Rutter recalls that for him and his brother Bill "joining the School in its second stage of evacuation at Windermere was undoubtedly the most momentous experience of our lives. I went there in September, 1941, and my brother a year later. I was a homeless wartime refugee from Belgium – where I was born and where my father lived and worked in the years between the wars – and we had 'come home' to Newcastle in November, 1939. It was like joining *The Fifth Form at St Dominic's* in real life. There were so many boys and so many had marvellous nicknames : 'Puggy' Scaife, 'Bull' Turnbull, 'Pud' Cannon, 'Toss'

[5]She had astonished everyone in 1928 by joining the Franciscan Order, and henceforth dressing in a brown habit. "She was fair and pretty", wrote Marjorie Coates, "and we missed her pretty clothes and especially her summer hats."
[6]This was probably the *Tern*, built in 1891 and still operating on the lake today. She was then steam-powered and was renamed H.M.S. *Undine* for her war service.

Walker, 'Punch' Elliott, 'Pluto' Arnot, the Wood Brothers ('Chips' and 'Splinter') and best of all – 'Potamus' Wear. My first term in a private billet was misery, but when, after the Christmas holidays, I was moved into the Boarding House or 'hostel' as it was often called, things just got better and better. I consider myself extremely fortunate to have experienced those years: they were unique. The camaraderie was greater, even than that which I experienced, later, as a National Serviceman in the R.A.F. The School was, at that time, just one big (reasonably happy) family."

Guides with handcraft outside the salvage depot, Millan's Park, Ambleside. L-R: Maureen Symington, Joan Wilson, Brenda Burke and Jean Craig.

In 1941, Miss Elliott "put into words a thought that had been in many of our minds for some time: 'What are we doing for the war effort?' A school committee was set up to look at the possibilities, and it was decided to form a Youth Squad, with three groups: the salvage group, the knitters and the gardeners." The first collected paper from houses and shops every Saturday morning and sorted it at the salvage depot. Sometimes the girls had the assistance of a horse and cart from the council, Stan the driver and Billy the horse. One sad day as they were leaving school, they saw the Salvage Depot was on fire and their recent paper collections with it. Dame Allan's Ambleside adopted a naval trawler based in Northern Scotland, already linked with Dame Allan's Fenham, and held dances and entertainments to raise funds to buy wool. This the knitters transformed into socks, helmets, gloves and scarves. If members of the salvage group spotted suitable books and magazines, they too were sent north. Was that trawler crew the best read and the best dressed in Scapa Flow? The girls certainly tried to make it so. The gardeners acquired an allotment in the park, and started to grow vegetables. The 3rd Ambleside (Dame Allan's) Girl Guide Company, based on the one started in Wigton but not developed because of severe weather and poor facilities, very soon flourished and had to operate a waiting list. They had good relations with the other Ambleside companies and took part in the parade in War Weapons week. Besides helping the salvage group, there was "a new line, the collection of nettles and other wild plants for the drug trade; rumour has it that we will be paid £5 per hundredweight for dandelion leaves." They also collected conkers in season: these were used for pig food, but some might have arrived in fragmented condition. Sadly, at the same time, waste paper collection in Fenham is said to have been responsible for the loss of much of the Schools' archives.

At Christmas, 1940, the older girls sang Christmas carols around Ambleside – "in a real Lakeland downpour", of course – poignantly finishing by singing French carols to some French refugees, who like the Holy Family, had been driven from their homeland. All the children at schools in Ambleside gathered in St Mary's Church for a carol service, and then the holiday began. Most girls returned to Newcastle; those who remained were well looked after. Most of the boys, too, returned home for the holidays. This was indeed a feature of the years of evacuation. There is no evidence that the Luftwaffe moderated their efforts during school holidays, and the inconsistency was widely accepted elsewhere in Britain.

There was, of course, full awareness of the war, and perhaps especially of the war in the air. There was a schoolboy competition for a poster to raise funds to buy aircraft. Brian Davison[7] delighted his peers with a picture of a Spitfire and a Messerschmidt with the slogan "Buy me and stop one", a variant of the ice cream slogan "Stop me and buy one".

One group of the Dame Allan's family not so far considered consists of those who went off to war. The most obvious first impact was the loss from the classroom of young masters. Although teaching was a reserve

[7]Brian Davison, later professor in the University of the West Indies: Deputy Lord Lieutenant of Glamorgan.

occupation for those over 25 (later over 30) some over that age chose to volunteer, and at least ten regular or temporary assistant masters were lost to the Boys' School over the course of the first year: the peacetime staff was ten. There was a rapid turnover of staff, until there was the clear recognition that it would be necessary to have women teachers to fill the gaps more satisfactorily. But it was amongst the Old Boys of the twenties and thirties that the impact was also clear. Some wrote to A.K. Wilson and the surviving members of staff at points during the war, with interesting and moving comments. One saw on his way to Shoeburyness something of the effects of the London Blitz two months after it had started. "The London area presents a shocking sight, and the East End that my train passed through seemed especially battered. I counted eighty smashed buildings in ten minutes on one side of the line. Overhead here (in Essex), wonderful foamy weaving designs of exhaust trail go on all day as the dog fighters tumble about the sky : several alerts sound daily: and it is a grand sight to see our men hunting for trouble in twenty-fours, and striding the blast miles up". One member of staff reported to AKW a meeting with an Old Boy, "the elder Ellison", in the Merchant Navy : "He is chief wireless operator on a benzine tanker bringing octane fuel from USA for the RAF. He seemed to think this a safer cargo than most in that tankers were hard to sink on account of the subdivided hull. He was at Singapore when the Folum Bridge was blown up, at Columbo in the Easter raids, at Alexandria at the time of Alamein, was torpedoed in the Mozambique Channel last October. I wonder if it was the same U-boat which drowned our daughter-in-law in the same place a month later."

One letter is worth quoting in full as typical of many.

> 149635 Lieutenant R.E.P. Marshall,
> 346 Company,
> Royal Army Service Corp,
> British Expeditionary Force
>
> 19.xi.42

Dear Mr Wilson,

A great deal of water has flowed under the bridge since I severed the link with Allan's and set out to make my way in the world. Sitting beside my truck last night, having the last pipe of the day, I began to think of the good old days and, naturally, my thoughts kept harking back to what I now know to have been the best days of my life – my last two years at the old school.

Somehow I seem to have lost touch with Newcastle and Allan's. I've been wandering around these desert sands for almost two years and so I'm writing to you in the hope that you can help me to pick up some of the threads of my old life. I've neither seen nor heard of any of my old associates since the outbreak of hostilities. I would very much like to know where some of my old friends are and what they are doing, and how and where I can get in touch with them.

I've had quite an adventurous time since I joined up in September '39. I went through the ranks in England, had a spell with the Commandos and was eventually gazetted as Second Lieutenant in the R.A.S.C. I arrived out here about two years ago, and have been through the Iraq and Syrian campaigns and the more recent shows in the Western Desert. On the whole, I've been more than extraordinarily lucky in the way of escaping serious injury. I've had my truck shot up by M.E.110's and come out of it with no more than a broken finger! I've had my driver shot through the head whilst sitting beside me, and have driven through a German tank convoy without having a single shot fired at me. Still, excitement is the spice of life, and apart from witnessing the horrible carnage and loss of life and seeing the decimating of the flower of three nations' manhood, I'm enjoying every minute of it. Now we are on the trail again and look like staying the course this time[8]. I sincerely hope so for grand fun as it is out here, I'm often filled with a nostalgic longing for the green fields and fogs and rain of old England.

---

[8]He refers to the advance of British troops from El Alamein to Benghazi, and perhaps to the Anglo-American advances eastward from the triple landings on 8 November in Morocco and Algeria.

Well, afraid there isn't much room left (on the Air Mail Letter Card). Sorry about my writing but I'm sitting on the ground resting this paper on my map board and it is really rather uncomfortable!

Do let me know what some of the other chaps are doing and send me any recent school mags that you can find.

Best wishes to Mrs Wilson and any of my old masters and old class-mates you may run across.

Yours very sincerely,
Pat Marshall

Interestingly it shows the mixture of adventure and horror that many others felt.

Others had a quieter time, of course. Another reported from India that he had "not fired a single shot since being on the rifle range at Prestatyn", and wrote vividly about his experiences and of his efforts to learn Urdu. Some had travelled widely and seen much of interest, almost as tourists.

Some became prisoners-of-war. Tom Ball (1928-34), navigator on a Lancaster, was returning from a raid on the Reich when his aircraft was set on fire by an enemy fighter, and he parachuted into German-occupied Holland near Breda. Of the crew of eight, six survived. He was imprisoned in the notorious Stalag Luft III, from which the "Great Escape" had been made earlier in the year. Seventy-six men escaped; fifty were shot on capture by Hitler's direct orders. Consequently escaping had been banned by the senior British officers, but nevertheless a new tunnel was being dug from the theatre. The principal enemy was boredom, and thus the theatre flourished to combat it - and to cover up work on the tunnel. Tom Ball had been involved in dramatics at church and at Dame Allan's, (he was in the first Gilbert and Sullivan there) and found the camp theatre a rewarding experience. The Red Cross had supplied musical instruments, and there was a flourishing orchestra. Another wrote to AKW apologising for "a long overdue letter, the more so in view of the fact that the present circumstances may seem inauspicious for a renewal of contact," sent from "Campo PG70, PM3300, No. 2 Compound, Italia." But there were other letters, too, that AKW must have dreaded getting. "It is with deep sorrow that I write to inform you of the death of my brother, Sergeant Robert Meikle RAF, on the 26th November, 1940, after only three weeks' active service." A tick in the corner indicates AKW had replied. At Windermere, the Armistice Day service was held annually, and the combined list of those who fell in the First World War, eight-four from Dame Allan's and twenty-seven from Windermere G.S., was read out. All hearers knew that a second tragic list was building up as the months passed. Every week there was a remembrance of Old Boys serving in the armed force, when each was named. By the end of the war Dame Allan's had lost two masters and forty-one Old Boys. The School has a book of honour detailing the service of its alumni.

As far as possible school traditions were maintained. For example, in 1941 Founder's Day was marked by a service in Newcastle Cathedral, led by the bishop, for the 110 Fenham pupils, while at the same time the vicar of Kirby Lonsdale conducted a similar service for the Lake District pupils in St John's, Windermere. Other traditions/ school events were not so successful. School magazines were suspended 'for the duration', but miraculously the Girls' School produced one issue in June 1941, covering the past two years and, covering the past two years, and others in 1942 and 1943. Young women were required to contribute to the war effort, sometimes doing jobs that had hitherto been the preserve of men. Many Old Girls were in nursing, but one, for example, reported that she was a full-time ambulance driver in the Bristol A.R.P. Casualty Service. Another had become a Land Girl, one had joined the Women's Auxiliary Air Force and two were in the Women's Royal Naval Service. One of the latter wrote: "Any crowd of girls can get all the fun they want out of the life and still be doing a real job – taking over a shore job and releasing a man to go to sea." She found the job fascinating, with plenty of free time and good food, but she was on duty for part of every day, had only three weeks' leave a year and was always in uniform.

One Old Girl recalls the years in Ambleside with considerable affection. The Smallwood hostel was cold and rather spartan accommodation, but "reverberated with care and love." At school, "books were in short supply, there was scarcely a chemical in the laboratory, and when your jotter was full, you rubbed it out to use it again." Another method was to fill the day book in the usual way in pencil and then turn it sideways and fill it again in ink. She, her sister and another girl were moved to live with a couple who "treated us with the utmost kindness and concern, despite the sacrifice it must have been for them to have taken us into their home. Our windows looked out on a stunning view of the hills which has remained with us all our lives." Above all she was aware of the commitment of the mistresses, "the splendid, selfless teachers, magnificent women who nurtured our minds and bodies for twenty-four hours a day. They took us for walks in the hills at weekends, and supervised homework in the evenings. The maths teacher, Miss Goodman, had two suits which she wore on alternate weeks. She demanded the highest standard from even those of us who were mathematically illiterate. But we all passed School Certificate, either from love, or fear of the consequences."

Several of the teachers stayed at the Vale View Hotel, but two were always in charge of the hostel, formerly Smallwood Private Hotel in Compson Road. As we have heard, the hostel was rather spartan, with only a piano in the lounge and no radio, but the matron, Mrs Hilling, taught embroidery and crafts. Jean Graham relates: "We slept mainly in double beds, up to six pupils in a room and had to use the washbasin in the room for a daily strip wash. Once a week we each had a bath (in not more than six inches of water!) on a strict timetable; my time was 4.30pm on Fridays. There were no laundry facilities and so we parcelled up our dirty washing at the end of the week and posted it home at a cost of 7d in time for Monday washday. The return parcel arrived on Wednesday, usually with a little treat enclosed. We also wrote a letter home each week. Our parents paid a fixed amount into an account from which we were paid one shilling a week pocket money, plus expenses for soap, shampoo, writing paper and so on. Not surprisingly, some girls managed to think up a lot of expenses to supplement their meagre pocket money. At weekends we were expected to be out of the hostel on Saturday and Sunday afternoons, but had to inform the mistress on duty of our intended plans so that she would know where to look for any absentees in the evening. Later, some of us acquired bicycles which widened the scope of our travels, but we were always forbidden to go beyond Troutbeck Bridge – because the Boys' School was at Windermere and never the twin shall meet. On Sunday mornings we all attended church, and had the option of Methodist or Church of England. Some of us attended confirmation classes run by the vicar, the Revd H. A. Thompson, and we were confirmed on 19 March, 1943, all in white dresses and our parents in the congregation. During the school holidays a special train took us back to Newcastle: were there no air raids in the holidays?"

She recalls swimming lessons at Waterhead on Lake Windermere as "very cold and stony. The changing huts were dilapidated wooden shacks full of spiders and cobwebs and without a proper roof. The teacher stood on the jetty, fully clothed, warm and dry, and we were attached to a rope by which she pulled us along in an effort to teach us to swim. I don't think anyone actually learned to swim until we returned to Fenham." With rather more pleasure she recalls the girl guide troop's picnics, when "we lit camp fires and cooked sausages on the end of twiggy sticks. The sausages turned out half-raw and half-burnt, but were always eaten with much enjoyment."

Audrey Smith recalled that the matron prepared the meals and ministered to the sick: "her favourite standby was cinnamon on sugar lumps administered liberally for impending colds. This was popular with those who liked cinnamon. One unusual institution was the canteen where we and several other schools had lunch in relays. We always complained quite unreasonably about the food, but the voluntary helpers who ran the place were most liberal with their second helpings. School houses flourished during this period, and we had the usual annual house events, with plays and parties. The first year, the staff supplemented this entertainment by producing a play of their own, which, as it included the appearance of Miss Elliott in a gym tunic, could not fail to be successful."

Education, despite all the problems, was rightly seen as what the Schools were principally about. Nevertheless, there were moments when the nation's needs were uppermost, as, for example, here for the boys. "As there was a shortage of farm labour, we were sometimes transported to neighbouring farms to help with potato picking. Although this was hard work, it was generally regarded as a welcome diversion from lessons, with the added advantage that we got paid, sixpence a day as I recall, which was a deal of money to us in those days. We were joined in potato picking by prisoners of war, both German and Italian. The Italians were quite friendly and most spoke a little English, but the Germans would not fraternise at all. Perhaps they were under orders not to speak.

"School lunches were awful, not just because of the wartime shortages but because they were brought some distance in supposedly insulated containers and were fairly cold by the time they were served (in a church hall in

Bowness, not at the school). The Headmaster and his wife used to suffer this with us, but Mrs Wilson was regarded by the boys as rather a dragon, constantly patrolling the room and instructing boys to eat up, not talk, tuck the elbows in, hold the knife properly and so on. It was no doubt invaluable in later years, but was not fully appreciated at the time.

1942—1943.
Headmistress :
Miss F. A. ELLIOTT, M.A.
Staff:
AMBLESIDE—Miss L. E. Goodman, M.A. (Second Mistress).
Miss M. M. Timson, B.Sc.
Miss E. C. Clark, B.A.
Miss E. M. Burton, B.A.
Miss J. M. Ball, C.S.M.M.G.
Miss I. Clegg, B.A.
NEWCASTLE—Miss S. I. V. Lippett, D.A.
Mrs. M. L. Damant, M.A.
Mrs. E. Hesk, B.A.
Miss M. Gray, B.A.
Miss N. E. Cook, B.Sc.
Miss R. Patterson, B.A.
Miss E. Wyles, B.A.
Miss E. A. Robinson, B.A.
Miss V. Burkett, L.R.A.M.

Girls staff 1942-43

"Rugby was played on two farmers' fields just off the main road. These were very wet and muddy, indeed worse, as they were used by cows between games, and we often had to chase them before we could play. At the end of the double games period, we would run back up to the school changing rooms in a completely mud-plastered condition. The changing rooms had very primitive showers, consisting of a long open trough with a spray bar over the top, and quite open. On one occasion I recall that we were a little late and one of our young lady teachers, Miss Dunn, waiting to take us in a nearby classroom, lost her patience and charged over to the changing room to chase us up. This caused consternation for twenty-odd boys in a communal shower, and a rather red face for Miss Dunn."

1942-1943

Head Master
A.K. Wilson

Dame Allan's Boys' School Staff Windermere		Windermere Grammar School Staff	
H. Mallinson	Science	R. Kissock	Senior Master, Science
E.G. Finch	French, Science	Mrs E. Purves	Latin
W.F. Little	Music, Science	Mr J. Friend	Art
Revd A.C. de P. Hay	Chaplain, R.E.		
Miss S. Boykett	Geography		
Miss I.C. Joslin	Science		
Miss M.P. Dunn	History, French, P.E.		

When Mallinson, Finch and Little returned to Newcastle in 1943, three additional members of staff were appointed to W.G.S staff, reflecting the changing balance of numbers of boys from each school.

In November, 1942, the Germans and Italians were defeated by the British Eighth Army at El Alamein. In February 1943, the German Sixth Army surrendered at Stalingrad, and in May the Axis forces in North Africa surrendered. The war in Europe was moving at last in the direction of the Allies. It was clear on Tyneside that it was not to be a major target for the Luftwaffe after all, and the trickle back to Newcastle of evacuees of all schools, starting as early as late 1941, became ever faster. No doubt the two heads of Dame Allan's heard many reasons for a transfer to Fenham, but none could be more poignant than this one.

"I feel sure you were shocked at the news that our dear John (a pilot officer) has gone on his

School Scouts provide guard of honour at the wedding of the Revd Charles Hay to Jean Humble, both teachers at the Boys' School, in 1944

last flight. It has been a terrible strain on us all and I hope you will understand that it will make it much easier for me if I have Timothy at home with me. I have today seen Mr Davies[9] and he says the boy can only start school

---

[9] C K Davies, the Spanish and Geography master, was left in charge of the school in Fenham during the early phase of evacuation. He taught at Dame Allan's from 1928 until December 1943.

at Fenham with your permission. This, I am sure, you will not withhold under the circumstances. Tim has taken the blow like a real little Briton, but seems nervy and on edge, and I think he will be better for immediate occupation at school."

It is interesting to observe that the Royal Grammar School followed a different path. It had been evacuated to Penrith – a very different place from Wigton – in September, 1939, and had not tried to return home in the spring of 1940. It too shared premises with another school on a shift basis, and this continued until their official return in 1944. There was no school in their Newcastle premises – they were used by the Army – and the consequence of this was a serious loss of pupils, and thus of income.

During 1940-41 only six girls transferred to Fenham from Ambleside. During 1941-42, five of eleven V Form girls, two out of eight Remove, ten out of 25 IV Form, four out of 23 III form and two out of 23 II form came home; seven also left to go to other schools. In Autumn 1942 the balance between Ambleside and Fenham was this: VI 9:10 ; V 7:24 ; IV 20:31 ; III 16:36 ; II 15:48. Twelve of the girls failed to return to Ambleside after Christmas, 1942, and to the governors and Miss Elliott there must have seemed no alternative but to recognise the reality of the situation. Miss Elliott was in Ambleside and most of her pupils were in Newcastle. She decided to return in 1943. Indeed, in June, she expressed the hope in the School Magazine that "it seems likely that nearly all the present girls will be back in Newcastle in September." In fact it was to take another year before all of the girls returned.

It seems that the boys were rather less affected by the drift, perhaps because they were receiving education in the combined DABS/WGS under A.K. Wilson. The policy of the Government had been throughout a strong recommendation for evacuation and this continued until the end of the war. However, as 1944 moved on and the allies landed in France on 6 June, Newcastle seemed safe. Even the start of the V.1 bombs on London a few days later was an event a long way away. Indeed London children were evacuated to Newcastle during July.

The extraordinary atmosphere of that last term in Windermere, attended by some very fine weather, was captured by a fifth former, Gwyn Bevan, who kept a diary which he illustrated with watercolours. In this, with the School Certificate examinations close at hand and the return to Fenham imminent, he wrote the following entries, prefaced by his recent recollections:

"It was a crucial time in the lives of my contemporaries and me. First there was the burgeoning of youth and a wonderful environment in which to take on the world. So much was vivid and thrilling. Evacuation, on which we had embarked mostly with excitement but with some foreboding too, had turned out to be a most wonderful experience in many different ways. In a broader context the war was entering a totally new phase when endless reverses suddenly themselves were reversed. My age group was preparing to join the fighting forces and we were training in such organisations as the Air Training Corps (my choice) and the equivalent army and navy schemes. Quite suddenly one could imagine that the war was capable of being actually won. We were able to lead idyllic lives in that fine summer; nothing could have been more life-enhancing then our experiences."

Two extracts from his diary recall the personal, national and international layers to those lives.
Sunday 28th May, 1944
Whit Sunday, Beautiful day. Morning Church.
At 7pm left Windermere on bikes with Chips, Splinter and Bob and cycled to Dunmail Raise, stopped half way up and left bikes under a bridge. Climbed 2000 feet up Dolly Wagon Pike and camped overnight in two bivouac tents. Beautiful sunset and my first night under canvas.
Monday 29th Whit Monday
Arose 5.20am and climbed to the top of Dolly Wagon Pike. Saw the sun rise over the Pennines: marvellous. Set off back to Windermere. Very hot, a beautiful day and fine ride back to the Boarding House, arrived in time for a breakfast at 9.15am. Painted four sketches. Letter from Father. Tired, and lazed about in the afternoon. In late afternoon had water fight on the sports field with water pumps. Bathed.
Sunday 4th June
Raining. Dirty day. Listened to Marion Anderson singing Saint Saens: *Sampson and Delilah*. Marvellous. Did quite a lot of work......

Sunset over Thirlmere

Long shadows at dawn

Our bivouac tents

Sunrise above Ullswater

28/29 May, 1944. A night on Dollywagon Pike (Chips and Splinter Wood, Gwyn Bevan and Bob Colston).Watercolour sketches by Gwyn Bevan

Monday 5th
ROME OCCUPIED
David Lumsden[10] absent ... Hylton Burrell[11] returned from a half-term visit to Newcastle where he'd been taken ill .... Cut grass on tennis court .... Rome fell after a 24-day offensive.

Tuesday 6th
INVASION OF CONTINENT
Air forces attack Le Havre; also struck at Normandy. Landings between Le Havre and Cherbourg. Great excitement. 11,000 planes in support, 5,000 tons of bombs dropped at night by heavy bombers. 4,000 ships and several thousand other craft in naval operations. 1,000 troop planes.

[10]Sir David Lumsden became Principal of the Royal Academy of Music
[11]He was later chairman of governors.

Napes Needle on Great Gable, climbed by Richard Laws

Richard Laws (6F) climbed The Mitre - and sketched it. 1944

Thursday 15th – saw experimental jet plane from dormitory window.
Friday 16th. Germans send first doodle bugs over south coast.
Wednesday 28th … Heard Leon Goessens playing Handel's Oboe Concerto …
July: Wednesday 19th, left Windermere for good.

Others too, in both Schools, realised that although it was good to be going home, they would miss the "wonderful environment" of the Lake District and all it had to offer to the thoughtful mind and the active body. Richard Laws[12] wrote shortly after the return to Fenham about a typical weekend on the hills. The following gives a flavour of the whole.

"We had with us four blankets and a small bivvy tent, a couple of loaves of bread, cheese, biscuits, tomatoes and a tin of stew. We left them at Sprinkling Farm and headed for Gable. Then along the Gable Traverse we went, past the red scree shoot, appropriately named Great Hell Gate, to the Napes climbs.

"First came the Needle which is probably one of the best known of all British rock climbs. Seven routes up the Needle are listed in the Fell and Rock Climb Guide Book, all of which are either "Very Difficult" or "Severe". We chose the Wasdale Crack and changed into rubbers, leaving our boots and rucksacks in the Needle Gully to be called for. The first pitch is a simple crack, climbed by inserting the left knee and foot into it and feeling for a toe grip with the right foot. The left is then inserted into the crack higher up, and so on to the top. We were now on the shoulder with only the final block in front of us, but no delay. To our right was a sheer drop of sixty feet. The route lies up the final block to the Mantleshelf, and a good balance is essential. If anyone disagrees, I suggest he tries climbing on to a mantelshelf five feet high and a good six inches wide. It is not very easy.

"We traversed along the Mantelshelf to the left hand corner, which overhangs Needle Gully, ninety feet below, and so to the summit. The descent was by Lingmell Crack. It was quite dark when we did reach the top of Great Gable. After sitting for twenty minutes watching a glorious sunset, we made our way down Great Hall Gate in

[12]Dr Richard Laws became a distinguished biologist and worked with the British Antarctic Survey, eventually becoming director (1973-87) and Master of St Edmund's College, Cambridge, (1985-96)

the dark. Then back we went over Styhead to the tent. Luckily the moon came out and we did not have to erect the tent in complete darkness. A hurried meal of bread and cheese followed, and then to sleep.

"We woke at seven thirty the next morning and had a bathe in the clear water of the tarn. Then breakfast of bread and cheese and the remains of the tomatoes, on which I had been sleeping! The clouds were down to about 2,500 feet on Great End immediately above us but we decided to climb South East Gully and over Broad Crags to the face of Scafell. South East Gully is, I think, the longest gully climb in Britain – 620 feet in all – though it does not provide continuous climbing. I was leading and we made height slowly, frequently stopping to feast on the berries which were so plentiful, and to admire the view. Cloud shadows were chasing across the bracken-covered hills around Derwentwater. Skiddaw was cloud-capped but there were rifts in the cloud through which came shafts of sunlight.

"After about 500 feet of climbing we were in the mist. There came a twenty-foot cave pitch and then we were soon on the top of Great End with visibility limited to about twenty-five yards. The tin of stew was opened and consumed by the two hungry climbers and then on again through the mist. By the time we reached Scafell Pikes the wind rose and the mists dispersed. We were confronted with a glorious view of Scafell Crags lit up by the morning sun, the shadows throwing the features of all the famous climbs into relief."

No one could pretend that Fenham was much like this, but there would be compensations too, and all realised that a new phase in their lives was beginning.

Chapter Ten

THE SCHOOLS IN FENHAM:
BUILDING ON FIRM FOUNDATIONS 1944 - 1970

In this chapter, the history of the schools will be considered in three sections; first the history common to both schools, second, the Girls' School under Miss Elliott and Miss South, and finally, the Boys' School under A. K. Wilson and B. C. Harvey.

It was clearly time to return to Newcastle and, in anticipation, the athletic sports were held in Fenham after a five-year break. At the end of the summer term, the boys said goodbye to Windermere and the girls to Ambleside. There were mixed feelings, of course. Some pupils had great affection both for those who looked after them and for the Lake District: some were heartily glad to be home and in Newcastle; most lay between the two extremes. One wonders how school work had been affected by the disruptions in the pupils' lives. For the most part they were very resilient, and in retrospect many felt they had gained more than they had lost. For example, Maureen Symington started in Fenham in 1937, went to Wigton, back to Fenham, on to Ambleside for three years and finally Fenham again. She rates the Ambleside years as the best, and retired there in 1985. Did it all hamper her education? In 1947 she gained a First in economics at King's College, University of Durham.

For the staff of the two schools a huge task lay ahead; they must have had a very short summer holiday. For A.K. Wilson there was first the task of handing over to his successor the headship of Windermere Grammar School and disentangling his D.A. boys from his W.G.S. boys, together with their books and equipment. For four years the W.G.S. boys had been as much his pupils as the D.A. boys, and he had treated them equally. The warmth of feeling between the two Schools is reflected in the March 1945 issue of the W.G.S. magazine, the first since the war began, when a correspondent wrote: "Of the many school minglings brought about by evacuation, ours must have been one of the most successful, and this must in large measure have been due to Mr Wilson, who was peculiarly well fitted for the difficult task of steering the joint schools. Two schools welded into one have divided the richer for this welding." A letter in that magazine from a senior boy in Fenham speaks of abiding friendships, of gratitude, of "the kindness of hosts and hostesses, of academic success together."

For Miss Elliott it was less complex, but still a considerable task to withdraw her girls from Kelsick Grammar School premises. The Girls' School soon settled down after September, 1944. As Miss Elliott wrote, "the most difficult patch in its history is over," and she had a full staff of sixteen mistresses plus two part-time teachers. Of the former, all academic teachers were graduates and most had diplomas in education; only two were married. Over the next two years there were to be quite a few staff changes, but the team clearly remained strong. House and form plays, the gardening club, the Barnardo Helpers' League, the junior and senior science societies, the junior and senior history societies and the sixth form debating society were quickly established or re-established.

Then there was the task of re-organising the Fenham buildings, currently occupied by the junior department and the mixed secondary school, to take the returning pupils, and return the Schools to their former segregated selves. It was vital that the re-opening in September should be well organised and the task of re-integration tackled vigorously. Fortunately the heads were not alone in the task; they were supported by energetic and committed staffs. Even so late in the war, teachers were required to do firewatching, viz, staying overnight in the Schools to guard against fires caused by enemy action. With three required each night, this was an extra burden after a day's teaching for a staff of the Head Master, eight mistresses and eight masters. Both Schools returned to the two-form entry established before the war. In December, after a lapse of six years, the Boys' School Speech Day was held in the Newsom Hall, overflowing into the Entrance Hall: the speaker was the Bishop of Newcastle. The Headmaster spoke of "the undoubted success of the time spent in the evacuation at Windermere – a success that was due to the wonderful hospitality of our hostesses and the friendly help and co-operation of all connected with Windermere Grammar School. Many boys have made friends for life in the kindly homes of the Lakes." He commented on the high academic standards achieved in the final year in Windermere. Amongst others, R.M. Laws had gained an open scholarship at St Catharine's College, Cambridge and D.J Lumsden an excellent School Certificate.

One play was in rehearsal in the spring term of 1945 for performance at the Girls' School Speech Day. It was Laurence Housman's *Victoria Regina*. The dress rehearsal was almost completed when "bedlam broke loose in the Boys' School and Miss Elliott appeared and announced that the war in Europe was over. A member of staff who was at the piano immediately, and with great abandon, struck up *God save the King*." Speech Day was the first casualty of peace: it had to be postponed because a national V.E. (Victory in Europe) holiday was declared.

However, the Schools had done more than return to their pre-war position with a development of prime importance. By the 1944 Education Act, three types of school were recognised: (i) those managed by the local education authority; (ii) those which received some financial assistance from central government, and were thus called direct grant schools, and (iii) those receiving no financial assistance and known as independent schools. To qualify for the second of these, a school had to show high academic standards, including the availability of advanced courses in the Sixth Form. Thus some pupils would be fee-payers and some would hold scholarships entitling them to free places. Both Schools satisfied the Minister of Education on the quality of education they offered. Similar status was achieved in Newcastle by the Royal Grammar School, Central High School, St Cuthbert's R.C. Grammar School and Sacred Heart R.C. School. This was an extremely important development for Dame Allan's Schools. One reliable authority says there was much local opposition, perhaps because it was perceived as attracting pupils away from the L.E.A. grammar schools.

There was, once more, a serious problem of accommodation and decisions had to be made. The Schools had started a preparatory department in 1942 "as a wartime proposal", and in a letter of late 1949 quoted above from the clerk to the Governors to Miss Elliott, he said it was intended that at some point it should be established as

Woodwork shop c1947; now drama studio

a "properly organised junior school". But at that time there were urgent problems for the Schools, and the decision was made in 1950 to close the 8+ and 9+ forms. The 10+ form survived because 10+ entry as well as 11+ had been established by the 1877 constitution. Forty years were to pass before the "properly organised junior school" came into being.

1953 saw the coronation of Queen Elizabeth II, and on the preceding

The Mikado, 1948. David Watson. The operetta was again given in 1963

Friday, the Schools held a service in their Parish Church of St James and St Basil. Each pupil received a Bible from the governors, and a coronation souvenir booklet from the City Council. Fifth and sixth formers received a copy of Sydney Middlebrook's *History of Newcastle, its Growth and Achievement*.

Academic attainment steadily improved in both schools during this period and the schools' reputation grew. Both Girls' and Boys' Schools benefited from the Direct Grant system. The wartime heads retired within a year of each other. A K Wilson left in the summer of 1953 and two terms later Miss Elliott also retired. Charles Hay, chaplain to both schools, suggested that a head should be appointed over the two schools but the governing body was not to make that change for another thirty-five years.

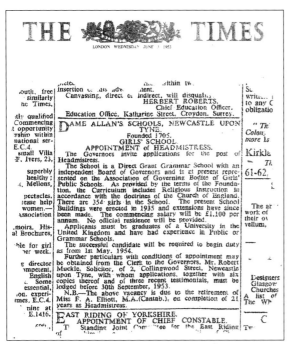

Front page of The Times, 3 June 1953. Not a picture of Queen Elizabeth II at her coronation, but the advertisement that caught the eye of Miss South

1955 was the 250th anniversary of the foundation of the Schools. The school shared some events, notably the Service of Commemoration in Newcastle Cathedral, when the preacher was an Old Boy, Canon V. A. Demant, Regius Professor of Moral and Pastoral Theology at Oxford. There were a governors' reception for parents and old pupils in the Old Assembly Rooms, and the annual Garden Fete. The Boys' School also held a cricket match with the Old Boys, an Open Day, athletic sports and a school outing. The principal events took place in July, close to the end of term.

The Sixth Form domestic science group volunteered to make a set of twenty St Nicholas Charity School costumes copied from the fine photograph of a group of girls in such costumes in 1877. One of the girls is named as Polly Bell, and the costumes are now called in the School "Polly Bells" or even "pollybelles", a common noun uniquely coined. These costumes, renewed as required, continue to be used on special occasions by prefects. Miss South records: "The domestic science department offered to make copies of the Boys' School uniform based on a similar photograph of 1867 of William Walton, but the offer was not taken up! As a lasting momento of the celebrations, every girl was given a 7/6 book token. There was a bumper Open Day on 19 July, including an exhibition of dolls dressed in various costumes throughout the time of the Schools' existence. The domestic science department also made a three-tiered cake, like a wedding cake, with the school crest, and every girl was given a slice the next day." The catering firm of Lockhart presented the School on long-term loan with a fine historical painting by Wilson Hepple (1853-1937) of Corporation Sunday, 1771. It was probably painted in his twenties or thirties when he executed many genre paintings. Prominent in the picture is a group of St Nicholas's Charity School girls, watching the procession arriving at the west door of St Nicholas's Church now the cathedral. The School later acquired the painting permanently, and it hangs in the dining hall. (See Chapter 2)

Miss Elliott had attended the major events of the year, and she opened the Parents' Association Garden Fete on the last Saturday of the summer term. Earlier in the year, in March, there were three performances of Bach's St Matthew Passion by a joint choir, and the girls gave performances of *Love's Labour's Lost* in May. Founder's Day had taken place as usual, with the added significance of the anniversary; the preacher was the Bishop of Newcastle, the Rt Revd Noel Hudson.

The Boys' School Speech Day, itself part of the 250th celebrations, had as its distinguished guest of honour Viscount Ruffside, High Steward of Cambridge University and, as Colonel Clifton Browne, a former Speaker of the House of Commons. This was the first Speech Day in the City Hall since 1929.

The school site also had to be developed. The austerity of the post-war years meant that there was no new building work other than the construction of an additional dining hall[1]. Pressure on space caused the governors

[1]This was situated behind the kitchens and was converted into four classrooms forty years later.

Milk Break in small Dining Hall, built 1947

to try to build more classrooms as early as 1946. The government restrictions and material shortages of the time, meant that the Schools had to wait until 1950 for the erection of a classroom block on the far side of the playground. These were five classrooms, A to E, with toilets, a cloakroom and an armoury for the cadets. They always had a temporary look to them, and were liable to be hot in summer and too cold in winter but were more spacious than existing classrooms. Having served the School well for a half-century, they were demolished in 2003 to make way for the Sixth Form Centre and the dance studio. The girls acquired two boys' classrooms behind the stage.

In October 1955 the newly furnished girls' library was opened by Professor Butt in memory of Miss Florence Moat (OA 1890-1895), a generous benefactor. The need for more laboratory space in the Girls' School was met by a block in the quadrangle, with a laboratory upstairs and a sixth form room below. The original plan was to build to the north, but local residents objected strongly and two appeals by the school were rejected. In 1958-59 extensions were completed and brought into use. They consisted of a new block in the quadrangle with two large and two small division rooms upstairs and extra staff accommodation downstairs. There was a new lecture room and a changing room and showers. For

Girls' quadrangle: Both this and the boys' quad have suffered from infilling because of the need for more accommodation and the difficulty of getting planning permission elsewhere on the site

the first time the offices for the Schools were separated by the provision of a new office for the girls. Sadly most proposed developments by the Schools in subsequent years were the subject of opposition from local residents who feared the noise and dust of construction, the mass, height or location of buildings, or the loss of light or view. Much of this has been understandable, but the Schools stand on a relatively confined site and building development is necessarily near to houses, especially those in Bolbec Road. Some plans have been rejected by the city authorities, some have been accepted after substantial or minor alteration, and some have been accepted immediately. In fairness, the local authority seems to have done its job impartially.

The increased demand for science in the Boys' School also called for an extension of laboratory provision. This led to a dedicated biology laboratory on the west side of the quadrangle, formerly for manual instruction. In 1957 an advanced chemistry laboratory was constructed above the former air raid shelter, now a scout storeroom largely paid for by the Industrial Fund for the Advancement of Science in Independent Schools. Building work continued in 1963 with an upgraded physics laboratory and a new senior physics laboratory. That year saw another development: the Orchestral Society became a joint society of the Schools, and the Annual Concert included several choral items by the combined choirs.

In 1964, some much-needed improvements took place in the Girls' School. A new art room with clay and kiln room was built, and the old one converted into a physics laboratory, when Lab D became a general laboratory.

The growth of the Sixth Form meant that common room provision was needed. For the boys, a block comprising a common room and adjoining prefects' room, was built on the south side of the Boys' quadrangle, with a music room and classroom above in 1964. In the same year, a smaller common room and a prefects' room were built for the Girls' School above the air raid shelter (by then used as a cloakroom) on the front of the school. A new girls' Music Centre (now the Ann Gillie Studio)[2] was built between the caretaker's house (now bursar's office) and the gate. This was not financed by the School Building Fund, but the £15,000 required was raised

[2] Ann Gillie (1906-95), for 65 years, "one of the North-East's most significant but least published artists." O.A. 1917-23 as Ann Philipson.

directly by a grant from the Parents' Association, by appeal and by many fundraising activities. Besides the main teaching room, there were practice rooms and instrument storage. At last music had a proper home and was on an equal footing with other subjects. It was opened on 30 April, 1969, by Dr Arthur Milner, OA 1903-09, and former music teacher to both schools. A new Dame Allan's Schools' Trust was established to facilitate the long-term plans for development for both Schools.

In 1947, the chairman of governors, the Very Revd G.E. Brigstoke, Provost of Newcastle, had moved to Durham as Principal of Bede College. Mr Brigstoke was unusual amongst chairmen of governors in that during the war years he taught scripture in the Schools. The Very Revd N. M. Kennaby succeeded him as Provost and as governor, and became chairman of governors. He retired from all these offices in January 1962 and he was succeeded as chairman by the vice-chairman, Col. A.D.S. Rogers, and as provost by the Very Revd C.C. Wolters, who became an *ex officio* governor. When in May, 1966, Col Rogers retired, Mr Wolters became chairman. 1962 saw the retirement of Robert Muckle, CBE, as clerk to the governors after thirty-seven years. He was devoted to the Schools, and played a large part in the acquisition of the Fenham site, the Schools' move there, the problems of tri-location during the war and negotiations for Direct Grant status. He was personally a generous benefactor, including the equipping of an office on site for his successor.

The Girls' School under Miss Elliott and Miss South

The return to Fenham was overshadowed by sadness as Miss Stella Lippett, the art mistress who had been in charge of the girls on the co-educational Fenham site, was forced to retire unexpectedly in September 1944 because of ill health. She died the following month aged 48; she had taught at the school for twenty-two years.

Marjorie Bowman recalled that shortages continued after the European and indeed after the Japanese wars had ended. "School uniform and books had to be sold from one generation to the next. Hockey and tennis were played only by the Senior School because of the difficulty of buying hockey sticks and tennis racquets. Gradually these difficulties lessened. School uniform became more readily obtainable and dress rules – which had been considerably relaxed since 1939 – became more rigid. Brown shoes were dyed black, grey stockings were worn by all and the School became much smarter. A serious setback occurred with the "New Look", when many of us tripped round the corridors with skirts almost catching our heels, feeling very smart, but this problem too was soon overcome.

"The introduction of 'the seven-day timetable' caused quite a stir. At a time when industry was clamouring for a five-day week, we were assembled in the gym and told that a seven-day week was to be introduced. There were immediate exclamations of 'I can't possibly come to school on Saturdays: I have a music lesson' and 'What about my Sunday School class?' Once we had been reassured that it would not mean any longer hours, we entered into the spirit of the experiment."

Joan Hodgson, who was a pupil at this time and was to be a biology teacher in the School for twenty-seven years, noted the difficulties inherent in the system. "You can imagine the problems it caused as far as lessons were concerned. The days, instead of being Monday to Friday, were labelled 1 to 7, the first day of a new term being day one. If that happened to be a Wednesday, say, then Friday was day three and the following Monday day four and so on, so Thursday of the second week would be a free activities afternoon. It was very difficult to remember what day it should be after a week and a day's half term! However, some of us considered the inconvenience worthwhile because of the group activities, which happened on every seventh afternoon. Most of the groups cut right across the age range. The first one that I joined was called 'Exploring Newcastle', run by Miss Muir. We went out on visits to such places as the Castle Keep, the Law Courts and the Central Police Station. Each time a new set of groups was about to begin, we would be told what was on offer and had to opt for the one we wanted to join, without having been told which members of staff were involved. After a term or two, one of the choices was to become a member of a new school Guide Company. I had been to a Brownie Pack meeting with a friend when I was about eight and had gone home afterwards and told my mother that I was not going back as the girls danced round a toadstool singing a silly song and that was not my cup of tea! However, the idea of Guides was a different matter entirely and so I put my name on the list, wondering which teachers would be running the

Company. Much to my surprise it turned out to be Miss Macdonald, the biology teacher, and as I had leanings in that direction even then, I was quite pleased.

"At that time clothes were still rationed after the war by a system of coupons, and uniform blouses were not available. An ex-army nylon parachute was obtained and we spent hours in the library during lunchtimes unpicking it. Someone on the staff dyed it Guide blue and cut out all our blouses. We took the pieces home and our mothers machined them together. We were able to buy navy berets and leather belts, so with our school skirts, our uniform was complete. We met in the gymnasium each day seven, in patrols named after birds and had a splendid time.

"I don't think the seven-day timetable lasted more than a year or so, but the Guide Company did continue for a while, becoming an after-school activity. In its second year, the 25th Newcastle (Dame Allan's) Guides joined the 34th Newcastle (Sacred Heart) Company for a week's camp under canvas, (bell tents I remember), at Budle near Belford. As I was sixteen I left Guides and joined the local Ranger Unit. Thus had begun my membership of the Movement, which lasted for several decades, as I later ran Guide and Ranger Units and was so keen on camping that I became a Camp Trainer. Many years later that experience led to me starting the Duke of Edinburgh's Award group in school."

Thus Miss Macdonald had influenced Joan Hodgson's academic interest, her career and her outdoor interests: a wonderful tribute to a fine teacher.[3]

Academic results were good, including in July, 1946, excellent Higher School Certificate results for Joan Graham, about whom we shall hear later. The following year Cynthia Wright was awarded the Mrs George M Smith Scholarship to the London School of Medicine, the first open scholarship to be won by a Dame Allan's girl. By 1948 there were fourteen Old Girls at university on degree courses, and many more on other courses of further education, especially at training colleges for teachers.

A great loss to the Schools was the retirement of Miss Janet B Ramage after twenty-seven years. "Bright and cheerful, ever ready to help or offer any kindness she could," she spanned College Street, Fenham, Wigton, Ambleside, Windermere (she was lent to the Boys' School) and Fenham again. She was head of geography and also of history for many years and served as Second Mistress for a year before the evacuation.

During the immediate postwar years, there was much suffering in Germany, and a collection was made for the Friends' Relief Service of clothes and toys following talks in school. One pastor wrote a letter of thanks to the staff and girls in moving terms about the gift of baby clothes: "We are a clergyman's family, and our home town is Stellin. The Russians took everything from us there. We had nothing to dress our little daughter. Just at that moment came charitable and gentle hands and calmed our hearts that were so troubled and fearful. And we were strengthened in our belief that in this wretched, suffering world there still is the salvation that conquers all hatred by brotherly love. So I thank all who have helped us in our distress."

Three changes took place that had an obvious impact, though two were not to survive for long. First the school houses were abolished on the grounds that (i) there was little general support for house activities, and (ii) where there was house enthusiasm it seemed to detract from school loyalty. They were reinstated some years later. We have seen that in September, 1946, there was the introduction of a seven-day timetable to allow for more subjects and free activities; this lasted for four years. The School Council started in 1938 and, suspended because of the war, resumed in September, 1948, and continues to meet to the present day. Miss Elliott said, "It acts in a consultative, not an executive capacity; nevertheless, many of its suggestions have been adopted and put into practice. It affords opportunities for the courteous airing of the grievances of all its constituent members: it allows each of us to hear the other's point of view and to discover that there are at least two sides to every question." There were two representatives from each form, and it met once a term unless there was need because of the volume of proposals for additional meetings. Anyone could attend as an observer.

[3]Miss Macdonald left Dame Allan's in December 1954, having been Head of Biology for eleven years and Second Mistress 1947 to 1949 and again from 1953. She went on to be Head Mistress of Queen Elizabeth Grammar School, Hexham, before joining a religious order and settling in the Convent of the Sacred Heart in Fenham.

As we have seen in September, 1948, the 25th Newcastle (Dame Allan's) Guide Company was formed as one of the senior activities allowed for in the seven-day timetable, and the following year a ranger patrol was formed. Other activities in 1948-49 were photography, plastics (making objects from sheets of plastic), weaving, cookery, chess, dramatic reading, play writing, Greek, shipping (ships and shipbuilding, especially on the Tyne), mothercraft, junior dramatics and bookbinding. Truly a liberal education. When the five-day timetable was resumed, these free activities were not immediately abandoned but put on the last two periods on one afternoon a week. Teaching accommodation was limited in this period and the quest for more buildings has already been noted. One of the Girls' School classes had to be conducted on the stage of the Newsom Hall, complete with rows of desks and a blackboard. Miss Elsbeth Evans (later Mrs Williams), the Head of English appointed in 1947, was given the stage as her classroom. Although one must sympathise with the limitations of the arrangement, it could be observed that Miss Evans's commanding personality must have been perfectly suited to the echo and dramatic ambience of the stage.

Foreign visits began in August, 1949, with a Swedish exchange, and the next spring a dozen pupils spent three weeks in Dusseldorf. No regular pattern was subsequently formed, but since that time overseas visits have become increasingly common, some (as these early ones) exchanges, some cultural/linguistic visits, some skiing trips and some team tours. At Easter, 1953, a party went to Paris. Half a century on, its priorities impress: "On Easter Day some of us got up at five o'clock and left the hostel at six so that we would reach the little English church near the Madelaine before seven o'clock. We went there, with Mr and Mrs Damant, to take Communion. The rest of the party went at nine o'clock."

The Girls' School inspection took place in March, 1953. There were now fifteen full-time and three part-time staff in addition to Miss Elliott. Of the 355 girls, 164 came from Newcastle, 74 from Northumberland, 82 from Co Durham, 32 from Gateshead and 3 from Sunderland. Of the 129 leavers 1950-52, 14 went to university, 27 to teacher training colleges, 30 to secretarial colleges and many into nursing and clerical employment. "It has required a great deal of very hard work," said the inspectors, "to raise the School from its former very unsatisfactory condition (in the College Street days), but with quiet persistence the Head Mistress, encouraged by the Governing Body and aided in recent years by dependable staff, has succeeded." The inspectors observed how the problem of early leaving, viz., before sixteen, noted in the previous inspection of 1936, had been completely solved, and moreover, there were now 45 girls in the Sixth Form. Miss Elliott, given a chance to put her school on the map by the new buildings and the direct grant status, had seized her opportunity.

At Easter, 1954, Miss Elliott retired after twenty-one years. She had taken over from Miss Dobson who had been head for nearly forty years, and was immediately faced with the exciting but demanding move to Fenham. Hardly had this been accomplished than the evacuations to the Lake District threw up new problems with new solutions to find. Then in 1944 came the rejoining of the two parts of the School. Even back in Fenham there were problems of space until further building work relieved the pressure. She suffered, too, from indifferent health, but remained always "calm and dignified". A contemporary tribute speaks thus: "A complete and steadfast faith in God enabled her to go forward with humility and confidence, and she devoted herself wholeheartedly to promoting the spiritual and temporal welfare of her school. Her alert mind was ever sensitive to the needs of others. She had complete confidence in her staff, and provided the freedom to plan and experiment". In her time the number of girls trebled, and the curriculum had broadened to include physics, chemistry, biology and German. Inspectors in 1953 had spoken of "her sense of purpose, her steady persistence and quiet humour", and had observed how she had raised the standards of her staff despite the difficulties of the war years. She lived in retirement for twenty-seven years, and died in 1981 at the age of eighty-five, remaining in touch with her old school to the last. To mark her years of service, a memorial service was held in the church of St James and St Basil, and the Old Girls presented the School with a set of books on the counties of England.

Miss Emily Marguerite South succeeded as Headmistress in April, 1954, with eighteen full-time and three part-time colleagues, of whom nine were married. She had held a State Scholarship and Classical Exhibition at Newnham College, Cambridge, where she had developed her love of classics. From this year the school began to keep a logbook of each year's events. This was maintained for over forty years. "One has only to read these

Log Books, so meticulously written by the pupils, supervised in dinner hours, breaks and after school by dedicated members of staff during the time of Miss South and Miss Graham, to realise the diversity of activities on offer to the girls – outings related and unrelated to subjects in the curriculum, holidays both enjoyable and instructive, courses to broaden knowledge of the wider world and its problems, visits to and by eminent personalities, plays, concerts and sports matches to be seen, heard, contested and produced charities to be supported, external trophies and prizes to be won for sport, music, literature, speaking foreign languages and understanding electricity – the furthering of the girls' education and the formation of their personalities through the Dame Allan's ethos is deeply impressive."

Miss South, Head Mistress, 1954-1970

Miss South recently recalled how, "when I was appointed, I was in charge of the kitchens and school meals, while the Head Master dealt with the grounds and groundsman, the caretaker, heating and cleaning." She of course delegated to "a long established cook" the actual catering, and soon afterwards the Eduacation Department required the employment of a qualified meals supervisor.

The School achieved a national triumph in 1955. It had become affiliated to the Electrical Association for Women, and in the Homeworkers' Examination in July, fifth and sixth formers did so well that they gained first place in the country and were awarded the trophy, the Miss Walter Rose Bowl.

As we have seen, drama has always been important in the girls' school. Most plays have far more parts for men than women, and it would be absurd to confine the choice of play to the rest. Likewise the borrowing of boys from next door would mean fewer girls would gain experience of acting, and those who did would largely have smaller parts. Casting the male roles needed great care on the part of the producer and great skill on the part of the actress. Costume plays were obviously easier; for a girls' school to do *Julius Caesar* in modern dress would not be sensible on several counts. The authors whose plays have been produced as the "School Play" during the past half-century have included Shakespeare, Euripedes, Barrie, Brecht, Shaw, Wilde, Sheridan, Gay, Marlowe, Gozzi, Miller and Schaffer. A succession of heads of department – Elspeth Williams, Richard Moore and Paul Lewton – keen on drama ensured very high quality, as did other members of the department.

Out-of-school activities continued to grow during the fifties. A fixture which has evolved over a half-century has been one with Galashiels Academy, in which the girls played hockey and the boys rugby, with local hospitality and a visit to Murrayfield. Reciprocal hospitality was of course given.

In 1955 a party of twenty spent a week in Paris, but two years later a liaison had been formed with Lycée Jeanne d'Arc in Rouen to promote, from the Dame Allan's point-of-view, better understanding of the French and their language. Girls were to spend three weeks of the Easter holiday in Rouen each year under the general supervision of Mrs Damant. The governors were determined that no girl should be excluded because of the cost from sharing in this valuable experience.

The increased size of the School meant that Speech Day had to be divided into junior and senior events and for several years this continued. It was, however, unsatisfactory that it was not possible to draw all the girls and their parents, as well as many grandparents and friends together in one place for so important an event in the School year, and in 1958 and subsequently it was held in the City Hall, generally in November.

The science department was growing and necessitating the development of laboratories mentioned above. In 1945 the first physics specialist, Mrs Esther Adams, was appointed. Many of the science teachers had themselves been engaged in scientific research[4] and one head of physics, Old Girl Judith Paul, later Mrs Farr, left the school

[4]This was true of Mrs Dorothy Towns, formerly a lecturer at King's College, Newcastle, Mrs Kathleen Earnshaw who undertook research work in microplantation and gained her MSc in the 1920s, and Mrs Mary Fleeting, a Mary Ewart Scholar at Somerville, and Mrs Jan Straughan who were both researchers in industry.

in order take part in spectroscopy research at Newcastle University. The science department was thus well served by a strong team of teachers and many girls were moving on to study science subjects at university.

The Old Girls' Association continued to flourish in these years. In 1956, for example, a hundred attended the annual dinner in the Crown Hotel, their usual venue. 1959 saw fencing and squash introduced to the Sixth Form P.E. programme, and the following spring a fencing team was formed. Marian Foster recalls its immediate success: having proved much too strong for King's College B team, Dame Allan's twice came close to defeating the A team.

The office of Second Mistress is more complicated at this time than its equivalent in the Boys' School. From 1936 to 1955, senior members of staff had undertaken two-year spells and then returned to the ranks. Mrs Margaret Damant, served for five years 1955-60, having also been in the post 1951-53. After 1960, three-year spells were instituted but Miss Mary Fawcett served only two years and Miss Catherine Durnford less. This was not satisfactory for a job that had become more complex with each passing year, and Mrs Margaret Johnson was then appointed (Easter, 1963) and served until her retirement, which was twenty-nine years later. This continuity served the Girls' School well, not least because of the clear vision of the person concerned. Miss Durnford left the school in the summer of 1963 to become an Anglican nun and teach in Africa. She kept in touch with the Schools, and her schools in Africa would receive support from Dame Allan's Girls' School in the years ahead.[5]

By 1962 the numbers had reached 416, of whom 93 were in the Sixth Form. The pressure for places was considerable. In 1960, for example, there were 585 candidates for 62 places at 10+ and 11+. Many of course were for Newcastle and Northumberland free places and were also entered for other girls' school examinations, but the competition ensured able entrants. Bright pupils from south of the Tyne, for whom there were no free places, as well as others, meant that some fee-payers were equal to the very best girls holding scholarships. Thus the School – and this was also true of the Boys' School – did not divide into two parts, and everyone was judged on character and ability. In the January 1963 entrance examination, two were awarded governors' scholarships, six Newcastle places and eighteen Northumberland places; the following year was similar.

In the winter of 1962-63, the School took part in the popular radio programme, *Top of the Form*. The team was unlucky to lose by one point to the boys of Hull Grammar School and by two to Norwich City Boys' School.

School magazines reveal a changing pattern in the lives of the mistresses. In 1962, for example, there were six new members of staff, all unmarried, but by the next September, two of them had married and were continuing to teach. Two existing members of staff also married, one of them continuing. But as yet there was no man on the staff. The first man to teach in the Girls' School since the war, was Claude Robinson. He had been head master of Jarrow Grammar School until his retirement in 1963, when he joined Dame Allan's to teach classics. He went part time in 1968 and retired the following year, aged seventy-one. One can assume from this remarkable record of service that the girls were keen students. In 1970 two men were on the staff, Ernest Fawcett, head of classics, and Jim Skipsey, head of physics and both would continue until their retirement.

In March, 1966, the School was inspected, thirteen years after its previous inspection. By now there were 432 girls drawn from seven education authorities; 127 were from Newcastle, 167 from Northumberland, 104 from Co Durham, 19 from Gateshead, 8 from Tynemouth, 5 from South Shields and 2 from Sunderland. For the first time in the School's history, the largest contingent was drawn, not from Newcastle but from Northumberland. Since 1953 the roll had increased by 77, which the report suggested had largely resulted from the increase of girls who entered the Sixth Form and went on to higher education. "This is a fine school which can provide a worthwhile course not only for the future university entrant but also for girls whose further education and training will be of a less academically exacting nature." Its only adverse criticism was with regard to accommodation – a familiar strain in the School's history. However, work began immediately to solve the problems revealed.

[5]Miss Durnford trained for the ordained ministry after the Church of England sanctioned the ordination of women, having already become a deaconess. She later became vicar of New Marske and honorary canon of York.

Alderman Mrs Kirkpatrick, Lord Mayor, pays the official annual visit to the Schools, 20 February, 1960. For almost 300 years, the Mayor/Lord Mayor was an ex-officio governor. The prefects wear the traditional costumes.

At the end of the summer term in 1966, Mrs Margaret Damant retired after a full quarter century at the Schools. She had originally joined the Boys' School in April, 1941, being transferred to the Girls' two years later. She was a caring and devoted school teacher, earning the respect of staff and pupils alike. Her charge of the modern languages department for fifteen years saw the teaching of French, German, Spanish and Italian in the school - she herself was fluent in the first three of these. The languages offered continued to grow and in 1967, Russian was offered in the sixth form, whilst Latin and Ancient Greek were still on offer for classicists.

The 1967 magazine gives a good idea of the activities of the Parents' Association which has so enthusiastically supported the Schools since its creation. Four of the five officers were men, the assistant secretary being the exception. There was a well-attended AGM, a Chairman's At Home, two demonstrations, a talk, fortnightly whist drives, a dance, twice-weekly badminton evenings, a golf section, a drama group, a weekly ladies' working party, a Christmas sale of work and the Summer Garden Fete. Perhaps this was the most active time in the association's history.

In the summer of 1968, DAGS was represented on the Commonwealth Institute's first sixth form cruise on the Nevasa to West Africa, with visits to Gambia, Ghana, Sierra Leone and French Senegal. With "an unparalleled body of lecturers" aboard and four weeks of cruising and land exploration, the students came back wiser than they had gone. This took place at the height of the Nigerian Civil War and rumours spread that the cruise ship was full of mercenaries going to fight. Miss Angela Crossfield and her party of Dame Allan's girls must have been the most unlikely mercenaries, but Port Harcourt was bombed as a result of the rumours and questions were asked in the House of Commons.

Games flourished and developed. Gymnastics continued to be popular, and the School teams held a display and took part in a competition, both for the first time. Tennis, hockey, fencing, netball, athletics, badminton and swimming all did well, while the acquisition of a trampoline was a great success especially on wet games days. A trampoline club for parents of pupils was started and was an immediate success, donations going to the building fund. Miss Dorothy Bluett, later Mrs Gibson, had specialist training in trampoline coaching as well as being a champion diver.[6]

[6]Miss Bluett was appointed in 1966. She was Ladies' Diving Champion of Northumberland, Durham and the North East of England. She kept up her enthusiasm and won the World Masters Diving Championship held in Munich in July 2000.

The Music Centre was opened in 1969 and the new facilities brought an increase in interest in musical activities, while other activities also blossomed. Elspeth Williams produced Brecht's *Mother Courage* with the help of boys; it was characterised by her own deep feeling for the text being transmitted to the cast. The Young Volunteer Force group continued its visiting of elderly people in their own homes, of young and old in hospital, and of deprived children in a Rye Hill centre. Orienteering began in 1968, and it proved popular with a few. Fencing continued well in these years, with events as far afield as Edinburgh (an honourable defeat by the international standard University A team) and London (Junior Schoolgirls' Competition). The juniors won every match, discovering in the process that "when fencing a boys' team no allowances are made" (by the girls?). The trampoline team won both junior and senior titles in the city championships, and third and second respectively in the north-eastern championships.

Miss South's retirement took place in the summer of 1970. A classical scholar with a deep love of her subject, Miss South was (and still is) a quiet, dignified lady with a welcoming smile and a gentle manner, in whose hands the welfare of the school, its staff and pupils flourished. At all times she encouraged her staff to broaden the girls' horizons beyond the classroom by participating in out-of-school activities whilst at the same time letting the girls know that only their best work was acceptable in the classroom. Of true Christian spirit, she was aware of girls with difficulties and helped them deal with their problems and make the most of their years at Dame Allan's. She worked tirelessly to raise money for the improvement of the school's accommodation, and was rewarded for her determination when she was able to see the completion and opening of the Girls' School Music Centre in April, 1969. When she retired, it was with very real sorrow that everyone at DAGS bade her farewell, for the school was losing a Headmistress who had demonstrated her genuine concern for the well-being of her pupils and staff throughout her sixteen years in office.

The Boys' School under A.K. Wilson and B.C. Harvey

The return to Fenham also marked the retirement of Ted Finch as Second Master. He had headed the co-educational school in Fenham during the evacuation of the boys to Windermere and the girls to Ambleside and had been the most constant and tireless of masters. He had studied medieval and modern languages at Christ's College, Cambridge, and won the Skeat Prize for Middle to Modern English in 1903. Before coming to Dame Allan's in January, 1924, he had served in the Egyptian Education Service for eighteen years and had been awarded the Order of the Nile. He had worked first under Brewer and led the school in the interregnum following his death, ending the detention and punishment book with "the salutary use of the cane", Bill Johnson was later to recollect, and "petrified boys until the fifth form when he imparted much worldly wisdom." He stayed at the school for one term after the evacuation ended, retiring at Christmas, 1944, three weeks after his sixty-fourth birthday. His successor as Second Master was Henry Mallinson.

The 72nd Newcastle Troop, the 6th Windermere and the 22nd Newcastle were united as the 72nd and in a few months presented Christmas Crackers to an enthusiastic audience. In the summer there was "a glorious month in the country" at Healey, helping once more with the harvest and forestry. Colonel Warde-Aldam's gratitude for this help during the war years resulted in the erection of a scout hut in 1947, and the beginning of a long connexion between the Warde-Aldam family and the Schools that has lasted until the present day. The "glorious month" had been preceded by victory in Europe on 8 May, and on 14 August, Japan too surrendered. The scouts also played a large part in the revival of the City Gang Show, and continued to do so for many years.

The Army Cadet Force re-formed its company, and in July, 1945, joined the First Battalion of the Northumberland Fusiliers in camp near Berwick. The Orchestral Society had languished during the Windermere years because of practical difficulties, particularly lack of instrumental tuition, but in the first month back in Fenham rehearsals started and by Speech Day three months later was fit to perform in public. The Operatic Society, which had likewise been unable to stage a full performance for the same reasons, resumed rehearsals a year later, and in January, 1946, produced *Ruddigore*, the Gilbert and Sullivan operetta last performed at Wigton before Christmas, 1939. The Dramatic Society was revived and soon had 152 members. It gave two one-act plays in December, 1945, and in April, 1946, performed Karel Capek's *R.U.R.*. Of this play it was written, "Effects in the last act, which depicts man being overrun by machine-made robots, were superb, more so when it is remembered that the boys carried out the whole thing themselves with only advice from the staff." Sport, too, with players drawn from both Fenham and Windermere traditions, soon returned to pre-war standards. The school houses were revived immediately in September, 1944, and house competitions resumed with their former keen rivalry. The First XV played twenty-two games in its first season, and won eighteen of them, one player scoring 168 points, thought a school record. *The Allanian*, suspended since 1939, resumed publication at Christmas, 1945, with a sober editorial on the grim years passed and "our serious duty to equip ourselves mentally and physically to take part now in the making of a brave new world, whence war shall be banished for ever."

An important distinction for the Boys' School was the election in 1946 of A.K. Wilson to the Headmasters' Conference, a body of the hundred top boys' schools in the country. The Headmaster of the Royal Grammar School was the only other day school member in the North East. This distinction was in no small measure a tribute to A.K. Wilson's personal standing in the world of education, but all successive headmasters have been elected to H.M.C. and this has played an enormous part in national recognition of the standing of the Boys' School.

With Direct Grant and H.M.C. status, the School's prestige and academic achievement rose steadily. At Christmas, 1945, five open scholarships and exhibitions are recorded; an old boy gained a rare Distinction in the Final Law Examination, and became the youngest solicitor in the country; another was President of the Dental Students' Society of Great Britain; a third became Director of Education of Somaliland. Two events that showed the continued gratitude of Dame Allan's to their former hosts in the Lake District were Speech Day, when the Director of Education for Westmorland, Mr Trevelyan, was the guest of honour, and the Founder's Day Service, when the preacher was Canon Smith, Vicar of St John's, Windermere. Both men did much for the two Schools.

Although the war was over, the Army Cadets were required for national work. The enemy now was a shortage of food, and the annual camp of 55 boys near Pontefract in 1946 was a Harvest Camp, fourteen days "on the land". Rationing was still in place, and was to remain in part for six more years; indeed bread, not rationed during the war, became so afterwards.

Scouts in Norway, August 1947. David Bates and Geoff Hall looking from the summit of Gaustatoppen (6178 ft) down on to town of Rjukan, where the heavy water plant had been attacked by commandos some years earlier (Telemark)

The Scouts entered a phase of great strength. A Senior Scout Troup for scouts over fifteen was formed with four patrols, and a Rover Scout Crew was added to the 72nd Group; both met at the historic Cordwainers' Hall in the Blackfriars. The main troop at school consisted of eleven patrols, and the Cubs numbered twenty-six. Over 140 attended all or part of a very wet camp at Healey. Conversely, the Cadets fell to only forty-six, perhaps a revulsion against the war, but since all fit boys had to serve in the armed forces for two years, experience in the Cadets was very valuable. There were twelve sixth form leavers in Summer, 1946; some gained immediate entry to university, while others did their National Service first. A year later there were sixty School Certificates, eleven Higher Certificates and four University Scholarships plus two awarded to O.B.s who had completed National Service. The scouts made their first overseas trip, with thirty-eight going to Norway for a fortnight, a school party went to Switzerland by train for twelve days, and two parties went to Paris for a week each. With the cadets at Catterick and scouts at Healey, Newcastle must have been curiously empty of D.A. boys that summer of 1947. The scouts in Norway spent a few days in Oslo with local scouts and their families, but most of the time were hiking in two parties, one between hostels in Jotunheim, the most mountainous part of the country, where they climbed Glittertind and Galopingen, the highest peaks, while a second party went to Telemark, with an ascent of Gaustatoppen. Friendships were made that have lasted to the present day.

During that year, the Science Society, the Arts and Crafts Society, the History Society, the Music Society and the Dramatic Society offered a wide range of excursions, lectures and activities. Joint activities by two societies were common, and a Junior Arts Club was born of a union of Music and Dramatic Societies. This club performed A Christmas Carol, "the first produced in the School by juniors". Sport too continued to flourish, with the usual ups and downs in interschool games. There were moments of great excitement: in one game against Hexham G.S. the School made only 66 runs and at one stage Hexham were 55 for 5, but the School bowlers then took the remaining wickets for 2 runs. In rugby, a number of players were picked for county teams. The Old Boys' Association suspended in 1939, was revived in late 1947, and in early 1948 over a hundred attended the A.G.M. It was decided to launch an appeal for a war memorial to match the existing one for the First World War. Cricket and golf were also revived.

In 1947 F Co of the Army Cadet Force was renamed as Dame Allan's Contingent of the Combined Cadet Force. It is interesting to observe that in the War Certificates "A" Examination Parts I and II, all passed. "L/Cpl Yeoman[7] gaining the highest result". The following year it had a total strength of 63, and got an excellent report in its War Office inspection. The Shooting Eight was just defeated by the R.G.S. 633 to 624. The Scouts had 125 members, the Orchestral Society over 60 and the other societies likewise flourished. The tradition of Bill Little's productions of Gilbert and Sullivan (this was his seventeenth) was maintained with *The Mikado*. The female roles were taken as usual by younger boys, and it is evident that they did not let down the show. "The most outstanding feature of this production, however, was the number of excellent performances put up by the younger members of the cast. W.Letts and A.Ridley sang charmingly (and clearly, an unusual thing in amateur shows) as Yum Yum and Nanki Poo. H. Buckham and D.Ward were two most vivacious and insouciant maids, both of whom made full use of movement and gesture, and of the stage. B. Reed was a most redoubtable Katisha, yet he managed also to indicate the essential pathos of this elderly and lonely lady." It is interesting to note that in the choral and Orchestral Societies review of 1950-51, in respect of a performance of Handel's Messiah Part One, it was feared that the tenors and basses, as "inexperienced choristers by virtue of their age" might be (though they were not) a problem, whereas "it is expected of the trebles that they should be good and they were." The Third Form boys had the singing of the alto part to undertake and ably led, they held their own. Masters, in particular Charles Hay and Bill Heal, played key roles in all G & S productions. One treble (the same A.Ridley who sang Nanki Poo) is praised for his "excellent rendering of *I know that my Redeemer liveth*." Sadly, with the earlier breaking of the voice and other factors such singing will never be heard again in the Newsom Hall.

In June, 1950, the memorial tablet to the forty-six Old Allanians killed in the Second World War was dedicated by the Bishop of Newcastle. It was symbolically given by the Chairman of the Old Boys' Association to the Chairman of Governors "for safe-keeping." The centre panel gives the names of the fallen, and the side panels list those who received medals or were mentioned in dispatches. Although the list of the dead was only half that of the First World War, the effect of the war fell on many others. Some were prisoners of war, some seriously injured, most suffered to a greater or lesser degree.

In a separate ceremony a month earlier before the pupils of both Schools, the Old Boys presented an oak lectern, designed by Bill Heal (art master) and made by Robert Thompson of Kilburn, for the Newsom Hall. It was dedicated by the Chairman of Governors, the Provost of Newcastle. The lectern has subsequently been joined by a table, a table lectern and a chair (the latter given in 2003 by the Old Boys in memory of Fred Wilkinson), all by Thompson's[8]. Despite – or maybe because of – this reminder of the price of freedom, the number of cadets in the C.C.F. rose to 102 by the following year, and, in conjunction with the R.G.S., naval and air force sections were in the course of being formed, the naval section based at the R.G.S. and the air section at Dame Allan's.

The School possesses a very moving volume in which A.K. Wilson recorded all he could learn of each serving Old Boy, with letters and press cuttings pasted in. They make interesting if chilling reading: "On one occasion he shot down three out of four Junkers 87 dive-bombers"; "Torpedoed in Caribbean Sea: 13 days on rafts; also mined and bombed off Scarborough"; "Was evacuated at Dunkirk"; "Body recovered from sea; buried in Holland"; "Paratrooper at Arnhem"; "Invalided out"; "Royal Marine Commando – Iceland, Dakar, Italy, Anzio, then with Tito's partisans. Twice wounded and lost leg."

---

[7] Alan Yeoman was to become a major-general.
[8] A further chair was presented by David Welsh on his retirement

Particularly poignant is an entry: "P.O.W. in Japanese hands in Borneo" prefaced in a different ink with "died as". A happier entry reads: "Missing from operations over Germany, Feb 21 1944" and below it: "Returned P.O.W. June 1945. A cutting from *The Evening Chronicle* of 22 September, 1944, tells another happy tale:

> 1918. Major Lawson, C.O. of the 2nd Battalion, Sherwood Foresters, liberated the Belgian village of Brugelette, near Ath. He billeted himself on the mayor and when he left he presented the mayor's son with a photo of himself.
>
> 1944, Sept 3. As the Guards Armoured Division raced to liberate Brussels in the swiftest advance the world has ever seen, the Revd Ernest Lawson, a divisional chaplain (and Old Allanian) fell out of the flying column to spend an hour in the district where he believed his father had been stationed in the Great War. Entering Brugelette by sheer chance, he was hailed as their liberator, for he was the first Englishman seen there for four years. The Mayor took him to his house to drink a glass of wine, and on the mantelpiece he saw a photograph of his father. The Mayor, son of the Mayor 25 years ago, announced the coincidence from the steps of his house. The dense crowd of villagers cheered themselves hoarse and rang the church bells in welcome."

A footnote. In 2003 Richard Adams, the author of *Watership Down* and numerous other novels, unveiled a plaque in the Newsom Hall to the memory of Alisdair Christison, who fought at El Alamein and was killed at Wadi Alharit on 6 April, 1943, aged 22. Mr Adams said at the unveiling, "He was the greatest friend that I have ever had." His C.O. in the Black Watch wrote to the father of Alisdair: "by far my most competent officer, invariably cool and unperturbable in battle and with the ability to turn his hand to whatever job required to be done." In particular he praised Christison's resourcefulness at Alamein and in the night advance at Marsa Brega. Christison's best school friend was Eric Rees, now a retired clergyman, who confirms the quality of friendship. School magazines and Speech Day programmes record his high intelligence and academic success. But he and the other forty-five were stopped from fulfilling their potential. As one father wrote to A.K. Wilson, "We are very proud of him and of all the other dear boys. May we all be found worthy of their sacrifice for a better world in which to live."

Other changes were taking place. School Certificate and Higher School Certificate were replaced by Ordinary and Advanced General Certificate of Education in 1951. A. K. Wilson said at Speech Day that he could not give "an unequivocal welcome" to the new system and that "the real needs of both schools and universities had not been met." However, the School's results had not suffered. It was recorded that the head of School, Peter Pilkington,[9] had been awarded an Open Exhibition at Jesus College, Cambridge, and Alan Yeoman had been accepted as a cadet at the Royal Military Academy, Sandhurst. Twenty were going to university, most to King's College, now Newcastle University but then a college of Durham University. Many Old Boys were doing their National Service in the armed forces. The Korean War was in progresss and there was still much of the Empire remaining, and so Allanians were in Korea, the Canal Zone, the Far East, Malaya, Germany, Iraq, East Africa, Kenya, Middle East and Holland, as well as one on the battleship *King George V* with the Mediterranean Fleet. Five others were pilot officers with the R.A.F. with no location given.

The same year there was a general inspection, after which the inspectors commented favourably on the vigour, industry and friendliness of the School community. The C.C.F. continued to flourish, and the R.A.F. section was much cheered to be allocated their own glider, a Slingsby Grasshopper. The groundsman was less enthusiastic. He found himself "keeper of an airfield as well as a playing field – and all the same hard-worked bit of grass." The Grasshopper had a wingspan of 39 feet and a length of 20 feet. When launched by winch, it could glide 150 yards and reach a height of up to 30 feet. It was possible to fly a circuit, carefully avoiding rugby posts and hockey goals – rare hazards on the average airfield. The thought that what goes up must come down must have played a part in everyone's thinking. The R.N. section met on board H.M.S. *Calliope* on Saturday mornings, and had cruises to Northern Ireland and the Baltic. The Cadets had also gained an armoury as part of the construction of the A-E

[9]Peter Pilkington, Lord Pilkington of Oxenford, housemaster at Eton, Head Master of King's School, Canterbury and High Master of St Paul's School. Chairman of Broadcasting Complaints Commission.

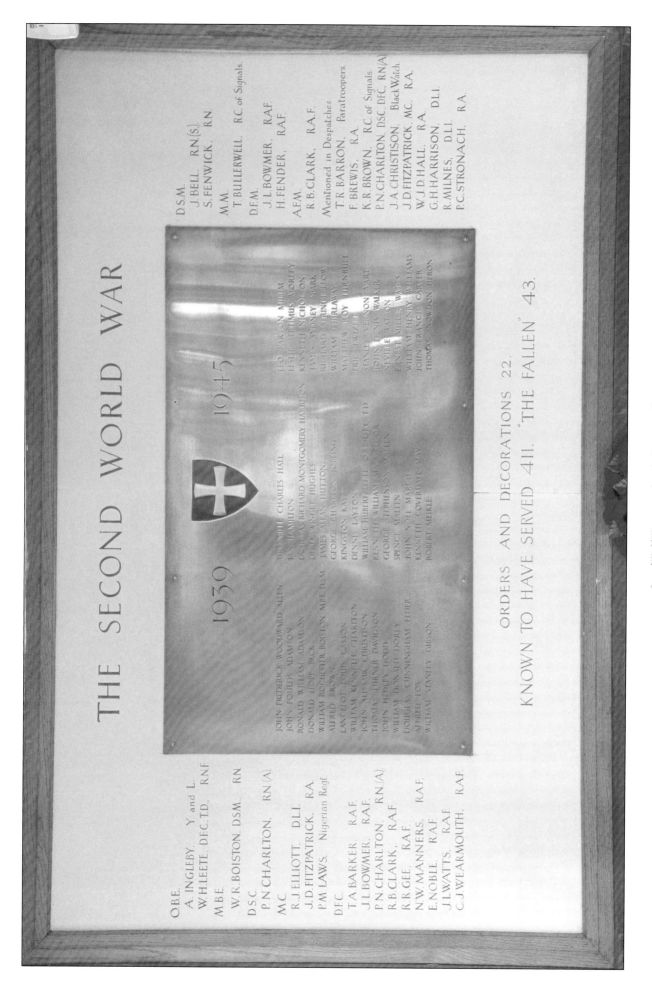

Second World War memorial in the Newsom Hall

block in 1950. Its massive steel door was to survive until the block was pulled down to make way for the current Sixth Form building. They also had a rifle range along the back of the school.

The Scouts continued their help with forestry at Healey, and Colonel Warde-Aldam offered them a site for a country headquarters of their own. A new activity in the early fifties was the annual camp of the Scottish Schoolboys Club in Perthshire. In the same year, an Old Boy, Superintendent E.G. Wright of the Kenya Police, was awarded the George Medal for his bravery and leadership when his small party was surrounded and attacked by 300 armed tribesmen.

In the summer of 1953, A. K. Wilson retired, and a phase in the history of the Boys' School came to an end. For twenty-six years he had worked to consolidate and enhance his school's standing. When he took over, there were six in the sixth form; when he left there were sixty. When he took over, his first task was to tighten discipline and instil a stronger sense of purpose. The accommodation at College Street was extremely inadequate and fundraising for the land and then the new buildings in Fenham was very difficult. No sooner did the Schools feel settled than evacuation came, and by autumn, 1940, he was head of DABS (Fenham), DABS (Windermere) and Windermere G.S. With peace came the two great successes of Direct Grant and H.M.C. A colleague recently described him as a "gentleman sustained by firm but broadminded Christian convictions ... blessed with a strong sense of humour and an infectious chuckle ... very shrewd, his Yorkshire directness and determination accompanied by an innate kindness."

A pupil in the thirties said, "The great thing about A.K. was that whoever you were and whatever you did, he always treated you as a gentleman." Another, Eric Rees, spoke of his "firmness but also genuine understanding". He rarely caned offenders and would not allow his colleagues to do so at all. The same pupil tells of his one obvious weakness. "He was nothing of a cricketer. He couldn't bowl, he was negligible as a fielder, and with the bat he had neither defence nor recognisable strokes. This made his regular participation in the Staff Match a problem for us. It was an understood thing among us that we wouldn't get A.K. out before he had broken his duck. On one occasion he snicked a ball into the slips just after he'd come in and a fielder absent-mindedly snapped up the catch. We were all horrified. Luckily, he realised what a dreadful thing he had done and dropped the ball to the ground like a hot potato. A few balls later A. K. hit a lucky single and we were able to apply ourselves to the business of getting him out. It didn't take long." He was almost certainly the School's greatest headmaster.

A. K. was always very supportive of the Music, Dramatic and Operatic Societies, and to mark his retirement they presented an original ballad opera, *The Thistle and the Rose*. The text, based on two border ballads on the Battle of Otterburn, was by R. Russell Craps and the music by Bill Little: it was a resounding success and a fitting tribute. It was a resounding success and a fitting tribute. The final stanza of the final chorus reminded the audience that it was Coronation Year.

Aye, there will come a time, aye, there will come a time
When the Rose and the Thistle our Sovereign shall bear,
And shoulder to shoulder we English and Scotsmen
Will pledge our true word to one Lady so fair.

On his appointment to a headship, Bruce Gaskin, a former history master at Dame Allan's, wrote to A. K. thanking him for the assistance he had given him in his career saying, "Not the least valuable assistance was the very happy introduction to teaching which I received at Dame Allan's. If my staff speak as well of me as your staff did - and no doubt still do - of you, I shall be very satisfied." He had helped many masters as well as boys with their careers. His own career was not to end with retirement. He went out to Kenya and taught maths there during the Mau Mau rising with a pistol on his desk.

A. K. Wilson's successor as Headmaster in 1953 was Barry Harvey, a classicist at Cambridge, who came to the School from King Edward VII School, Sheffield. During the war he had been in the Navy, and had become

Barry Harvey, Head Master 1953-70

Assistant Private Secretary to the First Lord of the Admiralty. His second master postponed his own retirement to ease the transition, but in December, Henry Mallinson departed to the considerable regret of colleagues and pupils. For twenty-eight years he had devoted his life to the School. Though Senior Mathematics Master, he introduced botany and zoology "with rapid and distinguished success". As *Major* Mallinson, he ran the School Corps and the Ponteland camps with great energy and efficiency. In Windermere he added the responsibilities of hostel warden to his other duties. His strength of personality and the high regard of his charges enabled him to adapt an informal approach to his "darlings, pets and clots." "His repertoire of sayings, some quotations, many pure Mallinese, but all apt in their context, is astonishing in its range and extent. Very many must have heard his timely warning 'Toute de suit — if not sweeter.' His tactful request for support, 'Do you all agree, Breth?' or his 'Any more for the Wappentake of Wansbeck?' addressed to his 'workers in the wine press' are recalled with delight into the present century. As one old boy recently said of him, he was "the most colourful of the lot, a universally loved and more-than-lifesize character to whom it is difficult to do justice on paper."

The success of *The Thistle and the Rose* showed that the School had its own Gilbert and Sullivan team, and in 1954 they produced another original operetta, *The Fortunate Traveller*, a further resounding success. Their own enthusiasm was transmitted to boys young and old, who wholeheartedly acted, sang, played instruments or worked backstage. It was a fine opening for the newly updated stage. The following year saw Aristophanes' *The Frogs* in translation and in a musical version, with some additions and alterations "to appeal to a modern audience that knew Newcastle."

In 1955, a School Tennis Team played a set of fixtures for the first time, and a sixth form badminton club came into being. Golf too became available to sixth formers. As has already been seen, science grew in strength leading to the development of the new laboratories. Lest it should be thought that this meant a weakening in the arts, it is worth observing that two concerts were held in 1956 to mark Mozart's bicentenary, the second including excerpts from *The Magic Flute* and *Mass No. 12*.

Throughout the late fifties, school activities continued to flourish. All three sections of the C.C.F. remained successful; drama, with *The Ascent of F6* and the very different *The Taming of the Shrew* did well; music by such composers as Bach, Handel, Beethoven and Mozart was performed; the Field Club gained from Earl Grey the use of a cottage close to the shore at Howick, near Craster; the scouts had nearly eighty members, and had camps in Northumberland and expeditions to Norway and the Pyrenees. Other school societies also put on interesting programmes, and of course games activities, with some impressive individual as well as collective achievements, were a source of constant mental and physical refreshment. Nor was any of this at the expense of academic success: in 1959, twenty leavers went to university, four on scholarships. Four Old Allanian's gained Firsts at Durham University alone, of whom one gained entry to the Administrative Grade of the Civil Service, the first to do so. David Stafford[10] gained a distinction in Advanced Level history, and David Waugh[11] scholarship level in geography.

As a classicist, Barry Harvey was keen to see this subject flourish and all of the heads of classics who served under him were Oxbridge-educated like himself. The qualities of these men were recognised in the impressive promotions that stole them from Dame Allan's-headships or deputies. Perhaps more impressive still were the subsequent careers of two heads of classics from the 1940s who pursued their vocations in the ordained ministry. John Suggit went on to South Africa where he firmly opposed apartheid and became Dean of Grahamstown and Professor of Theology at Rhodes University. His successor in the classics department, Roger Genders, also

---

[10]David Stafford, Professor of History at Centre of Second World War Studies at Edinburgh University, and author of numerous books and television programmes on the period.
[11]David Waugh, author of geography textbooks for schools. Since 1983, he has written 28 books and sold nearly five million copies worldwide, thought to be a record in Britain.

Combined Cadet Force: leading cadets in navy, army and air force. 1955

served the church overseas, becoming Principal of Codrington (Theological) College, Barbados, and then Bishop of Bermuda.

The sixties also proved a time of steady progress. In 1961, for example, five boys went to Oxbridge, eight to Durham, ten to Durham Newcastle Division and twelve to other universities. They studied eighteen different subjects of which the most popular were geography and chemistry (four of each), followed by English, electrical engineering and general arts (three). Four other boys went to institutions which today have university status. Sir Derman Christopherson, Vice Chancellor of Durham University and a governor, spoke of "the outstanding record of the Sixth Form." The very active societies covered history, science, natural history, classics, photography, chess, field, orchestra, orchestral concert going and debating, as well as scouting, play production and oversees visits. Individuals continued to add lustre to the School in all manner of ways with sports players representing the city, county and country. Unusual success came to a young member of the photographic society who won the National Challenge Trophy for Schools Photography (Colour Section) and Second Prize in the Photographic Information Council's Competition for Youth Organisations (The School Scouts), and had another photograph exhibited at the Fifth Annual Religious Arts Festival in Rochester, New York, over a period of two years.

In 1963 the Dramatic, Choral and Orchestral Societies performed Gilbert and Sullivan's *The Mikado*. "For one so young, G. Lawson as Katisha made a notable attempt at a difficult role to control. Special mention must be made of Yum Yum and her sisters. Those three young performers sang and acted extremely well. In particular, J. R. Henderson as Pitti-Sing made the perfect young lady." Apparently there were problems with the role of Katisha. The boy originally cast for the part was fourteen – and his voice broke three weeks before the production. A very brave ten-year-old took over the role, and at the dress rehearsal, hurt his wrist. After the three performances, it was found that he had actually broken it. The show can still go on with a broken wrist but not with a broken voice. Undeterred, the following year *The Pirates of Penzance* was performed, and audibility was praised: "The shape of the Newsom Hall is bad acoustically, a great deal of sound being lost to the sides, and not penetrating to the main body of the hall, yet few words were lost, even from the younger members of the cast." Adult singers take note. "At time it was difficult to believe that this (choral) singing was part of a school production."

Apart from the cadets and the scouts, there was a third outdoor activity, not of the School's creating, to supply its pupils with a holiday camp. Charles Hay introduced boys to the Scottish Schoolboys' Club, a strongly Christian organisation founded in 1912. The main camps were in the summer at Bruar and Dalguise, while short holidays and other events occurred between. As the name suggests, the other boys were Scottish, but they seem to have accepted the Tynesiders as almost Scottish. In 1969 the club was given a cottage at Garrigil near Alston by the parents of Stewart Wearmouth, who had tragically died the previous year. This was developed as a field centre and became widely available. When Charles Hay retired from the Schools, the link was broken and the holidays were shortly discontinued, but a link with another organisation, Holy Trinity Boys' Camp, was established through Eric Smith at the same time. It too was a Christian camp, based on the choir and boys' club of the huge parish church in Hull. It had no fixed venue and its annual camps rotated England – Wales – Scotland with a variety of sites in each country, the favourite in each being Hawes, Dolgellau and Aberfoyle. The Dame Allan's group became bigger than the Hull group, and in due course its name was changed to North Humber Camps to reflect this. The last was in 1998. A further annual outdoor activity was skiing, begun by Ted Baldry in the sixties. The venues were Hochsolden (Austria), Sauze D'Oulx (Italy), Le Mont Dore (France) and Crans Montana (Switzerland). In the mid-eighties, the trips became joint with the Girls' School – to the same four countries. Another regular excursion for over twenty years was for fourteen-year-olds to the Isle of Arran for a week's walking on the mountains and along the coast. All of these holidays, together with other one-off trips too numerous to record here, were much enjoyed and were of great benefit. One camper has since climbed a virgin Himalayan peak, and another has repeatedly broken his own record for the deepest cave descents in China, currently at minus 930 metres.

By 1965, the entry to university had risen to thirty-seven, with three others reading for degrees at technical colleges and three admitted to teacher training colleges. With great courage, *Hamlet* was chosen as the school play, but at least the hero had no need to be concerned that Ophelia's voice "like a piece of uncurrent gold, be not cracked within the ring," since she and Gertrude were played by girls. This was to establish a regular pattern of borrowing girls for Boys' School plays, and it made possible a wider choice of plays for school production. A year later came the first joint venture, *Most Loving, Mere Folly*, "a gallimaufry of songs, sonnets and scenes from Shakespeare." The scenes were concerned with love and marriage from eleven plays, interspersed with songs and sonnets and linked by a compere. This experiment was clearly a great success.

The next year saw the end of an age with Bill Little's final Gilbert and Sullivan operetta, *Trial by Jury*. This was his twelfth, plus two original operettas. He had joined the staff in 1929 as a part-time music teacher, became full time in 1935 and taught the subject to A Level until his retirement. He also taught English and R.I. to O Level and junior history and geography. He led or helped in cricket, rugby, school camps, school journeys abroad, orchestra, choir, cadets and scouts; the latter included many camps and gang shows. He was described as "one of those complete schoolmasters to whom so many owe so much. He never spared himself or asked or expected more for himself than the satisfaction of an idea fulfilled and a society enriched by what he has had to offer. He has always cared."

In 1969, of the leavers, thirty-two gained direct entry to seventeen universities, two to degree courses at colleges of technology and one to the Royal Naval College, Dartmouth. In June, five Old Boys at a single Cambridge college, Trinity Hall, achieved three firsts and two upper seconds. The Senior Tutor wrote: "The performance of your Old Boys has been very impressive … a remarkably satisfactory set of results, quite apart from the fact that they in their various ways seem to have contributed to the life of the college." Four others at Cambridge colleges obtained a first and three upper seconds.

In the summer of 1970, B. C. Harvey left Dame Allan's to become Deputy Secretary of the Headmasters' Conference and Headmasters' Association. When he came in 1953, he immediately seized the opportunity to continue the work of his predecessor, A. K. Wilson, and to make the School even better known, not simply in the North East but nationally. This was achieved by the encouragement of his pupils through his evident joy and pride in their academic and sporting success. The School's growing reputation was accompanied by a recognition in H.M.C. of his wisdom and clear-sightedness, and he was soon to hold office in that august body. His understanding of the situation of the Direct Grant members was especially appreciated. It was no surprise, he agreed to join its staff. One of his colleagues recalled his fondness for hillwalking especially in the Lake District and North West Scotland, in "antique boots, clinker and tricouni nailed, of great weight. Clearly he was possessed of great stamina. He was a good judge of character, a kindly man and sympathetic to boys."

Fenwick Allison played for England seven times in the 1950s at full back. Here, with the ball, against Wales at Cardiff Arms Park.

1988 Girls' production of As You Like It: Audrey and Touchstone. *Delightful oriental setting and costumes.*

Chapter Eleven

THE SCHOOLS IN FENHAM:
From Strength to Strength 1970 - 1988

The period began in 1970 with two new head teachers; both were historians, but neither could have known that they would find their own place in the history of the schools as the last headmaster and headmistress of Dame Allan's.

It is now necessary to look at the changing status of the two Schools.

In 1973 there was a major development, for both schools – and for the Central Newcastle High School and the Royal Grammar School – when first Newcastle and then Northumberland Education Authorities decided not to take up free places at Direct Grant Schools after 1974. The governors decided that they would award these places in order to keep the D.G. status, and if Wilson's Labour Government, as it seemed likely to do, withdrew the whole scheme, then the Schools would become independent and not be absorbed into the state system. The same policy was adopted by the Central Newcastle High School and the Royal Grammar School, but the two Roman Catholic schools had no alternative but to follow their Church's decision, made centrally, to become L.E.A. comprehensive schools. In 1974, the government announced the phasing out of the Direct Grant, viz., there would be no new pupils under the scheme but the existing ones would be allowed to complete their education. In 1976, the Schools reverted to their former status of independent schools. They had no real alternative if they were to continue, since it was not certain that the Newcastle authority even wished to retain them as an area comprehensive. Very sadly it meant that children whose parents could not afford the fees – apart from a few scholarship and bursary winners – would be unable to attend the Schools. Looking back on the withdrawal of the Direct Grant and also the loss of hundreds of fine grammar schools across the country, many people will see this as the starting point of a catastrophic decline in academic standards. For the Schools the emphasis had to be on creating a substantial bursaries fund, and the governors were able to provide a small number of scholarships and bursaries for the 1976 entry. From that point it has been a major concern to raise funds to provide help for children from less wealthy families.

It is interesting to note the increased level of joint activities in the Schools. Drama has already been mentioned when there was perhaps more the borrowing of personnel, the one from the other, than joint productions, because that was easier to arrange. However, a joint experimental Theatre Workshop produced a light-hearted revue called *Dilute to Taste* and a lively and original musical version of *Paradise Lost* entitled *Milton's Cosmic Wonder Show*. There was also a lively week of junior plays from the two Schools, not with mixed casts but with joint publicity and mutual support. Music, however, was a different matter and the rise of the joint orchestra and joint choir was a feature of these years. The major concert in the early summer was generally of the form of an orchestral first half and choral work in the second. The choir grew to a hundred strong, and delivered a powerful but controlled sound. In 1974, for example, there were works by Mozart, Brahms and Stamitz, followed by Pergolesi's *Magnificat* and Vivaldi's *Gloria*. In 1977 Haydn's *Nelson Mass* was the choral work; in 1979 Schubert's *Mass in G* and Haydn's *Te Deum in C*. In 1980 to mark Newcastle's 900th and Dame Allan's 275th anniversaries, the choir performed Haydn's *Creation* in the Newsom Hall and in Hexham Abbey. Both orchestra and soloists involved some invited adult performers to help the school members' remarkably high standards[1].

[1]One such school member was Catherine Lord, leader of the orchestra, who was the youngest ever to be awarded a violin scholarship at the Royal College of Music. She was the soloist with the Junior Philharmonic Orchestra in Khachaturian's Violin Concerto at the City Hall, and at nineteen played the Sibelius Violin Concerto at the Queen Elizabeth Hall in London. Several other girls became professional classical musicians, and one boy a countertenor.

St James' and St Basil's Church was always packed for the annual recital of Christmas music; despite many extra chairs sent from the Schools, some people had to sit on the floor or stand. In 1976, the choir recorded in the church a long-playing record, *Dame Allan's Schools Choir Sings Christmas Carols*. There were also a joint history society, Christian Fellowship, termly communion services in the parish church, interschool hockey matches, skiing holidays and much else. Sometimes the one school would organise events for both, particularly at the Sixth Form level, such as the annual visit to the Schools by Royal Shakespeare Company members, theatre visits, and science society.

Parents' Association Summer Fete: soaking a prefect c1974. The summer and Christmas fetes raise useful sums for extra equipment - minibuses, hall curtains, computers, stage lighting and so on.

The most spectacular joint events were perhaps the four sponsored walks. The Schools were themselves a charitable foundation, and, despite fundraising for their own building programme and for scholarships and bursaries, have not lost sight of giving to others. This is a feature that has grown steadily in both Schools since 1940. Conspicuous in the fundraising were four sponsored walks held jointly by the Schools. The first was in March, 1969, in aid of Shelter, when £1700 was raised and five families rehoused. The second was in 1974 for Help the Aged, then planning a residential block on Fenham Hall Drive. £5000 was collected and this released considerable grants towards the total cost. The block was named Allan House in honour of Eleanor Allan: one old woman had helped the young and the young were repaying their debt. The death in 1979 of a Lower Sixth boy from leukaemia, after a long brave struggle, provoked the Sixth Form into trying to raise £5000 for a two-year programme of leukaemia research at Newcastle University: the pupils of both schools raised £12,000, and funded a much larger programme. The fourth in 1987 was to raise funds for Matfen and Durham Cheshire Homes and this raised £9,000. These projects were largely conceived and planned by the Sixth Forms, and carried out by pupils of all ages. The first of these was on a route from the coast back to Fenham. The others used the Derwent Way from Shotley Bridge to Blaydon Rugby Club (10 miles), with the older ones who so wished doing 15 or 20 miles. Even in the years when these walks took place considerable sums continued to be raised for many and varied causes. The Junior Department's steady support for Guide Dogs for the Blind in recent years – again, not to the exclusion of other good causes – is certainly worthy of mention.

In 1981 the Department of Education and Science invited the Schools to join the Assisted Places Scheme, and allocated to each twenty-two places at 10 or 11, and five more for the Sixth Form. This scheme enabled far more parents of modest means to accept places at the Schools for their academically able children.

One of the main problems which faced the schools in the mid-70s was the condition of the buildings, for under the Direct Grant regulations such schools were not permitted to use their fee income for new building. A £250,000 Development Appeal, launched in 1977, eventually reached its target, though not without heroic fund-raising efforts by both schools. The Girls' School Domestic Science and Art rooms were completely refurbished and facilities such as a Careers Room, Medical Room and cloakrooms were added or updated.

In 1982 further building works began in the Girls' School on two new classrooms, a relocated junior library and improved staff accommodation. At the Boys' School work began on new music facilities largely for the boys,

Auditorium, 1983, built as part of the Lumsden Music Centre and primarily for the girls.

Lumsden Music Centre: main room

Boys' Library, 1985, formerly the Sixth Form Centre

and an auditorium largely for the girls. The latter was said to be primarily for drama, but was never satisfactory for that purpose.

In November, 1983, the new boys' music centre was opened by Dr David Lumsden, (Old Allanian), Principal of the Royal Scottish Academy of Music and Drama in Glasgow and about to become Principal of the Royal Academy of Music in London and be knighted. Built to a very high standard with handmade bricks of clay from a single pit, it consisted of a main teaching/performance room, a tutorial room, four practice rooms, an instrument store, staff toilet, and staff kitchen, with an auditorium primarily for the Girls' School, and a workshop and store for the caretaker/groundsman. Great care was taken on the acoustic properties of the main room, and there is no doubt about its qualities as a recital venue. For speech it seems better to face across the width rather than along the length – and to have a large audience. This facility allowed much internal movement in the Boys' School with consequent improvements for pupils and staff. The geography department moved to the old music room and its adjacent classroom, and a new senior library was created most successfully from the Sixth Form Centre to house the existing 14,000 volumes with space for considerable expansion. This in turn was to make possible a greatly improved staff facility. The former lecture room became a computer room. The caretaker's house became Sixth Form accommodation for the girls, and the caretaker was rehoused in Fowberry Crescent. Further building work saw new kitchens, a cafeteria system and the creation of four classrooms on the site of the smaller dining hall, no longer needed thanks to the cafeteria.

In 1987, the governors, through the Dame Allan's Development Trust, bought Matfen House, latterly the Mark Reay ice cream factory. The chance to acquire building land adjacent to the Schools simply had to be seized; no like opportunity could occur again. There were several possible uses for the site: Craft, Design and Technology were required for the core curriculum of a pending education act, and that seemed a possible use. However, the first proposal of a sports hall for both Schools was the most obvious, and was in fact adopted. The two sites did not quite touch, but by the purchase (and subsequent resale) of 15 Fowberry Crescent and re-alignment of its garden fence a little further north, direct access was achieved.

Fred Wilkinson, Head Master 1970-88

The Boys' School under Fred Wilkinson

Barry Harvey's successor was Frederick Wilkinson, educated at Furness Boys' Grammar School in his native Westmorland, and at St John's College, Cambridge. He came from High Pavement School, Nottingham, where he was deputy head and taught history.

The next year saw the departure of Canon Charles Hay, after thirty-five years, to take charge of the Wooler group of churches. He first joined the School part-time in 1937, but with the evacuation in September, 1939, became full-time. He became chaplain and head of history and religious education, founded the School scouts, formed a link with the Scottish Schoolboys' Club and took charge of rugby. In 1953 he also became deputy head. At the same time he was also vicar of Healey for five years and then of Heddon-on-the-Wall, also for five years. In 1970 he was made an honorary canon of the cathedral, in recognition of his many and varied services to the Church, joining Thomas Byrne an earlier head of history at Dame Allan's[2]. In all of these he was extraordinarily successful. As one who knew him well wrote, "He tackled everything with an exuberance that was infectious and an energy that seemed tireless. His wide range of activities and his varied experience gave him a profound knowledge of human nature, marked by a ready sympathy and a capacity to listen and understand." He provided continuity as the School developed, serving under three headmasters. He was succeeded as deputy head by Don Walker, head of geography and careers master, who had already been at the School for twenty-five years. The death of Douglas Turnbull in the same year, after twenty-four years teaching history and English, contributing generously to drama, scouting, the C.C.F, the library and much else, and possessing considerable pastoral skills, was a heavy blow to colleagues and boys. *Thunder Rock* by Robert Ardrey, chosen and cast by him from the Sixth of both Schools, was produced in his memory.

A new dramatic venture that year was junior plays, three one-act plays for fifty young actors. It was highly successful, and became an annual event. Initially the plays were produced by members of staff, but a welcome development was when Sixth Formers offered to produce. Further, as they became aware of the shortage of good material, boys from Fourth to Sixth wrote their own, and found these quite as acceptable to audiences as published plays, not because kindly parents admired the enterprise of original work – though they did, of course – but because they were genuinely better than many of those around. On at least two occasions, a version of *Pilgrim's Progress* and the ballad opera *The Ballad of Saloman Pavey*, the short plays were replaced by single works, but with large casts to involve as many as possible. The latter had music and a maypole dance, with fine homemade Elizabethan costumes.

In 1972, six went to Oxbridge, twenty-two to other universities, twelve to polytechnics to degree or diploma courses and nine deferred university entry until 1973; clearly the phenomenon of "the gap year" had arrived. The popularity of polytechnics is also interesting, with a rise from only two in 1969. The play that year, *A Midsummer Night's Dream*, was produced by Charles Stallard, the chaplain, with a cast drawn from both Schools, and was a resounding success. Another venture involving both Schools was the introduction of a weekly celebration of Holy Communion in the boys' library. The numbers involved were always small, but nevertheless these services continued for several years and were greatly valued.

1974 saw the death of Bill Heal, art master for twenty-six years. Besides his gifts for caricature (he regularly contributed cartoons for *The Evening Chronicle*) he was a competent linguist and excellent singer. His input in scenery and in singing to drama and G & S productions was immense. That year too Percy Stronach retired. As a boy in College Street he was a chorister at the cathedral and later became Head Boy. Soon after graduating, as a member of the Territorial Army he joined his unit in 1939 and was soon commissioned. With the rank of major,

[2]Thomas Byrne left Dame Allan's to train for the ministry in 1929. He became Inspector of Schools for the Diocese of Newcastle in 1938 and was made a Canon of Newcastle in 1969. They would later be joined by another former master, the Revd Walter Hatchley

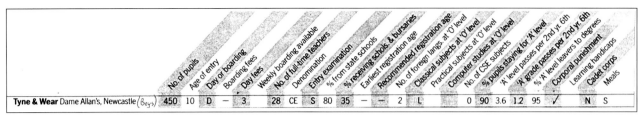

	No. of pupils	Age of entry	Day or boarding	Boarding fees	Day fees	Weekly boarding available	No. of full-time teachers	Denomination	Entry examination	% from state schools	% receiving scholarships & bursaries	Earliest registration age	Recommended registration age	No. of foreign langs. at 'O' level	Classical subjects at 'O' level	Practical subjects at 'O' level	Computer studies at 'O' level	No. of CSE subjects	% pupils staying for 'A' level	'A' level passes per 2nd yr 6th	'A' grade passes per 2nd yr 6th	% 'A' level leavers to degrees	Corporal punishment	Learning handicaps	Cadet corps	Meals
Tyne & Wear Dame Allan's, Newcastle (Boys)	450	10	D	–	3		28	CE	S	80	35	–	–	2	L				0	90	3.6	1.2	95	✓		N	S

The Sunday Times Magazine 1981

he took part in the Normandy operations and the Allied advance into the Low Countries and Germany, during which he was mentioned in despatches. He joined the staff in 1946 to teach mathematics and geography. His leadership of the C.C.F. until its disbandment in 1959, his headship of junior and then middle school forms, his link with the Old Boys' Association were aspects of a man devoted to his pupils and his classroom subjects. For years afterwards he was highly active with the Old Boys' Association – and golf.

Those years of the headmastership of Fred Wilkinson were to see the School rise to an astonishing level of academic achievement during the phasing out of the Direct Grant status. Little of this caught the public eye, since the comparative success of the School was revealed privately at H.M.C., and public league tables had still to be invented. Repeatedly the School was in or close to the top band on the old criterion of matriculation, viz. the requirement for university entry. In at least one year every single boy in the Upper Sixth qualified. However, the real high point came in 1981 when *The Sunday Times* sent questionnaires to all 720 independent secondary schools recognised as efficient by H.M. Inspectorate of Schools; about three-quarters replied. Information relating to about 400 was published in the newspaper's colour supplement. "Although most of the well-known public schools replied, there were a few notable exceptions, including Eton and Winchester." (*The Times*). The next day *The Times* listed "the top 19 independent schools ranked in order of the proportion of sixth form pupils going to university or doing other degree courses." Dame Allan's Boys' School was one of five schools with 95%, and was placed second by reason of its proportion of A grades (see table). There are various criteria for judging academic excellence, but this seems as good as any and better than most; in any case, *The Sunday Times/The Times* chose the criteria they thought best.

Although 1977-78 saw ten Oxbridge entries, including four open awards, it was in the total entry to all universities from a constantly growing Sixth Form that Dame Allan's shone. The academic results came from a strong sense of purpose and of community. The rich life of that community was always much more than classroom learning. Boys and masters saw each other in different and varied contexts. Games, whether weekly games afternoons, inter-house or inter-school fixtures, played a vital role. Additional facilities were acquired with the lease of the floodlit pitch at Hunter's Moor, and the purchase of tennis courts to the north of Fenham Hall Drive. In addition, while maintaining rugby as the winter game and cricket as the summer game, athletics grew in strength and a wider range of alternatives became available to the older boys.

We have observed too the other outdoor activities, the scouts, the S.S.C., the hiking/camping holidays, the ski and canal trips and the Pedestrian Society. We have seen how music and drama was generally of a very demanding quality, being the work of great composers and dramatists. School clubs – ornithologists, debating, history, stamps, railways, science, photographic, chess, film, alongside them – linked enthusiastic staff and enthusiastic pupils. Parents, pupils and staff worked hard to raise funds for the Schools through the Parents' Association. Pupils and staff raised many thousands of pounds for all manner of charities. In these contexts, clear of the classroom and academic interests, respect was heightened and the benefits carried back into the

The following table shows the results in percentage terms:	Pupils staying for A-levels	A-level passes per 2nd-yr sixth pupils	A-grades per 2nd-yr sixth pupils	A-level leavers to degree courses
King's, Chester ..	99	3.5	1.6	95
Dame Allan's, Newcastle ..	90	3.6	1.2	95
St Paul's Girls ..	94	2.9	1.0	95
Queen Elizabeth's Grammar, Birmingham ..	90	3.5	0.9	95
Bryanston, Dorset	95	2.6	0.4	95
King Edward's (Boys), Birmingham ..	95	4.0	2.1	90
Cheadle Hulme, Cheshire ..	98	3.2	1.1	90
North London Collegiate (Girls)	99	2.6	0.7	90
Exeter School, Devon	90	2.6	0.6	89
Leeds Grammar ..	92	2.7	0.6	87
Bradford Grammar	97	3.2	1.2	85
St Paul's Boys ..	99	3.0	1.0	85
Manchester Grammar	95	2.9	1.0	85
St Albans, Herts	95	2.8	1.0	85
Croydon High School for Girls	99	3.2	0.9	85
Charterhouse ..	98	2.8	0.7	85
Mount (Girls) York	90	3.2	0.6	85

Top 19 independent schools ranked in order of the proportion of sixth form pupils going to university or doing other degree courses.

The Times

classroom. Visitors to the School brought insights of the world outside: scientists, industrialists, clergy, historians, writers, professional people of all sorts gave their views. Two examples will suffice. Old Allanian Captain G. B. Jameson, M.C., spent a day in the School every year, taking a period each with a succession of forms. He told them of his earliest memory of Queen Victoria's Diamond Jubilee parade in Newcastle in 1897, of the return of the troops after the South African (Boer) War, of M. Bleriot's demonstration flight from the Town Moor, of his school days in College Street, and of his experiences of the First World War, which for him was 1914-19. Hundreds of boys felt history in the present. He continued his visits from Devon and later from Lincolnshire, always laying flowers to his old comrades on the war memorial and attending the Old Boys' Dinner, until he was 105, a year before he died. In that year the French Government made him a Chevalier of the Legion of Honour.

Many members of the Royal Shakespeare Company, as well as novelists and poets, have worked with sixthformers. Here Maurice Daniels, Newcastle Season Director with Juliet Stevenson and David Suchet to rehearse a scene from Measure for Measure. *Sketch by a sixthformer.*

A further example arose from the Royal Shakespeare Company's season in Newcastle each winter, when through the kind auspices of the Tour Director, Maurice Daniels, actors and actresses from the company worked, if possible, on an A level text with sixth formers of both Schools in the Newsom Hall. Juliet Stephenson, Barbara Leigh-Hunt, Michael Williams, Patrick Stewart and David Suchet were among them. Many theatre visits, especially to the R.S.C. through a School booking system, were arranged involving many of the staff, pupils and parents. In design competitions organised by the R.S.C., individuals and whole forms received prizes and hospitality.

The retirement in 1978 of Don Walker, head of geography from 1946 and deputy head from 1971, marked the departure from the School of one of its most outstanding teachers and scholars. He wrote *A Geography of Italy* (1958), *The Mediterranean Lands* (1960), a section of Shackleton's *Europe* and numerous articles for learned journals, and in 1962 was schoolmaster representative at a Council of Europe conference on geography textbooks. "The most convincing testimony of Don's outstanding abilities as a teacher is to be found, as it should be, in the acknowledgements of his past pupils who, with their experience widened and their judgement matured, can look back and regard it as a privilege that they were taught by him."[3] His patience, courtesy and kindliness, his willingness to listen, his wide knowledge, his lively sense of humour, his enjoyment of the simple things of life and his deep Christian faith were evident to colleagues and pupils alike.

Journey's End (R.C. Sherriff). 1979.

The growing burden of administrative duties was reflected in the development of the management structure of the school. Keith Moodie became Deputy Head assisted by George Bulmer, who was appointed to the new post of Senior or Second Master.

1979 saw the school play emulate the choirs, who for some years had given performances off the School premises, at Wooler Parish Church and at Matfen Hall. Jean Anouilh's *The Lark*, performed in the Newsom Hall in January, was taken on tour in August to the Edinburgh Festival Fringe, Hexham Abbey, Darlington Parish Church and The People's Theatre. It was an impressive production, and an exciting experience

[3]Including four professors of geography, and David Waugh (see above)

Murder in the Cathedral by T.S.Eliot. Newcastle Cathedral, 1981. Archbishop Becket preaches on Christmas Day, 1170 (Graeme Buttery).

for the cast. This success was to encourage three years later the performance of T.S. Eliot's *Murder in the Cathedral* in Newcastle Cathedral, in which the action took place around the audience seated in the pews, as though they were citizens of Canterbury in December 1170, and witnesses to Thomas Becket's murder. It was performed with much addition of mediaeval music, ceremony and processions. The cast was invited by the Hexham Festival committee to give further performances in the Abbey several months later. It was an ambitious undertaking in two magnificent venues, and was felt to be a great success. To mark the centenary of the Diocese of Newcastle in 1982, an even more ambitious production was also staged in the Cathedral. This was the N-Town Cycle of Mystery Plays in slightly simplified English, called *A Plaie Called Corpus Christi*. This version has not been published, and probably this was the first performance in the North-East of any version of this cycle. The play about Noah and the Flood was partly replaced by the only fragment of the Newcastle cycle to survive; this was almost certainly its first performance in the context of a cycle since the mid-sixteenth century. There was a large cast in mediaeval costumes, with numerous sets and many properties, appropriate music and some very memorable scenes, especially the Crucifixion. There were, too, some excellent individual performances, with Nicholas Johnson's Christ particularly good. The limitations of the school's proscenium stage, with or without the insecure platforms used as an apron, plus the Newsom Hall's tricky acoustics, caused some experimentation for *Oliver Twist* (and later *Macbeth*). The stage was abandoned, the action was on the floor of the hall and the audience placed on raised seats on three sides. For *The Ballad of Salomon Pavey* the performances were in the Music Centre and the audience placed on a single high rake.of seats. Several small-scale productions were also done in the Music Centre. Nevertheless, some very memorable performances took place on the stage: *A Midsummer Night's Dream*, *King Henry IV Part I*, *Twelfth Night*, *The Royal Hunt of the Sun*, *Journey's End* (the last two with splendid sets by Ralph Bell, the art department and the groundsman), the one with a gigantic sun that opened and revolved, the latter with a gloomy dugout on the Western Front in 1918). As with the Girls' School, the enthusiasm of members of the English Department – David Dunning, Ian Renwick, Jim Procter, Steve Hamilton and Eric Smith – ensured the best from their actors.

There were numerous varied developments around 1979-80. Perhaps the chief of these was the division into three forms instead of two of, first, the First Forms, and gradually the rest, resulting in classes of twenty-two.

A Plaie Called Corpus Christi: The Devil with Adam and Eve in the Garden. Newcastle Cathedral

This was not easy to achieve, but the benefits to everyone were very clear. German replaced Latin as a subject taken from the first year, and Latin was introduced in the second year. Computer studies became available in the Sixth Form.

With the help of the Parents' Association, a minibus was bought, and its value was immediately apparent. The acquisition by the Girls' School of another minibus the following year meant the Schools had gained a considerable asset, even if there were problems in taking a rugby team to another school with "Dame Allan's Girls' School" on the side of the minibus. One of the immediate beneficiaries of the acquisition of the minibus was the Duke of Edinburgh Award Scheme, started in 1980. By the summer of 1983, there were seven boys at the Gold Award level, ten at the Silver and fifteen at the Bronze. Not only was this a splendid start - and evidence of a real need for older boys – but its success continued for twenty years.

In 1982 came the retirement after thirty-four years of Bill Moses as head of games and an English teacher. A keen and skilled cricketer and rugby player, he encouraged players in both these sports, but by starting the annual swimming gala and introducing golf as a sport for seniors, he showed his regard for other sporting activities. In the classroom and in games "he refused to accept sloppy standards", but had great understanding for everyone who genuinely tried. Another retirement was that of Frank Curran, who taught classics for thirty-three years full-time, plus two more part-time. He was a man of formidable intellect, learning and wisdom, wit and kindliness, and "a teacher of great integrity, undemonstrative, quietly conscientious and sensitive to the needs of others." One story: to a headmaster who unwisely said in a corridor, "Late for a lesson?", he replied, "Don't worry, Headmaster, so am I."

Many distinguished Old Allanians corresponded with or visited the School in these years. General Alan Yeoman, Dr. Richard Laws, Professor Arthur Bell, Sir Michael Scott, Lord Pilkington, and Sir David Lumsden are mentioned elsewhere, but in addition there were Douglas Ridley, Commodore of Cunard, captain of the *Queen Elizabeth 2* and A.D.C. to The Queen, Alistair Baillie, the Governor of Anguilla, Jeoff Hamblin, chief executive of the British Tourist Authority, Ian La Frenais, the film and television script writer, and many others.

A development in school sport around this time was the extension of the geographical limits of inter-school games. Rugby and cricket matches had largely been limited to Southern Scotland to the north and Yorkshire to the south, but it was discovered that the French too enjoyed rugby, and some excellent tours took place. Alas, the French play little cricket, and so internationals had to wait a decade. Another compliment to the School's rugby was the selection of Farne Conway as captain of England U16 , first against Holland at Hilvesum near Amsterdam, then against Italy at Twickenham and finally against Portugal at the University Stadium in Lisbon. Another sport which gained popularity and achieved considerable success in the eighties was orienteering, in which boys competed in the National Schools, British and other major Championships, with some achieving gold standard.

The retirement of George Bulmer in 1985 after thirty-seven years – from 1953 as head of mathematics and from 1978 also as Second Master – was the end of a remarkable life of service to the School. His department's excellent examination results at all levels was one aspect of this service, but it was accompanied by his contribution to cricket and more significantly to rugby. (He had captained both at Durham University). For thirteen years he coached the First Fifteen, and then engaged in organisation and selection at county and international level. For twenty years he was an England selector, and for the last ten was the chairman. He was also for many years chairman of the County 19 Group. He was also a most kind and caring teacher and excellent colleague, with a ready smile and great skill in defeating problems.

The summer of 1988 brought the retirement of Fred Wilkinson as Head Master after eighteen years, essentially only the fourth head in a hundred years, and all of them dedicated to the good of their School. Those eighteen years saw many changes in the educational world outside the School, the work of politicians and educationalists with their own axes to grind, and changes to and pressures on society in other spheres, few of them good. He was naturally conservative and was keen to maintain "those high standards which have been built up over many years in this School – and which are nowadays seriously challenged by the temptations of mediocrity and sheer negativism." In his address to parents of new boys he would also say: "We seek not only to certificate but also to civilise..... to bring young pupils to maturity, a maturity which for the most part is seen in terms of Christian ideals." A man of deep faith, he was conscious of the School's Christian – and specifically Anglican – foundation, and was very active in church matters in the diocese, being at one time Lay Chairman of Diocesan Synod. In the world of education, he was for many years a member of the Court of the University of Hull, and served periods on the Council of the University of Newcastle and as chairman of the North East branch of the Headmasters' Conference. He had many other interests: music, drama, art, photography, and travel. As *The Allanian* tribute said, "All will know him as an unfailingly courteous gentleman who would have a friendly and interested word for everyone. He has a marvellous power of recall for people, events, facts; for faces, names and personal information... a moderate and reasonable man, extremely considerate, fair to a fault, slow to condemn though sometimes rarely tried... nothing was too much trouble for him." In such an atmosphere, "academic achievement reached an all-time peak around 1977-79."

He was never remotely a man for putting others down – rather for lifting them up – but on one occasion he was unable to resist the temptation – but gently done. At his first meeting of the Headmasters' Conference, when he was yet unknown, two heads of Victorian public schools were discussing their recent centenary celebrations. One rather condescendingly asked Fred if his school had had its centenary.

"Yes, we have," he replied.
"How did it go?"
"It was before my time, but not very well, I believe."
"Why was that?" enquired one a little too eagerly.
"It seems to have been overshadowed by the news from Cape Trafalgar," Fred replied.

The Girls' School under Miss Graham

Joan Graham, Headmistress, 1970-88.

Miss South's successor was Joan Graham, B.A., an Old Allanian, a London graduate in history, and head of history at Benwell School. She wrote at the end of her first year: "The weight of my responsibilities on my return to Dame Allan's was lightened by a pleasurable sense of coming home." It is interesting to note that when she went to university, she was one of only a handful; at the end of her first year as head it was eighteen, with thirteen to colleges of education, five to polytechnics and four to other colleges.

At Miss Graham's first Speech Day in 1970, the Vice-Chancellor of Newcastle University was the speaker, this honouring the long link between the two establishments. Half of the later speakers were distinguished academics. Clergy, including the Dean of Durham and the Provost of Newcastle, represented the church link, and there were speakers from law, including Judge Myrella Cohen QC, and business, including - enterprisingly - the managing director of Newcastle Breweries. Four were women, including Old Allanian Marian Foster, B.A., F.R.G.S., the very popular television presenter and later a governor. Each Speech Day evening followed the pattern of Chairman's remarks, Head Mistress' report, the distribution of prizes and address by the guest speaker and a vote of thanks by the Head Girl. There then followed a programme of music by the orchestra and choir or choirs, ranging from Northumbrian songs to Mozart. The printed programme listed all academic and sporting achievements during the past academic year. The physical education covered netball, swimming, athletics, fencing and trampolining in North-Eastern, Northumberland and Newcastle championships, in which the School regularly had considerable success.

It is instructive to look at a school magazine of the period to see the considerable contribution of girls of all ages to original creative writing. It contains thirteen prose pieces – short stories or essays – and forty-seven poems from first form to upper sixth; the variety in style and subject matter is very impressive.

-ATED

a. This school year has terminated
And we shall leave with hearts elated,
This school – a trifle antiquated –
Where we today are congregated,
From all the boys we're segregated,
It's really rather isolated,
We dare to say – a bit out-dated!

b. Our homework we've procrastinated,
And thus our prep's accumulated,
Our lessons we've appreciated
Or debated
Meditated
Contemplated
Cogitated
Overrated
Underrated
Or just hated.

c. By chemistry quite fascinated,
We've seen things precipitated,
Solutions have been evaporated
Wet things have been dehydrated
Even sometimes dessicated
Or thermally dissociated,
We've learnt how things are silver plated,
And all the while have been fumigated
By H_2S that's liberated.

d. In physics labs we've concentrated
On spiral springs which oscillated,
Heat waves being radiated,
Vapours which were saturated,
Light waves which illuminated,
Pendulums accelerated,
Electric currents generated,
And countless things being demonstrated,
Results we have well tabulated
And formulae well formulated.

e. Biology's held us captivated,
Seeing seeds being germinated,
Learning things so complicated
As how man originated,
How the birds and bees have mated,
How our insides have operated,
While frogs and fish we've mutilated
And their insides extricated.

f. How long it's seemed to us who've waited
Till this last term has culminated,
Now all and sundry are placated,
Our battles too have been abated,
And burdens much alleviated,
Until next term when renovated
Some of you, who are so fated,
Will return with hearts deflated,
While others who have graduated
Are soon to be emancipated.

Rosemary Kennedy VI.1

It's not Milton, but it's more fun. Furthermore, note that she is a scientist – and we all thought the polymath was an extinct species.

The resignation of Canon Charles Hay, the first chaplain to the Schools in 1971 was a sad event for the Girls' School as well as the Boys'. Joan Graham wrote: "He was a member of the staff of Dame Allan's when I was a pupil and it is hard to imagine the School without him, particularly the entrance hall undisturbed by his resounding laughter." Although most of his work had been based in the Boys' School, even in the Ambleside days, when he had had to travel from Windermere, he had taken very seriously his chaplaincy responsibilities to girls and staff. The Revd Charles Stallard was appointed chaplain to both Schools to succeed him.

In August, 1972, Miss Dorothy Hornsby retired after twenty-six years as teacher of Lower Second/1L. Though she could appear outwardly a little severe, she was very caring of her charges and taught them well.[1] Historically 10+ pupils derived from the 1877 constitution, but had been absorbed into a preparatory department in 1941 until accommodation pressure in particular caused the closure of the 8+ and 9+ forms. The preparatory department had been co-educational, and in day-to-day matters under the guidance of the Head Mistress. The 10+ form continued as a co-educational unit. At times the existence of the form, clearly an historical anomaly, must have been threatened by people of a tidy nature, but it survived, in no small way because of Dorothy

[1]One who remembers her warmly is Elizabeth Fallaize. She also recalls the arousing of her interest in French by Miss Brass, which eventually led to her becoming Professor of French Literature at Oxford and Pro-Vice-Chancellor of the University

Girls' junior plays: Tom Thumb. October, 1981.

Hornsby's skills but also because the evidence from the number of applications showed that the 10+ entry was in demand. It also had the advantage of keeping alive the hope that the junior school would be recreated. Later form mistresses made real efforts to make the boys feel a proper part of the Boys' School and not, as some of them had felt, an adjunct to the Girls' School. Gradually their situation improved, and was completed with the restoration of a full preparatory school.

There were several retirements of long-serving members of staff during the seventies. In 1974, Edna Best, who had taught principally mathematics, retired after twenty-nine years. "She was always calm and patient and did not rush her explanations," Joan Hodgson recalled. "She recited her punning motto to us:

> Good, better, best,
> Never let it rest
> 'Til the good is better
> And the better best"

The following year Elizabeth Marshall left after twenty years of teaching French and Italian, and Betty Lawson, head of history for many years, also retired. In 1978, Elspeth Williams, head of English and an inspirational teacher and play producer, retired after thirty-one years. Everyone, colleagues and pupils alike, found her a most powerful but caring woman. All of these ladies made a huge contribution to the School in their several ways.

The Speech Day programmes also list the governing body, and the changes in the constitution of the School are reflected in them. In 1970, at Miss Graham's first Speech Day, there were representatives of both Newcastle(3) and Northumberland(1) Education Committees, but in 1986 the Northumberland representative governor disappeared and the next year Newcastle's were reduced to two and not listed separately.

Music and drama continued to flourish over 1971-73, with another Brecht play *The Caucasian Chalk Circle*, and, as a pioneering joint venture, *A Midsummer Night's Dream* produced by the chaplain, and Gordon Jacob's choral work *Highways* and Britten's *Noyes Fludde*, all performed to the delight of their audiences and the satisfaction of their performers. High standards in games, music and drama helped produce academic success, with twenty-eight girls gaining entry to university in the summer of 1972. The academic achievement of these years is very impressive. In 1980 thirty girls went to university, four of them to Oxbridge. The next year saw that figure rise to forty, with eight for Oxbridge (all but one for Cambridge) and twelve for degree courses in polytechnics. In that year *The Sunday Times* did its survey of independent schools (see boys' section for details) and amongst the girls' schools Dame Allan's was in the top 5%. It was increasingly difficult to maintain such a standard as the bright pupils of less wealthy parents were excluded by political decisions at Westminster, but the girls continued to achieve high levels of performance under the guidance of the staff.

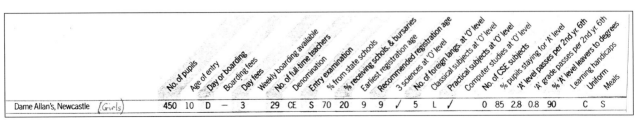

	No. of pupils	Age of entry	Day or boarding	Boarding fees	Day fees	Weekly boarding available	No. of full-time teachers	Denomination	Entry examination	% from state schools	% receiving schols. & bursaries	Earliest registration age	Recommended registration age	3 sciences at 'O' level	No. of foreign langs. at 'O' level	Classical subjects at 'O' level	Practical subjects at 'O' level	Computer studies at 'O' level	No. of CSE subjects	% pupils staying for 'A' level	'A' level passes per 2nd yr. 6th	'A' grade passes per 2nd yr. 6th	% 'A' level leavers to degrees	Learning handicaps	Uniform	Meals
Dame Allan's, Newcastle *(Girls)*	450	10	D	–	3		29	CE	S	70	20	9	9	✓	5	L	✓		0	85	2.8	0.8	90		C	S

The Sunday Times, 1981

Operetta and later musicals were introduced in the eighties; one, *The Tangled Web*, the text by the head of English, Richard Moore, received its first performance. Drama activities also included one-off productions, form plays, play readings and theatre visits, including an annual visit to Stratford for several days.

The Tangled Web: a sketch from DAGS magazine

Language exchanges continued to flourish and in 1983 a link was established with the Lycée Parc Chabrières in Oullins in the outskirts of Lyons. This joint venture with the boys was initiated by Charlotte Houlton of DAGS and Bill Lomas of DABS. This exchange has continued to the present and on the tenth and twentieth anniversaries of its inception, Dame Allan's staff and pupils were received as guests of the Mayor of Oullins.

Planning for the appointment of a principal necessitated changes in management structure. Miss Angela Crossfield became Senior Mistress, (she was the longest serving member of staff after the Deputy Head, Mrs Johnson), and Fred Bell became Senior Master. He had only arrived in 1975 but had a varied career before coming to Dame Allan's, culminating in being Assistant Director of Education for Northumberland. He was already head of History, Librarian and Exams Officer in the school.

With the retirement of Miss Joan Graham in 1988 came the end of a phase in the history of the Girls' School. Over a period of eighteen years she had seen the school through numerous upheavals – direct grant, independence, independence with assisted places; O levels to GCSE; fundraising and building works – and successfully maintained calm, so that pupils and staff did not suffer. Even the carpeting of the corridors made the place more homely and less institutional. It was her earnest endeavour to create a happy environment in which her pupils could thrive both personally and academically, and their success shows how well she accomplished this. Despite an ever increasing load of administration, she encouraged and supported with great delight the many extra-curricular activities that gave the School so much of its character. One of these was the Valentine's Ball, organised by the Parents' Association and the School and always a great success. The four major sponsored walks for charities, all initiated by Sixth Form boys, were promptly and enthusiastically supported as joint enterprises. She was much moved by the many tributes she received, and by the farewell events organised by the School, the Old Girls and the Parents' Association. Her continued interest in, and support of, Dame Allan's since her retirement has been much appreciated. So far as we know, she was the only Old Allanian to head either School in the three centuries of their existence.

Valentine's Ball, organised by Parents' Association

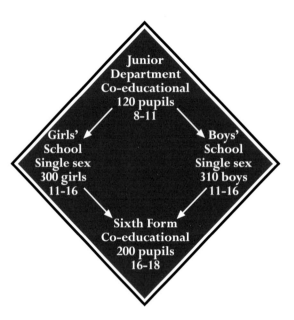

The structure of Dame Allan's

Chapter Twelve

ONE HEAD AND THE DIAMOND PATTERN 1988 – 2005

In this last chapter we are too close to the events and the persons to be objective, and it is the author's intention to sketch only the facts of this most recent period of the Schools' history. In Chapters 10 and 11 only teachers who retired after at least twenty years were commented on, though there were many who in a much shorter period made a considerable impact and will always be remembered by their pupils with deep gratitude. In this chapter even retired members of staff in the first category will only be listed.

The simultaneous retirement of Joan Graham and Fred Wilkinson enabled the governors to take a deep breath and look into the future. It was clear to them that a single principal for the two Schools had many advantages in drawing the Schools together. There had already been both formal and informal co-operation in many areas, even joint teaching where student numbers were low, but now the matter was wide open. The most radical change would have been combining the Schools into a mixed six-form entry unit. There were no doubt advocates of this, but a change so drastic, with its many ramifications, with the considerations that no mixed school ever did well in league tables and that many parents might well have chosen Dame Allan's Schools because they offered single-sex education in relatively small schools, seems to have been rejected quite early in the deliberations. However, at the sixteen plus level, with the opportunity to increase the range of subjects available, the idea of combining the two Sixth Forms was very attractive. With care, the sex stereotyping – girls do arts, boys do science, irrespective of their real talents – that affected many mixed schools would be avoided. "At the same time, especially below the Sixth Form, the separate identity and characteristics of each School will be carefully preserved," wrote Fred Wilkinson, in commending the historic change.

T.A.Willcocks, fiorst Principal, 1988-1996

The person chosen by the governors to carry this out as first Principal was Terry Willcocks, M.A., a graduate in modern languages of St Andrews. After teaching in Ipswich and at Edinburgh Academy, he had been deputy head at Nottingham High School for seven years. Despite the air of good will towards the changes, problems were inevitable, and it is a tribute to all concerned that these were not as great as they might have been. Parents of future sixth formers were consulted about the change, due a year later, and most were in favour. In September, 1989, the Lower Sixths were amalgamated, and the process was completed in September, 1990. At first, a mixed teaching group was taught in the one School or the other, and only after two years with integrated timetabling, was it possible to have a single group taught by members of both Schools. The Schools had different policies on examination boards, and agreement on a common policy was a first step. For pupils there was of course something of a cultural shock, but most recovered very quickly, as they had done in 1940. Initially, it was difficult to increase the range of subjects – that was to come later – but several subjects became immediately more viable. A further stage of integration was phased in over more than a decade. When a head of department retired in the one School, his or her counterpart became head of both departments, a logical development of having one principal. A sudden change would have produced years of illwill and/or expensive compensation.

Martial arts in the Junior School

"Macbeth". The cauldron bubbles as Macbeth and the witches listen to the Third Apparition

At the same time it was recognised that the Junior Department, lost in 1950, should be restored. First, a 9+ coeducational form, known as P2 was created; the former Lower 1 became P1. As has been noted earlier, the 10+ form was not the rump of the former Junior Department but a survival of a 10+ form of much older origins; it had become coeducational only in 1942 when the Junior Department was set up. In stages over the next few years an 8+ entry (P3) and a second form in each of the other two year groups were introduced, producing a junior department of approximately 100. Mrs Margaret Bindeman, the former Lo.1 teacher, assumed responsibility for the department, and in 2001 Andrew Edge took over as the head. The creation of a full junior department was a considerable achievement of these years. There was a plan to construct a junior school building between the pavilion and the sports centre parallel with the eastern edge of the field, but planning permission was refused, and the department was eventually concentrated at the north end of the Girls' School, largely on the site of the small dining hall.

H.M.S. Pinafore, December 1992. Previously performed by the Schools separately, but now a joint Sixth Form production.

Thus the diamond pattern of Dame Allan's Schools was created, unique in this part of the country, and possible because the starting point was two parallel schools sharing the site.

In the summer of 1996, Terry Willcocks retired. He could look back with satisfaction on what had been achieved over his eight years as principal. The two Sixth Forms had become one and the advantages of size had become clear. The curriculum had widened and some new subjects were to become popular, for example, politics. An ambitious development appeal had been successfully managed, resulting in an impressive science block, much more – and much better – teaching space had been created, and the junior department restored and developed. The two staffs had learned to work together for the good of their subjects and their pupils.

David Welsh 1996-2004

His successor was David W Welsh, M.A., who though born in Newcastle, was educated at Glasgow Academy and the University of St Andrews. He was head of modern languages at Eastbourne College and then head of general studies at his old school. He became assistant rector of Dollar Academy, and then moved to Woodhouse Grove at Apperley Bridge, Yorkshire as headmaster, where he stayed five years. His first task was to get to know people and to assess how the Schools were running. His previous experience as headmaster would have shown him where the buck stops. He had taken on the leadership of the schools with a sound academic standard, exemplified by the results of the Summer 1996 examinations. At least he did not have the worry of declining academic standards. The G.C.S.E. pass rate was 96%, with 88.6% of girls getting B grade or higher, and 75.6% of boys. At A-level, 72% of candidates got A to C grades (nationally 51%) and of these Grade A was 28% (nationally 16%). On Speech Day, Lord Pilkington, chairman of the Broadcasting Complaints Commission and an Old Allanian, commented on the new threat from the Labour opposition to abolish the Assisted Places Scheme. "I came from an ordinary and far from well off family," he said. "Naturally, to someone of my background, this proposed abolition is a tragedy as it prevents people like me today enjoying the advantages I enjoyed fifty years ago." The scheme was withdrawn when Labour came to power; the tragedy had come about.

A further step in the consolidation of the junior numbers was the acquisition of Linden Preparatory School in 1997. Linden was founded by William May in 1951. Mr May was an experienced teacher who converted Linden Villa his own large Victorian house in Forest Hall, into a small private school for his own grandchildren and their friends. It was immediately successful and four years later two classrooms were added. Illness forced him to retire in 1961, when the school was bought by Colonel A. K. Johnson, then of Whickham School. There were then forty-eight pupils. As numbers increased, more teachers joined the staff, and a parent-teacher association was formed. With parents' help, a hall, a toilet block and a classroom were soon added, and Bellingham Village School was bought and fitted out as an outdoor centre. In 1974 it was sold and Barlow School bought as a replacement. In both the children learnt about the countryside and its flora and fauna, and also learnt how to camp, canoe and orienteer.

Pupils travelled from a wide area – Amble, Acklington, Blyth, South Shields, Sunderland and Consett, as well as Newcastle and North Tyneside – as the School's reputation for discipline, good manners and old-fashioned standards of education spread. The school roll reached its maximum of 140 pupils, requiring a further portable classroom and, in 1994, the purchase of the adjacent house, which gave a pleasing sense of space.

Though proper attention was – and is – given to the 3Rs, the annual concerts in the People's Theatre and latterly the Whitley Bay Playhouse, the fine artwork around the School, the out-of-school visits, sports, the fund-raising for charities and a host of other activities show that a rich and varied education is the order of the day, and that it takes place in a happy community. To maintain continuity and the ethos of the School, Col. Johnson's daughter, Mrs Susan Inness, was appointed headmistress when Linden became part of the Dame Allan's family. It retained a semi-autonomous position, offering the special formula of education from three to eleven, with the opportunity to proceed to the boys' or girls' schools thereafter. On the retirement of Susan Inness in 2004, the head of the junior department, Andrew Edge, became head of both.

1989 was the fiftieth anniversary of the Schools' evacuation to Wigton, and forty-eight Old Boys and four Old Girls re-enacted the rail journey and the reception at Wigton station fifty years and one day after 1 September, 1939. They were less apprehensive than a half-century earlier, and the memories seemed little dimmed by the years between. The weekend's success led to another the next year to mark the 1940 evacuation to Windermere and Ambleside. The return from the Lake District in July 1944 was also observed in 1994.

Brussels, 1988. The plot is hatched: an evacuation reunion at Wigton, 1939-1989. Jack Castling, Bill Tobias and Gwyn Bevan

A decade after the first reunion at Wigton there was the diamond jubilee, again in Wigton, and a year later the same for Windermere/Ambleside. 2004 marked the sixtieth anniversary of the return to Fenham – but of course celebrated at Windermere. The origin of the reunion lay in a pleasant evening in Brussels in 1988 when Jack Castling, Bill Tobias and Gwyn Bevan recognised the significance in their formative years of Dame Allan's (Lake District) and sought to commemorate it. The above was the consequence of it. Somehow Dame Allan's (Fenham) pupils of the war years seem to have less to commemorate, but 1994 and 2004 were significant for them too. The Tercentenary Year is, however, the seventieth anniversary of the move to Fenham, and that is important to all.

The development of the buildings in the fifteen years between 1990 and 2005 has been extensive. The site is very restricted. There can be no development to the east of the drive without loss of playing area, and that is already tightly managed to accommodate its various uses. What seemed adequate in 1929 is not so today and further off-site facilities have had to be sought. Development to the west is prevented by the nearness of the houses of Bolbec Road, and from the first their privacy has been respected by single-storey buildings along the west side. This has meant that new construction has been essentially to the north or to the south. Earlier work – and car parking – had reduced the playground area for the girls, and the erection of the Lumsden Centre and workshops had taken the best site to the south.

Sports Hall, 1992

The acquisition in 1987 of Matfen House, latterly Mark Reay's icecream factory, was an important breakthrough, and the decision was made to build a sports hall on the site. This was opened in 1992 without ceremony, and has proved very satisfactory. It was the first building since the dining hall in 1938 fully for joint use. This left the two gymnasiums for re-development. The boys' gymnasium and senior chemistry laboratory were demolished and in 1994 a new biology block was constructed. It contains four biology laboratories, a general laboratory, two preparation rooms and a greenhouse to serve both Schools. It cost £1.65 million part funded by an appeal and part by the Schools' resources, and was opened by Professor Ian Fells, Newcastle University, the country's first professor of energy conversation and a father of two Allanians. The architects were Hesley Farthing. Some people feel that the prominent stone features do not sit well with the earlier buildings as the old gymnasium did. Inside, however, it is pleasant and spacious. The laboratories are square instead of the traditional rectangular form, and are very well equipped. The girls' gymnasium was retained, and their old laboratories were remodelled as four classrooms. The boys' old laboratories were converted into a Sixth Form Centre for both Schools.

The next major development was not a new structure but a refurbishment of the first floor of the front of the school. Two physics laboratories and three chemistry laboratories were entirely refurbished, and a new general

Biology block under construction, October, 1993

purpose laboratory, a new technology centre, an examination room and two preparation rooms were created. Thus in the space of six years the science facilities were brought right up-to-date. The development was formally opened by the Chairman of Governors, Mr Peter Gordon, M.B.E., in October, 2000.

The next stage was a problem. Four facilities were picked out as the most urgent. The first was a proper Sixth Form Centre, with teaching, study and common room space on two floors. The second was a dance studio to accommodate this highly successful examination subject. The third was a drama studio, since this too had become an examination subject under a specialist teacher. The fourth was art, with both Schools needing better facilities. There was no empty space to the west of the drive, and so where could it all go? The only possible answer was the demolition of the A-E classroom block, with its toilets, cloakroom, boiler room and old armoury. This was built in 1950 on the south side of the boys' playground, and had always looked rather temporary. Nevertheless, despite problems of keeping warm in the winter and a moderate temperature in the summer they were quite spacious and could accommodate classes of thirty-three in individual desk units with aisles between. They had served the School well for over half a century, and held fond memories for many. Their loss meant that new classrooms would have to be added to the building works on the west side of the playground. The playground itself, already small for current numbers, would be reduced in size.

Inevitably this development would impact on the lives of people in Bolbec Road and Nuns Moor Crescent, both during the building work and their privacy and outlook afterwards. The principal problem lay with the Sixth Form Centre because of its height and bulk. In order to reduce its height, the original plan to incorporate art studios with north lights in the roof space had to be abandoned and the pitched roof truncated. Windows were arranged to avoid intrusion on neighbouring houses, and the block was set as low as possible. Likewise the classrooms are single-storey and the windows placed low on the outside. The interior design of the centre is imaginative and practical, and the outlook to the Lumsden Centre enhanced by an attractive garden, accessible from the commonroom area. The dance studio, situated between the centre and the west boundary wall, is a fine space of good height, while the classrooms are very pleasing. The drama studio is a simple conversion of the former Sixth Form commonroom, which began in 1935 as a manual instruction (woodwork) room open to the

School dinners: twin queues for hot or cold alternatives

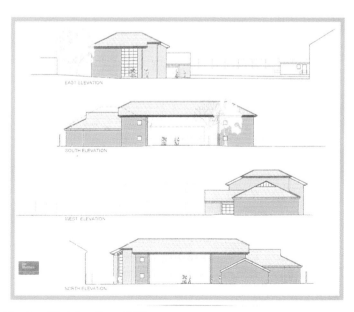

Elevation of Sixth Form Centre, 2004

roof and was subsequently underdrawn and equipped as the biology laboratory. The whole building project cost £2.4 million.

The next building development, which the Schools hope to launch in 2006, will be the extension of the Florence Moat Library (downstairs, north wing) into a single library for both schools, and the conversion of the former boys' library into a computer centre for general use. No doubt there will be more to do in the future, but recent years have seen the transformation of so much of the premises to keep abreast of good modern school accommodation.

Napoleon is reputed to have observed that an army marches on its stomach, metaphorically speaking. Food is almost as important to school-children: a good school lunch gives hope in the morning and satisfaction in the afternoon, allowing academic concentration in both sessions. The appointment of Richard Armstrong as catering manager saw the introduction of ever-increasing choice. It was made possible by great improvements to the kitchens, by a twin-track servery and the closure of the smaller dining hall. The dining hall serves 900 lunches a day, and has received several awards, including, as early as 1994, the first Heartbeat Award for healthy choices to be given to a city school. It has long provided breakfasts and afternoon teas, as well as catering for numerous special events from light snacks to four-course dinners.

Dance performance

Dance was first introduced into Dame Allan's in September, 1989. Jenny Skinner, head of girls' P.E., was anxious to create a balanced curriculum that offered a diversity of creative and physical activities, and Lynda Clough was appointed to develop dance.

It was impossible to foresee the impact that this new physical and visual art was to have on the Schools. Dance seized the imagination of the creative and presented a physical challenge for the active. The combined elements attracted large numbers and very quickly dance was offered as an extra curricular activity, growing from one Dance Club weekly to one Dance Club for each of the Year Groups from the Juniors through to Sixth form, ten groups in total.

It was an exciting time to be involved in dance. There were trips around the country to see highly acclaimed national and international dance companies. Numerous workshops and residencies with dance artists and dance companies fuelled the passion of the up and coming dancers as did visits to the many vocational dance schools in London.

The level of expertise, knowledge and artistry of some of the most talented dancers was beginning to attract attention. In 1992, after a performance at a local theatre as part of a Youth Dance Platform, the School received a telephone call inviting the dancers to enter a National Musical Theatre Competition sponsored by Barclays Bank. The group spent two years creating an original production which was written, produced and choreographed by both staff and students as a collective collaboration. The creative excitement was tangible. Regional auditions took place around the country. Only six works were to be chosen to take part in the final which was held at the Queen Elizabeth Hall on the South Bank, London. Dame Allan's was one of the six. The production *Who Opened the Box?*, focused primarily on choreography which was linked together by a script. Although live music was incorporated, singing was not included despite the category being Musical Theatre. The group were hoping to win the choreography category. The panel were so impressed by the ingenuity and originality of the whole production (theme, choreography, set and costume design and music) that despite there being a lack of singing it was awarded joint winners of best overall production. After this success, there was yet another surge of interest in dance including amongst the boys. The school built up links with other Youth Groups such as Gordonstoun School and an all-boys Youth Group in Peterborough. Dame Allan's dancers were invited to perform in Newcastle.

In 1995, after the introduction of both GCSE and A Level Dance, three girls were awarded places in top vocational dance school, London Contemporary School of Dance, the Laban Centre and the London Studio Centre. Hilary Stainsby emerged with First Class Honours and went on to achieve an MA. She is currently a professional dancer with Wayne McGregor's Dance, Random, one of the best contemporary dance companies. Claire Turnbull returned as a dance teacher to continue the tradition of dance at Dame Allan's in 1999.

The next generation of dancers were also to achieve major success. In 1997 the Senior Dance Performance Group was selected to perform at the Queen Elizabeth Hall. At regular intervals from 1998 onwards they were also invited to perform at the Northern School of Contemporary Dance in Leeds. In 2004, the Seniors were invited to perform in the Linbury Studio at the Royal Opera House, Covent Garden, in front of an extremely dance-literate audience. The performances included choreographies by the dancers themselves, a testament to their dance status.

In the latter part of the 1990s dance was introduced into the boys' PE curriculum. With this innovation came the opportunity for boys to study Dance at GCSE and A Level. The classes primarily consisted of the Rugby boys, who loved a physical challenge and the opportunity to learn new and demanding physical skills. In 2005 the number of boys involved in dance matches the number of girls and in some year groups exceed the number of girls. The new millennium has also seen one senior boy gain a scholarship at the London Studio Centre and another a place at the Liverpool Institute of Performing Arts.

Lynda Clough's energy and imagination have brought the Schools "a national reputation in dance", as the most recent inspection recognised.

Parallel with the success of dance has been the continued success of music and drama, often with elements of all three in a single production. In music there was increased diversity with groups such as the Ceilidh Band or Thingummyjiggers, inspired by Peter Hollins, and the Big Band, which began in a small way but eventually lived up to its name. The pattern of concerts and Christmas performances continued with the Senior Choir and various other choirs for younger pupils. Even classical composition had its successes, including a piece by Mark Deeks highly praised by Sir Michael Tippett. There were numerous drama productions of high quality: Jim Proctor's production of Tom Stoppard's *On the Razzle*, Paul Lewton's of Alan Bennett's *The Madness of King George* and Belinda Whitehouse's of *The Tempest* were three especially memorable and lively plays, full of imaginative touches and good acting. The advent of drama as a G.C.S.E. subject gave rise to studio performances such as *Abigail's Party* (Mike Leigh) in 2001, which had different casts for the two performances so that actors could be assessed for G.C.S.E. Junior plays also continued to be played to appreciative audiences. From 1990 some were written by the boys, the first being *Bypass the Bypass*, by Stephen Rose, a fourth former. The

Boys' junior plays. Bypass the Bypass, written by Stephen Rose (14). This was the first of the original plays written by boys. 1990

Girls' School festival of Shakespeare, with its considerable cast, continued to flourish.

Another addition to the cultural activities came in 1997. Public speaking had long been very successful in the Girls' School. In 1995, for example, they won the E.S.U. branch trophy, with Jill Davies and Susie Blundred winning the best speaker awards. The giving of talks had been for many years a feature of English lessons, but Belinda Whitehouse saw how it could be developed into a competition with a final before an audience of parents and friends. Initially this was a competition in the Boys' School only, but after several years Sixth Form girls joined their contemporaries in the senior section of the competition. The junior and middle sections of boys were joined by parallel sections of girls in 2005, with a total of five trophies awarded that evening. The standard of every competitor is amazingly high, with a maturity beyond their years. Serious matter is well researched and persuasively, even, on occasions, movingly delivered, and the amusing is given with professional timing and original humour. A further competition for under-fourteens is a reading contest of passages from *The Book of Common Prayer*, for a trophy given by the Revd David Johnson (O.A.) in memory of his father, Bill Johnson (O.A.), both brilliant speakers themselves.

In 1998 it was decided that the two magazines should be combined and called *The Allanian*. This would be in four sections to correspond with the four parts of the Schools, and would avoid repetition of news of the two parts that were coeducational. The resulting magazine, with a spine in perfect binding instead of staples, much use of colour and large format, is a handsome record of the academic year, plus original writing and artwork. It is supplemented by a newsletter, issued termly, and introduced in the summer of 1994.

During the period 1988 to 2005 there were numerous retirements of long-serving members of staff.

From the Boys' School they were:

1990	Frank Hume	Physics	37 years
	John Green	Music	23 years
1992	Keith Moodie	Deputy Head (Modern Languages)	31 years
1994	Ted Baldry	Biology	37 years
	Eric Smith	English	26 years
1995	Ralph Bell	Art	22 years
1996	Phil Balmer	Games	22 years
2000	Terry Shaw	Physics	28 years
2002	Maurice Swales	Mathematics	28 years
2003	Geoff Dent	Mathematics	32 years
	Mike Henry	History	30 years
	Jeanette Hutt	Politics, English	20 years
2004	John Blundred	Chemistry	32 years
	Peter Hollins	Geography	26 years

From the Girls' School they were:

1992	Margaret Johnson	Deputy Head (Religious Studies)	31 years
	Joan Hodgson	Biology	27 years
1993	June Reed	Music	23 years
1994	Jan Straughan	Chemistry	31 years
1995	Fred Bell	History	20 years
1996	Angela Crossfield	Deputy Head (Geography)	33 years
	Jim Skipsey	Physics	29 years
2000	Kate Thorpe	Chemistry	20 years
2004	Paul Lewton	English	21 years

As I list the above names, I am very conscious of what I said at the beginning of the chapter: there were many others whose contributions were enormous. Old Allanians can make their own supplementary lists.

At Easter, 2004, David Welsh also retired. He felt that either he stayed until after the Tercentenary celebrations, leaving his successor with a sense of arriving after all the excitement was over, or leaving early enough to allow his successor time to get his feet under the table before the Tercentenary year began. He nobly chose the latter course. In October, 2000, the Schools had had a full inspection. "Charged with maintaining separate high quality education for boys and girls between the ages of 11 and 16, whilst achieving overall improvements in the efficiency, consistency and cohesion of the schools taken as a whole, the principal provides well-conceived and perceptive leadership that has moved the schools forward and continues to make for the kind of improvement that will benefit all pupils." It speaks of a "civilised and civilising community. The ethos of mutual respect and concern for individual dignity is evident everywhere throughout the schools and is highly supportive of pupils' good progress and well being. A positive attitude to learning, and to the schools as a whole, is engendered in the pupils, who show this in their commitment to the schools and their exemplary behaviour. Attention to the personal development and pastoral care of the pupils is very good. The credit for much of this lies with the staff and particularly with the outstanding quality of leadership which the school enjoys." The inspectors' conclusions require no addition.

Dr John Hind, Principal since 2004

The governors' choice of a successor was John R Hind. Born in Mansfield, Nottinghamshire, he was educated at the Manor Comprehensive School, Mansfield Woodhouse, and read history at Downing College, Cambridge. He was assistant master at Exeter School, Devon, and then head of history and director of studies at Durham School. Whilst there he completed a Masters' degree in Education at Newcastle University and a PhD based on local history research at the University of Durham. From 1997-2004 he was deputy head of Kingston Grammar School in Surrey.

The academic performance over this period (1988 – 2005) has been pleasing to pupils, parents and staff. It is not profitable to try to compare current results with past results in terms of percentages because both the Schools and the examinations are on very different footings. The only possible test of present performance is in comparison with other similar schools and national standards, and in that Dame Allan's has done well. In 1999, for example, the A-level pass rate was 98%, 57% of all entries produced were A or B grades, and in G.C.S.E., Grades A*-C, the girls achieved 94.6% and the boys 95.1%. In 2001, the A-level pass rate was 99%, of whom 59% were A or B; at G.C.S.E., 96% of girls and 95% of boys achieved five or more A*-C. Individually, both boys and girls achieved one of the top marks in the A.Q.A. Board in a number of subjects. In 2002, Chris James actually achieved this both in English Language and in English Literature, while in Statistics, Chris Fairless and Karl Zammit-Maempel also gained a top mark despite taking the examination a year early. In the same year but at A-level, Thomas Riddick and Atif Salim were in the top five marks out of 11,000 candidates at Chemistry.

Christopher Fairless

Catherine Fairless

Christopher Fairless

Posters for the Tercentenary Concert

In that year, too, the pass rate reached 100% at A-level, 62% of them at A-B grades. Demanding courses at university did not put off able students; in 1998, for example, twelve went to read medicine or veterinary medicine.

Sport did not suffer from all this academic excellence, indeed for many pupils they supported each other. The development of overseas tours, both for boys and for girls, continued over this period. The acclimatisation and the playing away meant that games were not always won, but pupils learnt that the old adage about the playing being more important than the winning – sadly little understood by many professional players and their supporters – was actually true. That never prevented a win being a pleasing bonus, of course. The 1999 rugby tour of South Africa, with games in Johannesburg, Port Elizabeth, Cape Town and Durban, with two victories out of seven games, illustrated this. They came back a better team and more thoughtful people as a result of experiences on and off the pitch. In 2002, the Girls' U16 and U18 hockey squads and U14 and U16 netball squads found "the opposition tough but very friendly and hospitable" on a tour to Canada.

Individuals achieved national and international success. Rugby players have for half a century represented their country – and not always England, but Wales and Scotland too. In recent years with a wider field of activities, individual pupils have reached top levels.Harry Grigg, for example, held three British U21 weightlifting records in 2003, while in 1999, Matthew Gill won a national archery title, Stuart Haley won the British Schools U15 200 metres, James Denmark the U14 National Tennis Ladder title, and Philip Hines the National Tae Kwan Do championship with a first and a second. In 2004, Natasha Khatib was selected for the English Schools development squad for netball.

In 2000 Dame Allan's established a new and impressive record of a completely different kind. For a single year seven brothers, the Dickinsons from near Berwick, attended the School together, ranging in age from eight to seventeen. One must assume that the Revd and Mrs V.T. Dickinson are at least reasonably satisfied with what is on offer in Fenham.

Like the cadets earlier, the scouts closed for a variety of reasons, including a shortage of leaders who were willing and able to commit themselves to weekly meetings and to camps. It was also, perhaps, part of a move to something a little less formal. One very important activity that in some ways succeeded the scouts was the Duke of Edinburgh's Award. For many years this was run by Dave Bisset with great success at Bronze, Silver and Gold levels in Northumberland, the Lake District and the Isle of Arran. Joan Hodgson, for many years in the Guides, introduced the award in the Girls' School with similar success, and under Gill Maughan, this activity continues to flourish. Another annual out-of-school activity for boys in the First Form was a week on a multi-activity holiday at Lakeside led by Nick Glover. This was always fun but with a serious element: learning to do a range of outdoor activities *safely*.

One impressive enterprise in recent years has been the expeditions to remote parts of the world little troubled – or financed – by tourism. These World Challenge expeditions are organised and led by an experienced member of the organisation and include two or three members of staff. They are of three to four weeks' endurance, and have included Uganda, Kenya, Bolivia, Mongolia/China and in the Tercentenary year, the Indian Himalayas. On occasions the parties have reached over 16,000 feet and often been in very wild terrain. They have met local people, sometimes ones who had never or rarely seen a European man or woman before. All expeditions have a project to help some undertaking in a remote area, having paid for the equipment and materials in advance. The most common feeling after any of these trips is sheer amazement at the world's rich diversity and the great difficulties faced by many of its people. Whatever they had read or heard or seen on television could not quite prepare them for the real thing. Even the training and the money-raising enlarged their experience.

The Tercentenary celebrations began with the planting of three trees and the presentation of a mug designed by Christopher Fairless (outside design) and Polly Procter (inside design) to each member of the Schools. On 23 January there was a stunning dance performance at the Gala Theatre, Durham, and on 4 February there was a talent competition with more talent than it was reasonable to expect. In February there was an exhibition in the Central Library of items from the Schools' collection and borrowed material; it received many favourable comments. On 11 February, Founder's Day was commemorated in the presence of the Lord Mayor and Lady

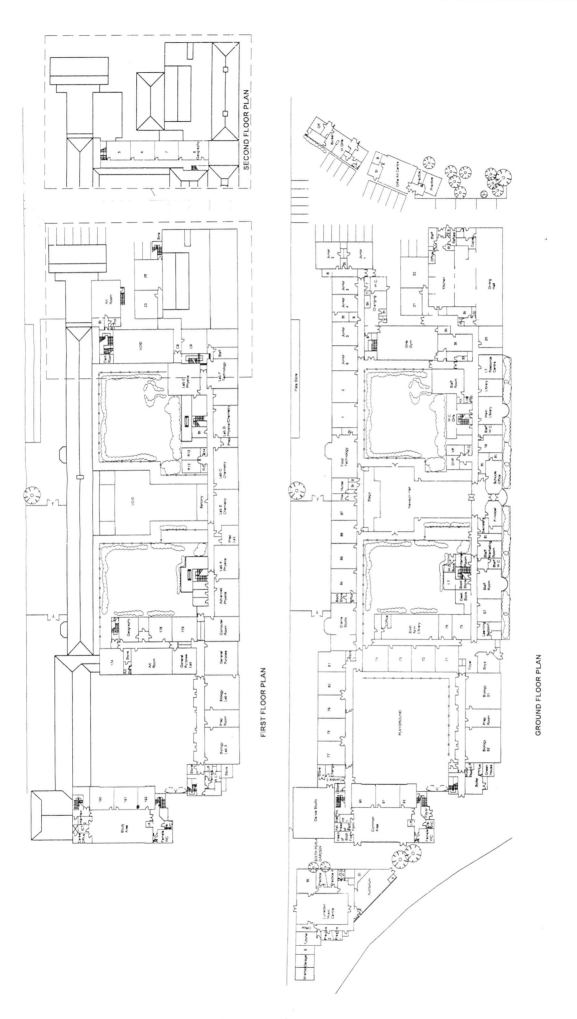

Dame Allan's Schools in 2005

Mayoress, the High Sheriff of Northumberland, the Lord Lieutenant, the Leader of the City Council, governors, friends, Old Allanians and the current members of the Schools. The preacher was the Bishop of Durham, Dr Tom Wright. His sermon exactly met the needs of the occasion and was greatly appreciated by the congregation. The director of music, David Tallent, conducted his own new anthem, *The Lord is the Everlasting God*, to words from the Book of Isaiah. There was a reception at the Schools afterwards and the cutting of a cake. The previous day there had been another commemorative service for the Junior School and Linden School in the parish church of St James and St Basil. This service was designed for the younger pupils. Next came the Tercentenary Public Speaking Competition, expanded this year to include sections for junior and middle girls.

On 10 April there was the Gala Concert at The Sage, Gateshead, with a very varied programme from pop to Handel, with many current and former Allanian performers. The youngest performers were the Lower School Choirs in a tribute to Admiral Nelson, *Hip Hip Horatio*, an entertaining and lively piece that was very well received. The Tercentenary Choir of 115 voices, accompanied by an orchestra of 43 players, performed a mixed programme, opening with Handel's coronation anthem *Zadok the Priest* and concluding with a medly from *Les Miserables*. John Scott sang a solo: he also sang one at the 250th anniversary concert. Music, so much fostered at school, became, he said, a most important part of his life. Susie Winkworth, who performed a cello solo by Bach, went further and is a professional musician. The guest of honour was Sir David Lumsden, formerly Principal of the Royal Academy of Music and an Old Allanian.

The Old Allanians held an Old Boys' Dinner and an Old Girls' Spring Lunch, and the Parents' Association held the Summer Fayre close to the end of term. Then the summer diaspora began, with forty Sixth Formers heading for India, girls' hockey and netball teams going to Canada, rugby teams to South Africa, a group touring the battlefields of the First World War in Belgium, and a party to the Mosel.

The Tercentenary year opened with the news that an Old Allanian, Dr Russell Cowburn, had become Professor of Nanotechnology at Imperial College at the age of 33. He was the subject of an article in *The Times*. He joined Ed Hinds, also an Old Allanian who is Professor of Physics there. Dr Stephen Rose (29) has been appointed Fellow of Hughes Hall, Cambridge, and awarded a Leverhulme Research Fellowship at Royal Holloway College, London; his subject is music. With relatively recent Allanians such as these, and the excellent examination results over the last few years, the Schools can look forward with confidence to their fourth century.

Eleanor and Francis Allan would be amazed at what their creation has become, and delighted at the spirit that still drives it, honouring the past and welcoming the future.

College Street building of 1883 today

APPENDIX 1

CHAIRMEN OF TRUSTEES
1705-1877

From the foundation of the Schools until 1877, the chairman of the trustees was always the Vicar of Newcastle; during an interregnum the acting chairman was probably the next senior cleric. After 1877, the Vicar of Newcastle was not always the Chairman of Governors, but always served on the governing body.

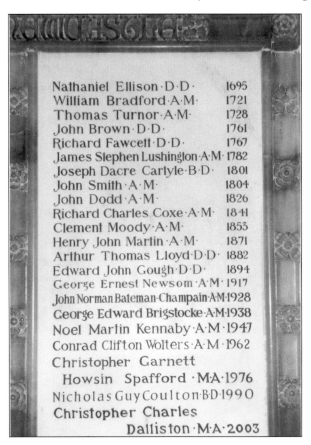

Nathaniel Ellison·D·D·	1695
William Bradford·A·M·	1721
Thomas Turnor·A·M·	1728
John Brown·D·D·	1761
Richard Fawcett·D·D·	1767
James Stephen Lushington·A·M·	1782
Joseph Dacre Carlyle·B·D·	1801
John Smith·A·M·	1804
John Dodd·A·M·	1826
Richard Charles Coxe·A·M·	1841
Clement Moody·A·M·	1853
Henry John Martin·A·M·	1871
Arthur Thomas Lloyd·D·D·	1882
Edward John Gough·D·D·	1894
George Ernest Newsom·A·M·	1917
John Norman Bateman-Champain·A·M·	1928
George Edward Brigstocke·A·M·	1938
Noel Martin Kennaby·A·M·	1947
Conrad Clifton Wolters·A·M·	1962
Christopher Garnett Howsin Spafford·MA·	1976
Nicholas Guy Coulton·B·D·	1990
Christopher Charles Dalliston·M·A·	2003

CHAIRMEN OF GOVERNORS
1877-2005

1877 - 82	Revd Canon H Martin MA, Vicar of Newcastle
1883 – 96	W D Cruddas, MP, JP
1897 – 98	R G Hoare, JP
1899 – 1900	E A Hedley, JP
1901 – 15	Revd Canon J Moore Lister, DD, Vicar of St Andrews
1916 – 17	Alderman Sir Walter Plummer, JP, DCL
1917 – 28	Revd Canon G E Newsom, MA, Vicar of Newcastle
1928 – 38	Very Revd J N Bateman-Champain, MA, Vicar and Provost of Newcastle
1938 – 47	Very Revd G E Brigstocke, MA, Provost of Newcastle
1948 – 62	Very Revd N M Kennaby, MA, Provost of Newcastle
1962 – 66	Colonel A D S Rogers, OBE, TD, MA
1966 – 76	Very Revd C C Wolters, MA, Provost of Newcastle
1976 – 82	J E Miller, LL.B
1982 – 87	Professor A L Crombie, MB, ChB, FRCS. (Ed)
1987 – 93	M Bird
1993 – 95	H R Burrell, MA
1995 – 2000	R P Gordon, MBE, DL, MA, FIB
2000 –	Mrs D J Salmon

Appendix 2

THE ALLAN FOUNDATION

MASTERS   MISTRESSES

St Nicholas's Charity Schools

		1705/6	Mrs Alice Wild
1709	James Dixon	1709	Mrs Dorothy Wild
1710	John Watson	1723	Mrs Ramsay
1712	Samuel Mowbray	1729	Mrs Rodham
		1738	Mrs Hannah Hall
1743	? Hall	1743	Mrs Elliott
		1754	Mrs Bulman
		1760	Mrs Brown
c1774	William Umfraville	1766	Mrs Keenleyside
1775	Anthony Charlton	1784	Mrs White
1785	Ralph Dees	1791	Mrs Henzell Usher (m.1789)
1807	Thomas Charlton	1817	Mrs Margaret Baxter
		1834	Mrs Ann Waters
1838	John Findley	1836	Miss Margaret Hownam
		1844	Mrs Findley (m?)
1847	Michael Wilson	1846	Miss Elizabeth Jane Read
1851	John Brockbank		
1854	William H.Thorn (U) & Holland Eckersley (L)*		
1855	George Lake (U) & Holland Eckersley (L)*		
1861	William D Norris (July - Sept)		
1861	John D Stubbs (until 1878)	1866	Mrs Jane Anderson (until 1878)

Allan's Endowed Schools / Dame Allan's Schools

1883	Thomas Merrick	1883	Mrs Catherine Landells (m)
1893	Edward B Moffatt MA	1886	Miss Emma M Mousley
1896	Frederic W Brewer MA	1894	Miss S Elizabeth Dobson LL.A
1926	Francis M Osborne MA MA	1933	Miss Florence A Elliott MA
1927	Alfred Kenneth Wilson MA		
1953	Barry C Harvey MA	1954	Miss E Marguerite South MA
1970	Frederick Wilkinson MA	1970	Miss Joan Graham BA

PRINCIPALS

1988	Terry A Willcocks MA
1996	David W Welsh MA
2004	John R Hind MA, MEd, PhD

*From 1854-1861 there were separate masters for the upper, "U", and lower, "L", schools.

APPENDIX 3

DEPUTY HEADS
Since 1883

Deputy Heads are variously styled Senior Master / Mistress, Second Master / Mistress, Deputy Headmaster / Headmistresses and from 2000, Vice-Principal. Note: most of these were already members of staff before becoming Deputy Heads.

Girls' School

1883-Dec 85	Unknown
Jan 86-c. 94	Miss Mary F Heylin (Edinburgh)
c.1894-1896	Miss Agnes H Hawthorn (Edinburgh)
1896-c.1900	Miss Agnes M Young (London)
c.1900-1907	Unknown
Jun 07-1936	Miss Edith L Buxton (London)
1936-1938	Miss Jessie N Dodd BLitt (Durham) LLA (St Andrews)
1938-1940	Miss Janet B Ramage LLA (St Andrews)
1940-1944	Miss Stella I V Lippett DA (Gray's School of Art, Aberdeen) Fenham
1940-Dec 42	Miss Elizabeth E Nobbs BA (London) Ambleside
1943-1945	Miss Louisa E Goodman MA (Cambridge) Ambleside
1945-1947	Miss Elinor C Clark BA (London)
1947-1949	Miss Rose M McDonald BSc (Durham)
1949-1951	Miss Janice V R Cooper BA (London)
1951-1953	Mrs Margaret L Damant MA (Durham)
1953-Dec 54	Miss Rose M McDonald BSc, MEd (Durham)
Jan – Sep 55	Miss Janice V R Cooper BA (London)
1955-1960	Mrs Margaret L Damant MA (Durham)
1960-1962	Miss Mary Fawcett BSc (Durham)
1962-Apr 63	Miss Catherine Durnford BA (Durham)
Apr 63-1992	Mrs Margaret Johnson BA (Durham)
1992-1996	Miss S Angela Crossfield BA (Durham)
1996-2001	Mrs E Deirdre Wheeler BA (Durham) MSc (Econ) (L.S.E.)
2001	Mrs M Janet Middlebrook BA (Leeds)

Boys' School

1883-1898	Alexander Begg Noble Certificated Master (London)
1898-1923	Arthur Goodacre BA (Royal University of Ireland)
Autumn 1923	George A Harding BA (London)
1924-1944	Edwin G Finch ON MA (Christ's College, Cambridge)
1944-1953	Captain Henry Mallinson MC BSc (Leeds)
1953-1971	Revd Canon A Charles de P Hay MA (St John's College, Cambridge)
1971-1978	Donald S Walker MA (St Catharine's College, Cambridge)
1978-1992	J Keith Moodie MA (Gonville & Caius College, Cambridge)
1992-2000	Kenneth E Jones MA (Jesus College, Cambridge)
2000	William J Lomas BA, MA (Newcastle)

Appendix 4

CHAPLAINS

1939-1971	Revd Canon A Charles de P Hay MA
1971-1974	Revd J Charles Stallard MA
1974-1979	Revd Sydney C Jones MA
1979-1985	Revd Cecil B Dick MA
1985-1988	Revd Peter R Hestleton MA
1988-1995	Revd John Hazelton MA MLitt BPhil

HONORARY CHAPLAINS

1998-2001	Revd Alison E Harrison B.Ed
2001-2004	Revd Sue Wilson BPharm PhD
2004-	Revd Canon Joan Dotchin

APPENDIX 5

INDENTURE

Indenture made the twentieth day of February in fourth yeare of the Reigne of our soveraigne Lady Queen Anne over England Annoque Domi 1705 Betweene Ellinor Allan of the Towne and County of Newcastle upon Tyne, Widdow, of the one part, and William Proctor Esq., George Henderson Esq., and John Ord Esq of the said Towne and County of Newcastle upon Tyne, Gents, of the other part.

Reciting – of Lease under Seal of the Dean and Chapter of Durham bearing date on or about the 20th day of July in the 12th year of the reign of the Late King William the 3rd unto Francis Allan of Newcastle upon Tyne aforesaid, Merchant deceased, executors and assigners of
All that their tenements, ffarmhold and husbandry at Wallsend with the exception of the Woods, Mynes and Quarrys and liberty to dig – and work the same, for the lease 21 years from the 26th day of June then last part yielding and paying £34 7s
Reciting Will of the said Francis Allan containing Devise to the said Ellinor Allan of
All his goods, chattels and Estate whatsoever of what nature or kinde soever and did appoint the said Ellinor Allan sole executrix, and shortly after died
And also reciting that the said ffrancis Allan in his lifetime did purpose and intend in case the said ffrancis Allan dyed unmarried that he would settle, assine and convey the said ffarmhold and premisses and the rents, issues and proffitts thereof to the said Ellinor Allan for her life and that then that the same should be and goe for a charitable use, and that the said Ellinor Allan being willing and desirous to perform the intencon of the said Francis Allan.

The indenture witnesseth that the said Ellinor Allan did give, grant, bargaine, sell, assyne, transfere and give over to the said William Proctor, George Henderson and John Ord their executors.

All that said in part recited lease mentioned above in trust for the said Ellinor Allan for her life and a payment weekly to Alice Wild and payments for fines, rents etc and upon this further trust and confidence that in the next place the overplus surplussage or remainments anyways over and above such disbursement outlays and payments as foresaid should from time to time, and at times thereafter by the said William Procter, George Henderson and John Ord and the survivor of them the executors of such survivors be lodged and deposited with and paid unto the Right Warsll the Maior of the Towne for the time being, the Vicar of the said Towne for the time being, the Lecturer or afternoon preacher of the parish church of Saint Nicholas in the said Towne for the time being, the Minister of the parish church or Chappelry of All Saints in the said Towne for the time being, the Lecturer or afternoon preacher of the said parish church of All Saints for the time being, the Minister of the Parish Church or Chapellry of Saint Johns in the said Towne for the time being and the Minister of the Parish Church or Chappelry of Saint Andrews in the said Towne for the time being, that they or any four of them should lay out and disburse the same to the several uses intents and purposes thereafter mentioned, that is to say – First of all, for procureing and hireing a master to teach and instruct fforty poor boys inhabitants within the said Parish of St Nicholas and Parish or Chapellry of St Johns or either of them to read and write English and soe much of Vulgar Arithmetic as to ffit and qualify them for mechanick-trades and in the next place for procureing and hireing a Mistress to teach and instruct twenty poor girls the inhabitants of the said parish of St Nicholas and parish or Chappelry of St John's or either of them, the said Girls to be taught and instructed by the said Mistress to read and knitt and sow plaine work and the master to be obliged to teach the said Girls to write

And upon this further trust that the said Trustees or any four of them should lay out imploy disburse and pay all and every the rest and residue of the said moneys so to be by them had and received out of the rents issues and proffitts of the said tenements ffarmhold and Husbandry from time to time in the putting out of the said boys apprentices and the said Girls to service and in such other charitable and necessary uses in and about the said school and the Edication and teaching of the said children as they the said Maior and Vicar for the time being and the said Lecturers and Ministers or any four of them shall think fitt or necessary so as they exceed not the sum of three pounds in the bindeing apprentice or putting out to service one of the said boys or girls to be taught and instructed as aforesaid –

And upon this further Trust and confidence that the said school so to be sett up for teaching the said Boys and Girls and the moneys to be received in about for teaching or concerning the same in all and every matters and things any manner or way relateing thereunto and not herein otherwise ordered directed and set downe should for ever hereafter be governed visitted and managed in the same manner method and forme and according to the rules and orders prescribed and sett downe (and now remaining or a coppy thereof remaining in the hands or custody of the Right Worshipfull the Maior of Newcastle upon Tyne the Vicar Ministers and Lecturers or some of them for the Direccon Government and ordering of the school lately erected and sett up or intended to be erected and sett up in the said parish and Chapellry of St Johns within the said Towne of Newcastle teaching thirty four boys or girls of that parish or Chapellry to read English.

Here follow the usual covts

Appropriate extracts from the St John's Charity School rules referred to in the indenture above

Copy of the Rules referred to in the above in part abstracted Indenture Novr ye 19th 1705

Rules for the Foundation of a Charity School for 34 poor children in the Parish of St John's Newcastle as they were sent in Lettrs to Dr Robert Thomlinson Lecturer of St Nicholas Rector of Whickham and Prebendary of St Paul's in the years 1705 and 1706

[The Master]
[The trustees named above] may have the naming appointing and removing a master and the putting in and removing the poor children… In your choice of a master I desire that you would have regard to the following Qualifications, viz.,

1. That he be a member of the Psent Establish'd Church of England, several call their churches the Church of England but I call (and mean) the psent Establish'd Church so and no other.

2. That he be of a sober life and conversation and of a humble and meek Behaviour.

3. One that frequents the holy Communion, I mean other than at the three great festivals, unless casually prevented.

4. A young man of a healthy constitution and prefer one that has had experience in teaching if equally qualified.

5. If a young man cannot be had, then one married, but then let him be one that keeps good order in his family, his wife being a member of the same Establish'd Church of England, for though I have charity for men of all perswasions, I cannot think that a married man whose wife is not of the Establish'd Church fit for this purpose.

6. If a young man unmarryed be chosen and hearafterwards marry, I would not have that adjudg'd a just cause of turning him out in case he have behav'd himself to the content of the Overseers and marry a sober woman, a member of the Psent Establish'd Church of England.

7. If a master be a freeman or otherwise qualified to give a vote for election of members to serve in Parliament I do order that he shall be displac'd, if he gives any vote on such occasion, for hereby he may draw illwill upon himself and consequently upon the Design he's concern'd in.

8. That he be well grounded in the principals of Christianity so as to give an account thereon to the visitors.

9. That he understand the grounds of Arithmetick so as to be able to teach the Golden Rule and write a plain fair hand. The school shall consist [of the children of freeman of the parish, and failing them, those of non-freemen, and thereafter of other parishes].

[The Children]
4. As soon as any child can well read English (of which the overseers or any 2 to be judges) can say the Church Catechism by heart, and write and cast accounts, then to be remov'd and another to be plac'd in his or her Room, and at such Removals to have given the Whole Duty of Man bound, and a Bible and Common Prayer Book bound together.

5. If they come not constantly after their first Entry, to be remov'd, I mean constantly being absent above one half day in a week. If more and the excuse not allowed by the Overseers or some of them, to be remov'd. The school hours to be in Winter from 8 to 11 and from one to 4, and in Summer from 7 to 11 and from 1 to 5. All church and state Holidays to be observed by the master's carrying the children to church.

6. The names of all children admitted to be enter'd in a Roll to be hung up in the school with the Days of their admittance and Removal or Departure.

7. The master to take an account every day of the absent and present them to the overseer who visits that week.

8. [The trustees or overseers] to visit each in his turn every week, and as he shall see occasion to exhort and reprove and inspect the progress of the scholars and the performance of the master, and on the first Monday of every Kalender month all the overseers to meet and endeavour the progress of the Design, for the prospect is now melancholy of a new generation coming up not less ignorant (than their Parents) of the end of their Creation and the common principles of Christianity and it may be hop'd that some good Christians of your Parts will contribute to rise and make this sort of Charity more general. The Law has provided for the Indigent but not to instruct the poor and ignorant.

9. At any of the monthly meetings the overseers or any 4 or 5 of them to have power to make such good orders for the better Government of the school (not contrary to these) as they shall think fit and at any such monthly meeting the visitors having all notice to be present, the major part shall have power upon great misdemeanor which they or the major part shall adjudge so to remove the master and appoint a new one. And in this case I would have no .... the major part of the visitors present to have the power, having all had personal notice or notice left at their respective abodes, two days at least before the meeting.

10. The master to take ten scholars more, but not to exceed upon any pretence whatsoever. If he does after a second admonition from the visitors or any two of them to be remov'd and this part to be dispens'd with or for it to be, either wilfully or negligently, I declare it directly opposite to my Design.

11. The master to say a short prayer, concluding with the Lord's Prayer every morning and evening, and every scholar every Day of the Week (if capable of it) to learn a part of the 119 Psalm in the reading Psalms without book but not to be made repeat above 6 or 8 verses at a time.

12. The master to have £15p.ann to be paid him Quarterly, at Xtmas, Ladyday, Midsummer and Michaelmas, and twenty shillings every Martinmas day to make provision for Winter, but if the overseers think it better to pay him weekly they may.

13. The master to receive no measure of Satisfaction or Reward from the Parents or Friends of the children for by such means many free schools are become the most chargeable of any, the good Endowments generally drawing men who (not free from covertousness) take Rewards or Wages above the Foundation and thereby the children of the poorer sort are either neglected, or their forc'd beyond their abilitys to equal the rich in their presents or Rewards, otherwise the children are discouraged, and the Design of the Founders quite altered, who design'd by their Endowments that Learning should be taught at the easiest price to all that would come, and in suffering this I shall think the Visitors guilty of a great Breach of Trust[1].

14. Twenty pounds clear is set apart for this work; £16 whereof for the master, 40s to be employed for a stock to buy books and in other charitable uses about the school, the other 40s to bind one or two of the boys to sea or to Shipbuilders, or to put one or 2 of the Girls to an apprenticeship or to some honest service at the Direction of any 4 or five of them [the overseers or visitors].

What remains is for you to correct what you think convenient or to make any alterations not in substance differing from these. Many amendments no doubt you may make and some necessary additions; all of which I submit to. (But the principal matter will be a house for the Master, which need but consist of one large Room for the school, a Room above for the master and a Garret above that. And I hope this Design and the Charitable Disposition of your magistrates and Common Council will prevail upon them to build and maintain upon some waste spot of Ground.[2]) Your Corporation's eminent Charitys no doubt have been a means of its long Prosperity and Preservation against the attempts of its Enemies and if the Report be true that all the great Revenue of your Corporation is employed in Works of Charity and munificence I must not doubt of their forwardness to nourish this poor Design which without them will expire and die upon the Front of the House when they build one. Let their Charity be remember'd and the poor Children be put in mind to all Posterity to rise up and pray for the long Prosperity and Welfare of your Charitable Corporation as will always your Faithful Friend

---

[1] Much the same argument appears in a 1706 report of the S.P.C.K. (Society for the Propagation of Christian Knowledge): "he shall content himself with his salary."
[2] This is probably only applicable to St John's School

APPENDIX 6

SCHEMES OF GOVERNMENT OF THE SCHOOLS

1705/6	Scheme according to will of Eleanor Allan. Eleanor Allan's Charity: St Nicholas's Charity School
1795	Amended
1824	Scheme : Clergy Jubilee School
1877	(11 July) Scheme: Allan's Endowed Schools
1895	(3 October) Amended
1899	(26 September) Amended
1901	(4 November) Amended
1909	(20 October) Scheme
1917	Scheme ("An efficient secondary school")
1921	(7 February) Scheme : Dame Allan's Schools
1930	(16 October) Amended
1957	(8 March) Amended
1966	(27 June) Modified
1987	(17 February) Scheme
2000	Scheme
2004	(18 August) Amended

ACKNOWLEDGEMENTS

Many old pupils and members of staff and even people with no real link with the Schools have contributed to this book, some very generously. I have had to be selective to achieve some balance between different periods and between the two Dame Allan's Schools. However, nothing is to be wasted, since all material will be deposited in the Schools' archive for the benefit of future researchers. There is certainly material for further investigation. I am very grateful to them all.

I am, however, especially grateful for a number of individuals. First, I have been sustained by Mr Welsh and Dr Hind who have encouraged and helped. Second, their secretary, Mrs Lorraine Stephenson, has been unfailingly cheerful in the face of my hand-writing and changes of mind. Mr Tom White has taken numerous photographs and digitally enhanced much material. Two Old Allanians have given many hours in researching material, and their contribution has made for greater knowledge and thus a more substantial book. They are Dr Aidan Lawes of the National Archives at Kew, and Mr Stephen Davies. The latter has ferreted out much fine detail, and has acquired an encyclopaedic knowledge of the Schools at all periods. We owe these two gentlemen a great deal.

I am also grateful to the staffs of the National Archives, Newcastle Central Library, the Tyne and Wear Archives, Morpeth Records Office and Newcastle Cathedral; to the archivists of St Catharine's, Queens', Newnham and Fitzwilliam Colleges and Hughes Hall, Cambridge; to Ms Margaret Moncrieff and the Revd Dr Alan Munden; and to Mr Peter Jokelson, Mr Paul Hart and other staff of Prontaprint Newcastle.

Finally, despite the endeavours of all of us, there will be errors in this book. Please send any corrections to the author, care of the Schools, so that they may be recorded in a revised copy to be kept in the archives.

E.D. Smith